OF

ness

e

Alamo

Revised Edition

WITHDRAWN

by Bill Groneman

Republic of Texas Press

Library of Congress Cataloging-in-Publication Data

Groneman, Bill.
    Eyewitness to the Alamo / Bill Groneman.-- Rev. ed.
        p. cm.
    Includes bibliographical references (p.) and index.
    ISBN 1-55622-846-5
    1. Alamo (San Antonio, Tex.)--Siege, 1836--Personal narratives.   I. Title.

    F390.G85 2001
    976.4'03--dc21   2001019400
                                            CIP

Printed in the United States of America

ISBN 1-55622-846-5
10 9 8 7 6 5 4 3 2 1
0103

All inquiries for volume purchases of this book should be addressed
to Wordware Publishing, Inc., at 2320 Los Rios Boulevard, Plano,
Texas 75074. Telephone inquiries may be made by calling:
(972) 423-0090

For my wife Kelly
and my daughter Katie

The task was a laborious one because eyewitnesses of the same occurrence gave different accounts of them as they remembered, or were interested in the actions of one side or the other.

—Thucydides

Contents

Foreword

C. L. Sonnichsen, that grand old man of southwestern history who passed away several years ago, would have loved Bill Groneman. Sonnichsen, who as president of the Western History Association and as a mentor to me in the Western Writers of America greatly influenced my own views on academic historians and so-called "popular historians," was a champion of what he called "grassroots historians." Although "Doc" Sonnichsen, as he was called by his many admirers, had a Ph.D. from Harvard, he despaired of an academe where "highly specialized scholars have left the busy world behind, communicate only with each other, and speak a private language understood only by themselves." Doc wrote those words back in 1981, before the academic community, and especially practitioners of western history, descended to far more pathetic levels of self-congratulation and total isolation from the interests of the intelligent reading public.

Sonnichsen defined "grassroots historians," and he considered himself one of them, as "amateurs, untrained enthusiasts, buffs, and ordinary citizens who want to know about some special corner of the past—'grassroots' types who spend long hours, happy and exciting to them, in county courthouses, old newspaper files, state archives, and regional libraries. Not all of them are either humble or obscure. There is a wide gray area between the black of the academic specialist and the white of the busy buff."

Bill Groneman is the perfect exemplar of Doc Sonnichsen's "grassroots historian." Unlike so many who labor in the fields without recognition, Groneman has had a profound impact upon Texas history and, most especially, the study of the epic battle of the Alamo. When, in 1994, Groneman published a provocative little volume entitled *Defense of a Legend*, arguing that the Alamo journal of Mexican officer José Enrique de la

Peña, published in 1975 by Texas A&M University Press, was a fraud, he stirred up a firestorm. (One minor brushfire was his psychological interpretation of this historian in the following: "When Professor Paul Andrew Hutton, a leading proponent of the execution theory, wrote an article on Crockett for *Texas Monthly* magazine, he proclaimed that when he began writing his article, he sought to 'dismantle him, to free myself from the shackles of childhood hero worship.' Professor Hutton was one of the major voices decrying everyone else's 'fragile psyches,' yet it was he who seemed to be trying to purge himself of childhood demons.") Groneman and I met soon after his book was released and struck up a friendship based on our mutual obsession with Crockett and the Alamo.

While I continued to disagree with his interpretation of the Peña document, I could not help but admire his love of history and his passion to uncover the truth. He raised serious questions about the document that have never been completely answered despite rather savage attacks by academic rivals and a conference on the Peña journal at the University of Texas that studiously avoided inviting Groneman to participate.

Groneman's work stirred up a grand debate that is ongoing, created a cottage publishing industry around the questions he raised, and helped to enhance the career paths of his academic critics by adding new lines to their vitaes. All this swirling controversy he faced with a remarkably dry sense of humor and a determination to force his opponents to produce real evidence to back up their interpretations. He also no longer stands alone, for some other noted authors, such as the historian William C. Davis and the novelist Stephen Harrigan, have often sided with him.

Groneman and I have shared a few debate platforms, where I learned firsthand the subtle bite of his dry wit. In one particularly clever exchange in the February 1999 *Wild West* magazine, he was asked "when taking a historian like Hutton to task, weren't you intimidated?" He responded, with classic Groneman style, "Not really, because we were Alamo buffs, members of this Alamo Society. I wasn't thinking about his national reputation. I didn't know he was that famous at that time. I didn't know he was that famous until he told me."

The Crockett debate brought Groneman and *Defense of a Legend* considerable notoriety, but he has done other important history work including *Alamo Defenders* in 1990, *Battlefields of Texas* in 1998, and *Death of a Legend* in 1999. All this has been accomplished while pursuing a career with the New York City Fire Department, where he currently ranks as Captain.

Groneman's most impressive work—and most useful to the student of the Alamo or casual reader interested in exploring this story in more detail—is the book you hold in your hand—*Eyewitness to the Alamo*, first published in 1996. It is rather remarkable that an eminently useful anthology such as this had not been previously published. John Rios' *Readings on the Alamo* (1987) took a historiographical approach, while Timothy Matovina's *The Alamo Remembered* (1995) dealt only with Tejano accounts central to the formation of an ethnic consciousness. Groneman's careful selection of contemporary accounts of the storied battle, both authentic and fanciful, still stands alone as the best single volume of its kind available.

Groneman's thoughtful commentary on these narratives adds considerable value to the book. His organization is straightforward and clear: Part one deals with letters written at the time of the battle by participants; part two with accounts given immediately after the battle; part three with nineteenth-century memoirs; and a final section with twentieth-century appearances of previously unknown accounts. It is extraordinary just how much new material on the battle is only now coming to light. Future research in Mexican archives will undoubtedly yield even more of value. All of this new material, as Groneman makes clear, is fundamentally changing our understanding of what was once assumed to be a well-known story. Much of this new research and many of the new questions now being asked are the result of the new interest in the topic inspired by Groneman's books.

Yes, indeed, Doc Sonnichsen would have loved Bill Groneman.

Paul Andrew Hutton
University of New Mexico

Acknowledgments

I would like to thank and acknowledge all of the following: My wife Kelly, son Billy, daughter Katie, and dalmatians Dotty and Glennis. My friends at Republic of Texas Press, Russell and Dianne Stultz, Ginnie Bivona, and the rest of the fine staff. The past and present staff of the Daughters of the Republic of Texas Library at the Alamo who are always more than helpful, Director Elaine B. Davis, former Director Cathy Herpich, Martha Utterback, Jeannette Phinney, Warren Stricker, Jana Bomersbach, Rusty Gamez, Linda Edwards, Sally Koch, and Dora Guerra. Those who provided help, encouragement, inspiration, advice, illustrations, or examples of their own work: Chris Anderson; John Anderson of the Texas State Archives; Dorothy Black, former Alamo Chapel Hostess; David C. Bowser; Bill and Debbie Chemerka; Ann Fears Crawford; Ed Dubravsky; Ray Esparza; Jack and Yetta Fauntleroy; Don and Terry Griffiths; Angela Hamrick; Dr. Todd Harburn; Cyde Hubbard; Paul Andrew Hutton Ph.D., Walter Lord; Timothy M. Matovina Ph.D.; Tom Munnerlyn of State House Press; Joe Musso; Ma and Mikey Novak; Dorothy Perez; Etna Scott; Tom Shelton of the Institute of Texan Cultures; Bob Strong; Rod and Jean Timanus; Terry Todish; Tim Todish; Tonia J. Wood of the Texas State Archives; the staff of the Malverne Public Library; the Alamo Society, and Firefighter Steve Cox, Engine Company 308, FDNY for his help with the computer.

I especially thank my friend Tom Lindley of Austin, who has shared the results of his intense research on the Alamo and the Texas Revolution.

Introduction

The siege and battle of the Alamo took place from February 23 to March 6, 1836. Today it is a well-remembered and much-celebrated event. However, immediately following the battle on that bloody Sunday morning many years ago it was not quite so. There were not many people anxious to, or in a position to, actually remember the Alamo. Virtually all of the combatants on the Texan side of the conflict had been killed. There were a handful of noncombatant survivors within the fort and a greater number of combatant survivors among the victorious Mexican soldiers, but at the time no attempt was made to piece the story together through their testimony. There was no official inquest into the battle since both sides were waging war and had more pressing matters to attend to. To the survivors the siege and battle of the Alamo was a violent, bloody tragedy, not the glorious historical event as it is seen today. It is likely that they would have preferred to put the traumatic details of the battle behind them.

Still, eyewitness or alleged eyewitness accounts of the siege and battle have emerged over the years. They come from the small group of survivors within the Alamo, Mexican soldiers, civilian witnesses, and couriers who had been sent out before the final battle. These accounts have been set down in the form of official correspondence, letters, memoirs, alleged diaries and journals, oral family tradition, books, newspaper articles, and even in the form of communications from the commanders of each side during the siege. These are the people to whom the saying "Remember the Alamo" truly applies. When we remember the Alamo today it is through the words and writings of later historians and researchers who have interpreted, reinterpreted, and sometimes heavily edited the accounts of the participants or alleged participants.

Eyewitness testimony is very compelling. Whether it is given in a courtroom or in a history book, it carries a great deal of weight. Unfortunately eyewitness testimony relies on human memory, and despite an unflagging confidence in our own memories and the general belief that human memory is an efficient recorder of data, it is actually a very frail mechanism. Elizabeth Loftus, Ph.D. and Katherine Ketcham explain the situation in their book *Witness for the Defense*:

> Even if we are careful observers and take in a reasonably accurate picture of some object or experience, it does not stay intact in memory. Other forces begin to corrode the original memory. With the passage of time, with proper motivation, or with the introduction of interfering or contradictory facts, the memory traces change or become transformed, often without our conscious awareness. We can actually come to believe in memories of events that never happened.[1]

The pages that follow offer a variety of eyewitness or alleged eyewitness accounts of the battle of the Alamo. They or parts of them have been cited in works on the Alamo many times before. Sometimes they have been presented in condensed form, at other times edited or merely interpreted by later authors.

There are problems with many of these eyewitness accounts that continue to confound historians and researchers. Very few of the accounts are consistent with one another, even those given by the same individual at different times. This most likely can be attributed to the problems of memory mentioned above. Other accounts are attributed to people whose identities cannot be verified or whose presence at the Alamo during the time period they are speaking of is not confirmed by any documentation. Some accounts have appeared many years after the fact with no record of authenticity. Some have been dismissed as fakes already while others are highly suspect.

The accounts presented here include some of these bogus accounts as well as the suspect ones since all have served as primary source material for the telling of the Alamo story in the past. Familiar scenes that have found their way into various renditions of the story originate in these sources. Comments will be included with some of these accounts, but the final decision as to whether or not any of them are of historical value is left up to the reader.

Once an account is woven into the fabric of history, it is difficult to raise questions about its authenticity or accuracy. Some writers, researchers, readers, and historians tend to react on an emotional level. One example is the case of John Sutherland (accounts #3.10 and #3.37). Sutherland's dramatic account, in its various forms, has served as the opening scene to the siege of the Alamo in books, articles, and films for years. Recently, Austin researcher Thomas Ricks Lindley found evidence that Sutherland had made a land claim years before his account first appeared, and in that he made no mention of his links with the Alamo on the first day of its siege. Also, Lindley found documentary evidence of Sutherland having been in San Antonio before the siege began, but no evidence of him there on February 23, 1836. Lindley explained this to another historian who understood all of the points Lindley was making. The other historian's reply was something to the effect, "Well, if we eliminate the Sutherland account, then we won't have any account of the beginning of the siege." Exactly! The point of this is, generally, people feel that a questionable, inaccurate, or false historical account is better than no account at all.

There is a problem with presenting so many accounts from such a wide variety of sources. The ideal situation would be to put the words of the account giver between quotation marks as if this person was giving the statement directly to the reader. In most cases this is impossible since the thoughts and words of the reporter of the account are so intermixed with those of the alleged eyewitness that they cannot be distilled from one another. Some of the accounts presented are edited to focus primarily on the siege and battle of the Alamo, and in almost all cases the accounts are from longer narratives. Those interested are urged to go back to the original source in order to evaluate any particular account in its original context. In some cases I have made minor adjustments in spelling. In the case of proper names, some are spelled in more than one way, sometimes in the same account. I have tried to leave these names as they were written. In the cases where accounts appear in the form of letters, the salutations and closings of these letters are dispensed with and just the text as it applies to the Alamo is given.

I have changed the headings of the accounts as they appeared in the original printing of this book. Before each account I give the name of the person the account is attributed to. As in the original book, this does not mean the account actually originated with this person. I also include the manner in which the account came to us; for example, via a newspaper interview or by one person passing the information to another, etc., and the date or year the information generally became public. I have numbered each account to reflect the chapter and sequence of the account in that chapter. For example, an account numbered "1.7" means the account is in chapter 1, and it is the 7th account in the chapter. Hopefully, this will help in cross-referencing different accounts by various individuals.

The correct spelling of many of the Spanish names include accent marks. I have left these marks out if they had been omitted in the original documents. I have also left the spelling of names of people and places as they appear in the originals. Therefore, there will be a variety of spellings of the names of any given person or place.

Chapter one presents letters written as the Alamo siege progressed. They give a brief but firsthand glimpse as to what transpired at the scene. These letters are presented in chronological order according to the dates they were written. The accounts in the other chapters are presented in the order in which they first appeared. It is important to present them in this fashion since even though the eyewitness' or alleged eyewitness' memory dates back to the event itself, the order in which the accounts were made public may have influenced later accounts.

Finally, too much handling of some of these accounts may be inadvisable. They are like the marine animals described by John Steinbeck in his introduction to *Cannery Row*—animals so delicate that they are "...almost impossible to capture whole, for they break and tatter under the touch." One must allow them to "ooze and crawl of their own will onto a knife blade..." in order to capture them. Following Steinbeck's lead it may be best to present these accounts as he did in writing *Cannery Row*, "...to open the page and let the stories crawl in by themselves."[2]

Chapter One

THE SIEGE

Remember the Alamo

— Sam Houston (and others)

Letters or communications written by participants provide our first look at the Alamo siege and battle. They are the initial eyewitness accounts written, or believed to have been written, as the drama unfolded rather than in the form of memoir. Along with patriotic rhetoric and pleas for assistance, some early details of the siege and battle come to light. Regarding the letters of February 23, there is no way to know in which order they were written. The order of their presentation here is strictly by the choice of this author.

1.1
William Barret Travis, February 23, 1836
From a message to Andrew Ponton

The enemy in large force is in sight. We want men and provisions. Send them to us. We have 150 men and are determined to defend the Alamo to the last. Give us assistance.[1]

William Barret Travis (1809-1836) was born in South Carolina and raised in Alabama. In 1831 he emigrated to Texas where he practiced law in San Felipe. In December of 1835 he was commissioned a lieutenant colonel in the newly formed Texan cavalry and in the following month was ordered to San

Travis's letter of February 23 to Andrew Ponton
was his first message from the besieged Alamo.

(Yale Collection of Western Americana, Beinecke Rare
Book and Manuscript Library, Yale University)

Antonio de Bexar, the location of the Alamo, to reinforce Colonel James Clinton Neill's meager force of Texan revolutionaries. Travis became interim commander of the forces stationed at Bexar when Col. Neill left in early February 1836 to raise money, supplies, and reinforcements for his garrison. Travis ultimately commanded the Texan forces during the siege and battle of the Alamo. His letters provide us with the earliest look at the Alamo during the siege.

1.2
William Barret Travis and James Bowie, February 23, 1836
From an alleged letter to James Walker Fannin, in Henry Stuart Foote's book *Texas and the Texans*, published in 1841.

We have removed all our men into the Alamo, where we will make such resistance as is due to our honour, and that of the country, until we can get assistance from you, which we expect you to forward immediately. In this extremity, we hope you will send us all the men you can spare promptly. We have one hundred and forty-six men, who are determined never to retreat. We have but little provisions, but enough to serve us till you and your men arrive. We deem it unnecessary to repeat to a brave officer, who knows his duty, that we call on him for assistance.[2]

This letter first appeared in Henry Stuart Foote's *Texas and the Texans* in 1841 as a letter to James Walker Fannin. Its inclusion in his book contained no citation as to an original letter.

1.3
James Bowie, February 23, 1836
From a message to the commander of the invading force below Bejar

Because a shot was fired from a cannon of this fort at the time that a red flag was raised over the tower, and a little afterward they told me that a part of your army had sounded a parley, which, however, was not heard before the firing of the said shot. I wish, Sir, to ascertain if it be true that a parley was called, for which reason I send my second aid, Benito Jameson, under guarantee of a white flag which I believe will be respected by you and your forces. God and Texas![3]

James Bowie (1795-1836) was born in Kentucky and later lived in Louisiana. He emigrated to Texas in 1828. Bowie was commander of the volunteer troops among the Alamo garrison, elected by popular vote upon the departure of Col. Neill. By mutual agreement he shared command of the garrison with Travis for a short time. His role in the siege and battle of the Alamo was limited due to the fact that he was incapacitated by illness early on. It is unknown why Bowie acted unilaterally in calling for a parley at this point. If Travis had been upset by such a move, he seems to have responded by sending out a messenger of his own to converse with the Mexican officers. (See the journal entries of Juan N. Almonte in account #2.7).

1.4
José Batres, February 23, 1836
From a message to James Bowie

As the Aid-de-Camp of his Excellency, the President of the Republic, I reply to you according to the order of his Excellency, that the Mexican army cannot come to terms under any conditions with rebellious foreigners to whom there is no other recourse left, if they wish to save their lives, than to place themselves immediately at the disposal of the Supreme Government from whom alone they may expect clemency after some considerations are taken up. God and Liberty![4]

Colonel José Batres was an aide-de-camp to General Antonio Lopez de Santa Anna during the Texan campaign. He was killed at the Battle of San Jacinto on April 21, 1836.

1.5
William Barret Travis, February 24, 1836
From a letter to the "People of Texas and all Americans in the world"

I am besieged by a thousand or more of the Mexicans under Santa Anna. I have sustained a continual Bombardment & cannonade for 24 hours & have not lost a man. The enemy has demanded a surrender at discretion, otherwise, the garrison are to be put to the sword, if the fort is taken. I have answered the demand with a cannon shot, & our flag still waves proudly from the walls. I shall never surrender or retreat. Then, I call on you in the name of Liberty, of patriotism & every thing dear to the

Travis's letter of February 24, 1836. The most dramatic and
well known of the communications from the Alamo.

(Courtesy of the Archives Division—Texas State Library)

American character, to come to our aid with all dispatch. The enemy is receiving reinforcements daily & will no doubt increase to three or four thousand in four or five days. If this call is neglected, I am determined to sustain myself as long as possible & die like a soldier who never forgets what is due his own honor & that of his country. <u>Victory or Death</u>.

P.S. The Lord is on our side. When the enemy appeared in sight we had not three bushels of corn. We have since found in deserted houses 80 to 90 bushels and got into the walls 20 or 30 head of Beeves.[5]

This letter is the most well known and the most dramatic piece of correspondence associated with the Alamo. What is considered to be the original of this letter appeared in 1891 when John G. Davidson, a great-grandson of Travis's daughter Susan Isabella, placed it on temporary loan with the Texas Department of Agriculture, Insurance, Statistics, and History. Two years later he sold it to the state for $85.[6]

There are slight differences in wording between this letter and earlier versions of it that had been printed in contemporary newspapers and broadsides. This version did not begin to appear regularly in writings on the Alamo until well into the twentieth century.[7]

1.6
Launcelot Smither, February 24, 1836
From a message to "All the Inhabitants of Texas"

In a few words there is 2000 Mexican soldiers in Bexar, and 150 Americans in the Alamo. Sesma is at the head of them, and from the best accounts that can be obtained, they intend to show no quarter. If every man cannot turn out to a man every man in the Alamo will be murdered.

They have not more than 8 or 10 days provisions. They say they will defend it or die on the ground. Provisions, ammunition and Men, or you will suffer your men to be murdered in the Fort. If you do not turn out Texas is gone. I left Bexar on the 23rd. at 4 P.M.[8]

Launcelot Smither (1800-1842) emigrated to Texas from Alabama in 1828. He made his living as a horse trader and amateur physician to the Mexican garrison at San Antonio de Bexar before they were driven out of Texas. He left San

Antonio on the first day of the Alamo siege, but it is uncertain whether he left on his own or as an official messenger of Travis.

1.7
Albert Martin, February 25, 1836
From a postscript to Travis's letter of February 24, 1836

Since the above [Travis's letter of Feb. 24] I heard a very heavy Canonade during the whole day think there must have been an attack made upon the Alamo We were short of Ammunition when I left. Hurry on all the men you can in haste.

When I left there was but 150 determined to do or die tomorrow I leave for Bejar with what men I can raise [?] will [?] at all events - Col Almonte is there the troops are under the Command of Gen Seisma [Sesma].[9]

Albert Martin (1808-1836) was born in Providence, Rhode Island, and emigrated to Gonzales, Texas, in 1835. Martin was the emissary sent by Travis to treat with Col. Juan N. Almonte on February 23, 1836. Martin carried Travis's message of February 24 from the Alamo. He returned with the relief force from Gonzales on March 1. He died in the Alamo battle five days later.

1.8
William Barret Travis, February 25, 1836
From a letter to Sam Houston printed in the *Arkansas Gazette* April 12, 1836

On the 23rd of Feb. the enemy in large force entered the city of Bexar, which could not be prevented, as I had not sufficient force to occupy both positions. Col. Batres, the Adjutant-Major of the President-General Santa Anna, demanded a surrender at discretion, calling us foreign rebels. I answered them with a cannon shot upon which the enemy commenced a bombardment with a five-inch howitzer, which together with a heavy cannonade, has been kept up incessantly ever since. I instantly sent express to Col. Fannin, at Goliad, and to the people of Gonzales and San Felipe. Today at 10 o'clock A.M. some two or three hundred Mexicans crossed the river below and came up under cover of the houses until they arrived within point blank shot, when we opened a heavy discharge of grape and canister on them, together with a well directed fire from small arms which forced them to halt and take shelter in the houses about 90 or 100 yards from our batteries. The action continued to rage about two hours, when the enemy retreated in confusion, dragging off many of their dead and wounded.

During the action the enemy kept up a constant bombardment and discharge of balls, grape and canister. We knew from actual observation that many of the enemy were wounded - while we, on our part, have not lost a man. Two or three of our men have been slightly scratched by pieces of rock, but have not been disabled. I take great pleasure in stating that both officers and men conducted themselves with firmness and bravery. Lieutenant Simmons of cavalry acting as infantry, and Captains Carey, Dickinson and Blair of the artillery, rendered essential service, and Charles Despallier and Robert Brown gallantly sallied out and set fire to houses which afforded the enemy shelter, in the face of the enemy fire. Indeed, the whole of the men who were brought into action conducted themselves with such undaunted heroism that it would be injustice to discriminate. The Hon. David Crockett was seen at all points, animating the men to do their duty. Our numbers are few and the enemy still continues to approximate his works to ours. I have every reason to apprehend an attack from his whole force very soon; but I shall hold out to the last extremity, hoping to secure reinforcements in a day or two. Do hasten on aid to me as rapidly as possible, as from the superior number of the enemy, it will be impossible for us to keep them out much longer. If they overpower us, we fall a sacrifice at the shrine of our country, and we hope posterity and our country will do our memory justice. Give me help, oh my country! Victory or Death![10]

1.9
Antonio Lopez de Santa Anna, February 27, 1836
From a letter to General Vicente Filisola

On the 23rd of this month I occupied this city, after some forced marches from Rio Grande, with General D. Joaquin y Sesma's division composed of the permanent battalions of Matamoros and Jimenez, the active battalion of San Luis Potose, the regiment of Dolores, and eight pieces of artillery.

With the speed in which this meritorious division executed its marches in eighty leagues of road, it was believed that the rebel settlers would not have known of our proximity until we should have been within rifle-shot of them; as it was they only had time to hurriedly entrench themselves in Fort Alamo, which they had well fortified, and with a sufficient food supply. My objective had been to surprise them early in the morning of the day before, but a heavy rain prevented it.

Notwithstanding their artillery fire, which they began immediately from the indicated fort, the national troops took possession of this city with the utmost order, which the traitors shall never again occupy; on our part we lost a corporal and a scout, dead, and eight wounded.

When I was quartering the corps of the division a bearer of the flag of truce presented himself with a paper, the original which I am enclosing for your Excellency, and becoming indignant of its contents I ordered an aide, who was the nearest to me to answer it, as it is expressed by the copy that is also enclosed.

Fifty rifles, of the rebel traitors of the North, have fallen in our possession, and several other things, which I shall have delivered to the general commissary of the army as soon as it arrives, so that these forces may be equipped; and the rest will be sold and the proceeds used for the general expense of the army.

From the moment of my arrival I have been busy hostilizing the enemy in its position, so much so that they are not even allowed to raise their heads over the walls, preparing everything for the assault which will take place when at least the first brigade arrives, which is even now sixty leagues away. Up to now they act stubbornly, counting on the strong position which they hold, and hoping for much aid from their colonies and from the United States of the North, but they shall soon find out their mistake....[11]

Antonio Lopez de Santa Anna (1794-1876) was born in Jalapa, Mexico. He entered the military in 1810, and by 1833 he was elected president of Mexico as a liberal. Once in power Santa Anna quickly moved toward despotism. At the outset of the campaign against Texas, he left the leadership of the Mexican government in the hands of others and personally led the Mexican army into Texas. (For other accounts by or attributed to Santa Anna see #1.11, 1.15, 3.1, 4.31, and 4.33.)

1.10
Philip Dimitt, February 28, 1836
From a letter to James Kerr

I have this moment, 8 P.M., arrived from Bexar. On the 23d, I was requested by Colonel Travis to take Lieutenant Nobles and reconnoiter the enemy. Some distance out I met a Mexican who informed me that the town had been invested. After a short time a messenger overtook me, saying he had been sent by a friend of my wife to let me know that it would be impossible for me to return, as two large bodies of Mexican troops were already around the town. I then proceeded to the Rovia and remained till 10 P.M., on the 25th. On the 24th there was heavy cannonading, particularly at the close of the evening. I left the Rovia at 10 P.M., on the 25th, and heard no more firing, from which I concluded the Alamo had been taken by storm.[12]

Philip Dimitt (1801-1841) was born in Kentucky and emigrated to Texas in 1822. He was a merchant and trader operating from his own post, Dimitt's Landing. He had been ordered by Sam Houston to raise a company of at least 100 men and reinforce the garrison at San Antonio de Bexar in January 1836. He proceeded to San Antonio even though he could not raise the specified number of men.

1.11
Antonio Lopez de Santa Anna, February 29, 1836
As an order to General Joaquin Ramirez y Sesma

…Informed of the news that was communicated I say to you: That it is very good, go out in search of the enemy assuming that they are to be found so close by; but I judge the need to take with yourself the Jimenez battalion, and at the same time ten large boxes of rifle cartridges: since ammunition is never superfluous. Try to prepare yourself to fall on them at daybreak, and in a way that you are able to surprise them.
In this war you know that there are no prisoners.[13]

This information comes in the form of an order issued from Santa Anna to General Joaquin Ramirez y Sesma, who commanded the Mexican cavalry. Its focus is not directed toward the Alamo, but to activities outside of the fort in the surrounding territory. The Alamo battlefield encompassed the town of

San Antonio as well as the area around both the fort and the town. Regarding the impending Alamo battle, this message clearly illustrates Santa Anna's policy towards prisoners of war. He would enforce this policy in the aftermath of the Alamo battle and other battles of the Texan campaign. (For other accounts by or attributed to Santa Anna see #1.9, 1.15, 3.1, 4.31, and 4.33.)

1.12
William Barret Travis, March 3, 1836
From a letter to the Texas Constitutional Convention published in the *Telegraph and Texas Register* March 24, 1836

From the twenty-fifth to the present date the enemy have kept up a bombardment from two howitzers, one a five and a half inch, and the other an eight inch, - and a heavy cannonade from two long nine-pounders, mounted on a battery on the opposite side of the river, at a distance of four hundred yards from our wall. During this period the enemy have been busily employed in encircling us in with entrenched encampments on all sides, at the following distances, to wit: In Bexar, four hundred yards west; in Lavallita, three hundred yards south; on the ditch, eight hundred yards northeast, and at the old mill, eight hundred yards north. Notwithstanding all this, a company of thirty-two men from Gonzales, made their way in to us on the morning of the first inst. at three o'clock, and Colonel J.B. Bonham (a courier from Gonzales) got in this morning at eleven o'clock without molestation. I have fortified this place, so that the walls are generally proof against cannon balls; and I shall continue to entrench on the inside, and strengthen the walls by throwing up dirt. At least two hundred shells have fallen inside of our works without having injured a single man from any cause, and we have killed many of the enemy. The spirits of my men are still high although they have had much to depress them. We have contended for ten days against an enemy whose numbers are variously estimated from fifteen hundred to six thousand men, with General Ramirez-Sesma and Colonel Batres, the aid-de-camp of Santa Anna, at their head. A report was circulated that Santa Anna himself was with the enemy, but I think it was false. A reinforcement of about one thousand men is now entering Bexar from the west and I think it more than probable that Santa Anna is now in town, from the rejoicing we hear.

Col. Fannin is said to be on the march to this place with reinforce-ments, but I fear it is not true, as I have repeatedly sent to him for aid without receiving any. Colonel Bonham, my special messenger, arrived at La Bahia fourteen days ago, with a request for aid, and on the arrival of the enemy in Bexar, ten days ago, I sent an express to Colonel F., which arrived at Goliad on the next day, urging him to send us reinforcements; none have yet arrived. I look to the colonies alone for aid; unless it arrives soon, I shall have to fight the enemy on his own terms. I will, however, do the best I can under the circumstances; and I feel confident that the determined valor and desperate courage, heretofore exhibited by my men, will not fail them in the last struggle; and although they may be sacri-ficed to the vengeance of a Gothic enemy, the victory will cost the enemy so dear, that it will be worse for him than defeat. I hope your honorable body will hasten on reinforcements, ammunitions and provisions to our aid so soon as possible. We have provisions for twenty days for the men we have. Our supply of ammunition is limited. At least five hundred pounds of cannon powder, and two hundred rounds of six, nine, twelve, and eighteen pound balls, ten kegs of rifle powder and a supply of lead should be sent to this place without delay, under a sufficient guard.

If these things are promptly sent and large reinforcements are has-tened to this frontier, this neighborhood will be the great and decisive ground. The power of Santa Anna is to be met here or in the colonies; we had better meet them here than to suffer a war of devastation to rage in our settlements. A blood red banner waves from the church of Bejar, and in the camp above us, in token that the war is one of vengeance against rebels; they have declared us as such; demanded that we should surren-der at discretion, or that this garrison should be put to the sword. Their threats have no influence on me or my men, but to make all fight with desperation and that high-souled courage that characterizes the patriot, who is willing to die in defence of his country's liberty and his own honor.

The citizens of this municipality are all our enemies, except those who have joined us heretofore. We have three Mexicans now in the fort; those who have not joined us in this extremity, should be declared public enemies, and their property should aid in paying the expenses of the war.

The bearer of this will give your honorable body a statement more in detail, should he escape through the enemy's lines.

God and Texas - Victory or Death.

PS The enemy's troops are still arriving, and the reinforcements will probably amount to two or three thousand.[14]

1.13
William Barret Travis, March 3, 1836
From a letter to an unidentified friend, published in the *Telegraph and Texas Register* March 24, 1836

I am still here, in fine spirits and well to do, with 145 men. I have held this place 10 days against a force variously estimated from 1,500 to 6,000, and shall continue to hold it till I get relief from my countrymen, or I will perish in its defense. We have had a shower of bombs and cannon balls continually falling among us the whole time, yet none of us has fallen. We have been miraculously preserved. You have no doubt seen my official report of the action of the 25th ult. in which we repulsed the enemy with considerable loss; on the night of the 25th they made another attempt to charge us in the rear of the fort, but we received them gallantly by a discharge of grape shot and musketry, and they took to their scrapers immediately. They are now encamped in entrenchments on all sides of us.

All our couriers have gotten out without being caught and a company of 32 men from Gonzales got in two nights ago, and Colonel Bonham got in today by coming between the powder house and the enemy's upper encampment.... Let the Convention go on and make a declaration of independence, and we will then understand, and the world will understand, what we are fighting for. If independence is not declared, I shall lay down my arms, and so will the men under my command. But under the flag of independence, we are ready to peril our lives a hundred times a day, and to drive away the monster who is fighting us under a blood-red flag, threatening to murder all prisoners and make Texas a waste desert. I shall have to fight the enemy on his own terms, yet I am ready to do it, and if my countrymen do not rally to my relief, I am determined to perish in the defense of this place, and my bones shall reproach my country for her neglect. With 500 men more, I will drive Sesma beyond the Rio Grande, and I will visit vengeance on the enemy of Texas whether invaders or resident Mexican enemies. All the citizens of this place that have not joined us are with the enemy fighting against us. Let the government declare them public enemies, otherwise she is acting a suicidal part. I shall treat them as such unless I have superior orders to the contrary. My respects to all friends, confusion to all enemies. God bless you.[15]

1.14

Juan Valentine Amador, March 5, 1836, 2 o'clock P.M.

From an order to Generals, chiefs of sections, and commanding officers of the Mexican force

Being necessary to act decisively upon the enemy defending The Alamo, the Most Excellent General-In-Chief has ordered that tomorrow at four o'clock the attacking columns, placed at short distance from the first trenches, undertake the assault to begin with a signal given by the General by means of the sounding of a bugle from the North battery.

General D. Martin Perfecto de Cos will command the First Column. If he cannot, I will. The Permanent Battalion, Aldama, with the exception of the Grenadier Company and the three first Active Companies of San Luis, will form the First Column.

The Second Column will be commanded by Colonel D. Francisco Duque. If he cannot, by General D. Manuel Fernandez Castrillon. The Active Battalion, Toluca, and the three Active Rifle Companies, San Luis, with the exception of the Grenadier Company, will form this Second Column.

Colonel D. Jose Maria Romero will command the Third. If he cannot, Colonel D. Mariano de Salas. The Rifle Companies from the Permanent Battalions, Matamoros and Jimenez, and the Active Battalion, San Luis.

The points from which these columns will mount their attacks will be designated by the General-In-Chief at the opportune time, and then the Column Commanders will receive their orders.

The reserves will be formed by the Sapper Battalion and the first Grenadier Companies from the Permanent Battalions, Matamoros, Jimenez and Aldama, plus the Active Battalions, Toluca and San Luis. The reserve force will be commanded by the General-In-Chief at the moment of attack; but the gathering of this force will be carried out by Colonel D. Augustin Amat, under whose orders the reserves will remain from this afternoon until they are placed in positions to be designated.

The first Column will carry ten scaling ladders, two crowbars and two axes; the same number by the second; six ladders by the third, and two by the fourth.

The men carrying the ladders will sling their rifles on their backs until the ladders are properly placed.

The Companies of Grenadiers and Scouts will carry ammunition at six rounds [packages of cartridges] per man and at four the riflemen, and two flints in reserve. These men will not wear cloaks, carry blankets, or anything else which will inhibit them to maneuver quickly. During the day all shako chin-straps will be correctly worn - these the Commanders will watch closely. The troops will wear shoes or sandals. The attacking troops will turn in after the night's prayers as they will form their columns at midnight.

The untrained recruits will remain in their camps. All armaments will be in good shape - especially the bayonets.

As soon as the moon rises, the riflemen of the Active Battalion, San Luis, will move back to their quarters to get their equipment ready; this will be done by leaving their stations in the line.

The Cavalry, under the command of General D. Joaquin Ramirez y Sesma, will occupy the Alameda and will saddle up at Three o'clock in the morning. Their duty will be to guard the camp and keep anyone from deserting

Take this into consideration: Against foreigners opposing us, the Honor of our Nation and Army is at stake. His Supreme Excellency, the General-In-Chief, expects each man to fulfill his duties and to exert himself to give his country a day of glory and satisfaction. He well knows how to reward those brave men who form The Army of Operations.[16]

General Juan V. Amador was a member of Santa Anna's staff. These orders appear in a number of books on the Alamo and in a variety of translations each with slightly different wording. For instance the sentence that spells out the duties of the cavalry under Gen. Ramirez y Sesma calls for them to "...guard the camp and keep anyone from deserting." In other versions their duty is to "...scout the country, to prevent the possibility of an escape."[17] Although these orders lay out the plan of attack in this fashion, it does not necessarily mean the attack went off this way. Newly uncovered evidence indicates that changes were made.[18]

1.15
Antonio Lopez de Santa Anna, March 6, 1836
From a letter to José Maria Tornel

Victory belongs to the army, which at this very moment, 8 o'clock A.M., achieved a complete and glorious triumph that will render its memory imperishable.

Antonio Lopez de Santa Anna

[Lithograph based on a ca. 1850 daguerreotype] From Albert C. Ramsey, *The Other Side: Or Notes for the History of the War Between Mexico and the United States* (New York: John Wiley, 1850). (Courtesy of the Institute of Texan Cultures)

As I had stated in my report to Your Excellency of the taking of this city, on the 27th of last month, I awaited the arrival of the 1st Brigade of Infantry to commence active operations against the Fortress of the Alamo. However, the whole Brigade having been delayed beyond my expectation, I ordered that three of its Battalions, viz: the Engineers - Aldama and Toluca - should force their march to join me. These troops, together with the Battalions of Matamoros, Jimenes, and San Luis Potosi, brought the force at my disposal, recruits excluded, up to 1400 Infantry. This force, divided into four columns of attack and a reserve, commenced the attack at 5 o'clock A.M. They met with a stubborn resistance, the combat lasting more then one hour and an half, and the reserve having to be brought into action.

The scene offered by this engagement was extraordinary. The men fought individually, vying with each other in heroism. Twenty-one pieces of artillery, used by the enemy with most perfect accuracy, the brisk fire of musketry, which illuminated the interior of the Fortress and its walls and ditches - could not check our dauntless soldiers, who are entitled to the consideration of the Supreme Government and to the gratitude of the nation.

The Fortress is now in our power, with its artillery, stores, &c. More than 600 corpses of foreigners were buried in the ditches and entrenchments, and a great many who had escaped the bayonet of the infantry, fell in the vicinity under the sabres of the cavalry. I can assure Your Excellency that few are those who bore to their associates the tidings of their disaster.

Among the corpses are those of Bowie and Travis, who styled themselves Colonels, and also that of Crockett, and several leading men, who had entered the Fortress with dispatches from their Convention. We lost 70 men killed and 300 wounded, among whom are 25 officers. The cause for which they fell renders their loss less painful, as it is the duty of the Mexican soldier to die for the defence of the rights of the nation; and all of us were ready for any sacrifice to promote this fond object; nor will we, hereafter, suffer any foreigners, whatever their origin may be, to insult our country and to pollute its soils.

I shall, in due time, send to Your Excellency a circumstantial report of this glorious triumph. Now I have only time to congratulate the nation and the President, ad interim, to whom I request you to submit this report.

The bearer takes with him one of the flags of the enemy's Battalions, captured today. The inspection of it will show plainly the true intentions of the treacherous colonists, and of their abettors, who came from parts of the United States of the North. God and Liberty![19]

Santa Anna apparently felt it necessary to exaggerate the losses of Texans at the Alamo while downplaying his own. Traditionally the Texan losses are given as 182 – 189, but new evaluation of sources indicates the number was probably closer to 250 – 260. Still, Santa Anna's number of 600 is unrealistically high.[20] (For other accounts by or attributed to Santa Anna see #1.9, 1.11, 3.1, 4.31, and 4.33.)

Chapter Two

1836

We also are compassed about with so great a cloud of witnesses
— Hebrews XII 1

2.1
Susanna Dickinson, March 24, 1836
From an article in the *Telegraph and Texas Register*

At daybreak of the 6th inst. the enemy surrounded the fort with their infantry, with the cavalry forming a circle outside to prevent escape on the part of the garrison: the number consisted of at least 1000 against 140! General Santa Ana commanded in person, assisted by four generals and a formidable train of artillery. Our men had been previously much fatigued and harrassed by nightwatching and incessant toil, having experienced for some days past a heavy bombardment and several real and feigned attacks. But, American valor and American love of liberty displayed themselves to the last: they were never more conspicuous: twice did the enemy apply to the walls their scaling ladders, and twice did they receive a check; for our men were determined to verify the words of the immortal Travis, "to make the victory worse to the enemy than a defeat." A pause ensued after the second attack, which was renewed on the third time, owing to the exertions of Santa Anna and his officers: They then poured in over the walls, "like sheep:" the struggle, however, did not even there cease- unable from the crowd and for want of time to load their guns and rifles, our men made use of the but [sic]-ends of the latter and continued to fight and to resist, until life ebbed out through their numberless wounds and the enemy had conquered the fort, but not its brave, its matchless defenders: they perished but they yielded not: only one (Warner) remained to ask for quarter, which was denied by the unrelenting enemy....

[At this point the editor of the article added his own unabashed praise for the defenders of the Alamo. The narrative continues below:]

From the commencement to the close the storming lasted less than an hour. Major Evans, master of ordnance was killed when in the act of setting fire to the powder magazine, agreeable to the previous orders from Travis. The end of David Crocket of Tennessee, the great hunter of the west was as glorious as his career through life had been useful. He and his companions were found surrounded by piles of assailants, whom they had immolated on the altar of Texas liberties. The countenance of Crocket was unchanged: he had in death that freshness of hue, which his exercise of pursuing the beasts of the forest and the prairie had imparted to him. Texas places him, exaltingly, amongst the martyrs in her cause. Col. Travis stood on the walls cheering his men exclaiming "Hurra my boys" till he received a second shot, and fell: it is stated that a Mexican general (Mora) then rushed upon him, and lifted his sword to destroy his victim, who, collecting all his last expiring energies, directed a thrust at the former, which changed their relative positions: for the victim became the victor, and the remains of both descended to eternal sleep: but not alike to everlasting fame.

Travis's negro was spared, because, as the enemy said, "his master had behaved like a brave man:" words which of themselves form an epitaph: they are already engraved on the hearts of Texans, and should be inscribed on his tomb. Col. James Bowie, who had for several days been sick, was murdered in his bed: his remains were mutilated.

Suspended animation has returned to the instrument of our narration, and we continue. Mrs. Dickinson and her child, and a negro of Bowie's, and as before said, Travis's were spared.

Our dead were denied the right of Christian burial; being stripped and thrown into a pile, and burned. Would that we could gather up their ashes and place them in urns!

It is stated that about fifteen hundred of the enemy were killed and wounded in the last and previous attacks.[1]

Susanna Dickinson (1814-1883) was the wife of Almeron Dickinson, who served as an artillery officer in the Alamo garrison. She survived the Alamo battle with her infant daughter Angelina. This first account of the fall of the Alamo appeared in the newspaper the *Telegraph and Texas Register*

Susanna (Dickinson) Hannig survived the Alamo battle and gave several accounts of it in later life.

(Courtesy of the Archives Division — Texas State Library)

published in San Felipe de Austin by Joseph Baker, Gail Borden Jr., and Thomas H. Borden. The paper had been in publications since the previous October. The issue in which this account appeared was the last issue before the editors were forced to flee to Harrisburg before Santa Anna's army. The account is interspersed heavily with editorial comments by the publisher, and the actual information provided by Dickinson is scant. Much of the information in this account is repeated later in accounts by Travis's slave, Joe. Some of the statements attributed to Joe actually originated with Susanna Dickinson. (See the account of Joe, #2.6. For other accounts by or attributed to Dickinson see: 2.5, 3.18, 3.20, 3.22, 3.23, 3.28, 3.29, and 4.22.)

2.2
Unidentified Mexican Soldier, April 5, 1836
From an article in *El Mosquito Mexicano*

Dear brothers of my heart; God our Lord receive thanks, because the triumph of our forces are multiplied. The ungrateful and proud colonists who made us suffer so many days of unpleasantness in the previous campaigns have now succumbed to the fate brought about by their imprudent rashness. After thirteen days of continuous fire, his excellency the President ordered at 2:00 A.M., the night before last, that the fortifications at the Alamo be attacked: to make this effective four columns were readied, being commanded by General Cos and Colonels Juan Morales, D.N. Duque de Estrada y Romero. I was under the orders of General Cos and therefore will relate what I saw at close range. After a roundabout approach we stopped at 3:00 A.M. on the north side, about 300 paces from the enemy's fort and there the column which consisted of the Aldama and part of that of San Luis Potosi. We remained on the ground until 5:30 (the morning felt quite cool) when the signal to march was given by his Excellency the President, from his battery situated to the northeast. Immediately Mr. Cos yelled - on your feet! and placing himself at the head of the forces, we ran to the assault. Ladders, beam, bars, pick axes &c were carried for that purpose; although the distance was short, we suffered through cannister shots that shot down more than forty men: the tenacious resistance of our enemy was to be admired and the dauntless steadiness of all the generals, chiefs, officers and troops: it seemed as though the shot and bullets from the cannons, muskets and rifles of the enemy found their mark on the chests of our soldiers, who ceaselessly shouted Long Live the Mexican Republic! Long Live General Santa Anna! I assure you that all signs of fear or terror disappeared at the sight of so many brave men by ladders, by batteries, by embrasures and even over one another clambered over the walls. The four columns and the reserves as if by a charm at the same time climbed the enemy's wall and threw themselves inside his enclosure after about three quarters of an hour under horrible fire which when ended was followed by a horrid battle at sword point; and afterwards a pitiful but unavoidable massacre of the ungrateful colonists took place, some throwing down their arms and attempting to flee or hide.

Miserable ones! They no longer exist: they all died, all and up to now I have seen burned (to avoid putrefaction) 257 bodies not counting the previous ones of the thirteen days, or those being caught, who attempted to escape. The chief they called Travis died like a brave man with his gun in his hand, in back of a cannon; but the wicked and boastful Santiago Bowie, died like a woman, almost hidden under a mattress. On our side we suffered heavy losses both of officers and troops, and about 200 wounded, a regrettable loss but small if one considers the strong position of the enemy and its kind. The former insult which we have received has been avenged. His Excellency the President made a beautiful speech to all of the divisions inside the Alamo in view of the dead enemies, and is pleased with everyone's behavior.[2]

The true identity of this Mexican soldier has never been established. There has been some speculation that the writer was José Juan Sanchez Navarro, a scion of the largest land holding family in Mexico. The reason for this writer's anonymity also remains a mystery. (See Sanchez-Navarro's account #4.29.)

2.3
Joe, April 11, 1836
From a letter by an unidentified correspondent to the editor of the *New Orleans Commercial Bulletin*

...The Honorable Davy Crockett died like a hero, surrounded by heaps of the enemy slain. Colonel James Bowie was sick and unable to rise. He was slain in his bed: the enemy allowed him a grave — probably in consideration of his having been married to a Mexican lady, a daughter of the late Governor Berrimundi [Veramendi]. The enemy had made daily and nightly attacks upon the place for 10 days. The garrison was exhausted by incessant watching; at last the enemy made a final assault with 4000 men, half an hour before daylight, on the morning of the 6th instant. It was dark, and the enemy were undiscovered until they were close to the walls, and before the sentinels had aroused the garrison, the enemy had gained possession of a part of the ramparts. The garrison fought like men who knew there was but a brief space left them in which to avenge the wrongs of their country's possession. When driven from the walls by overwhelming numbers, they retired to the barracks, and fought hand to hand and man to man until the last man was slain — no, there was a man yet left; a little man named Warner had secreted himself among the dead bodies, and was found when the battle was over, and the dead men being removed without the walls of the fort. He asked for quarters; the soldiers took him to Santa Anna, who ordered him to be shot. The order was executed, and the body was taken out and burnt with the heroes who deserve as bright a remembrance as those who died on the pass of Thermopylae.[3]

Joe (1813 or 15 - ?) was the slave of William Barret Travis and accompanied Travis into the Alamo. He participated in the Alamo battle as an active combatant but survived with minor wounds. He was last reported in Austin, Texas, in 1875. Joe was briefly detained by Santa Anna following the Alamo battle and then was permitted to travel to the Texan forces. He gave his story of the battle to Texan officials, and his words were interpreted and passed on by some of those who heard them. This first letter is included since it has been cited as one of Joe's firsthand accounts in the past, and the writer states, "I learnt these facts from a negro boy, the servant of Colonel Travis." Apparently no anthropologist, the writer also explains that Joe's life was spared "probably in consideration of his kindred blood [to the Mexicans]."[4] This letter should not be construed as Joe's exact words. It is obvious that the account has been heavily edited by one or perhaps more newspaper editors. (For other accounts by or attributed to Joe see #2.4, 2.6, and 4.13)

2.4
Joe, April 12, 1836
As reported by George C. Childress
in the *Memphis (Tennessee) Enquirer*

The servant of the lamented Travis, says his master fell near the close of the siege. That the Texians had picket guards stationed some hundred yards around the Alamo, (as the fort of San Antonio is called,) and upon its walls; that on Sunday morning about 3 o'clock the guard upon the wall cried out, "Col. Travis the Mexicans are coming!" Whether the picket guards were asleep or killed is not known; they were not heard, if they sounded any alarm. The Mexicans were encamped around the Alamo, out of the reach of its cannon. Col. Travis sprang from his blanket with his sword and gun, mounted the rampart and seeing the enemy under the mouths of the cannon with scaling ladders, discharged his double bar-reled gun down upon them; he was immediately shot; his gun falling upon the enemy and himself within the fort. The Mexican General *leading* the charge mounted the wall by means of a ladder, and seeing the bleeding Travis, attempted to behead him; the dying Colonel raised his sword and *killed him*! The negro then hid in one of the apartments of the fort, until the spirit of bravery was entirely quenched, when he heard a voice enquire if there "were no negroes here." The negro replied "yes here's one," and came out; a Mexican discharged a gun at him, but did him no injury; another ran his bayonet at him, injuring him slightly, when the Mexican officer speaking English interposed and saved him. This officer conversed freely with the negro as also did Santa Anna; this general was there, and made the negro point out Col. Travis; by which conversation he knew his master had killed the general leading the siege, as their blood then congealed together. The body of Col. Travis and his little yet great band were burnt by order of Santa Anna....[5]

This version of Joe's account comes to us through the observations of George C. Childress, who had been the editor of the *Nashville Banner*. Childress was present at Washing-ton-on-the-Brazos, Texas, when Joe reported the fall of the Alamo to Texan officials. He claimed to receive this account personally from Joe and described him as being "intelligent and known to be faithful and honest."[6] (For other accounts by or attributed to Joe see #2.3, 2.6, and 4.13.)

2.5

Susanna Dickinson, April 29, 1836

**As reported by William Parker to the
editor of the *Mississippi Free Trader***

...of the five [Alamo defenders] who, for a moment survived their companions, and threw themselves on the victor's clemency, two were pursued into her room, and subjected in her presence to the most torturing death. They were even raised on the points of the enemy's lances, let down and raised again and again, whilst invoking as a favor, instantaneous death to terminate their anguish, till they were at last too weak to speak, and then expired in convulsion.[7]

This account comes to us third hand from a letter written by William Parker, who had traveled to Nacogdoches, Texas, in an attempt to determine the fate of his son Christopher A. Parker, who had died in the defense of the Alamo. According to his letter, Parker obtained Susanna Dickinson's story from William Hadden, a private in the Texan army who had escaped the mass execution of Colonel James Fannin's troops at Goliad. Hadden was found half starved along the Colorado River by Major Benjamin J. White, who brought him to the settlements along the Brazos River. While on his way, Hadden crossed paths with and obtained this account from Dickinson. (For other accounts by or attributed to Dickinson see #2.1, 3.18, 3.20, 3.22, 3.23, 3.28, 3.29, and 4.22.)

2.6

Joe, May 25, 1836

**From a letter from a correspondent of the *Fredericksburg Arena*
to the editor of the *Frankfort (Kentucky) Commonwealth***

The Garrison was much exhausted by hard labor and incessant watching and fighting for thirteen days. The day and night previous to the attack, the Mexican bombardment had been suspended. On Saturday night, March 5, the little Garrison had worked hard, in repairing and strengthening their position, until a late hour. And when the attack was made, which was just before daybreak, sentinels and all were asleep, except the officer of the day who was just starting on his round. There were three picket guards without the Fort; but they too, it is supposed, were asleep, and were run upon and bayonetted, for they gave no alarm that was heard. The first Joe knew of it was the entrance of Adjutant Baugh, the officer of the day, into Travis' quarters, who roused him with the cry — "the Mexicans are coming." They were running at full speed with their scaling ladders, towards the Fort, and were under the guns, and had their ladders against the wall before the Garrison were aroused to resistance. Travis sprung up, and seizing his rifle and sword, called to Joe to take his gun and follow. He mounted the wall, and called out to his men — *"Come on Boys, the Mexicans are upon us, and we'll give them Hell."* He immediately fired his rifle — Joe followed his example. The fire was returned by several shots, and Travis fell, wounded, within the wall, on the sloping ground that had recently been thrown up to strengthen the wall. There he sat, unable to rise. Joe, seeing his master fall, and the Mexicans coming near the wall, and thinking with Falstaff that the better part of valor is discretion, ran, and ensconced himself in a house, from the loop holes of which he says, he fired on them several times after they had come in.

Here Joe's narrative becomes somewhat interrupted; but Mrs. Dickenson, the wife of Lt. D., who was in the Fort at the time, and is now at San Felipe, has supplied some particulars, which Joe's state of retirement prevented him from knowing with perfect accuracy. The enemy three times applied their scaling ladders to the wall; twice they were beaten back. But numbers and discipline prevailed over valor and desperation. On the third attempt they succeeded, and then they came over *"like sheep."* As Travis sat wounded, but cheering his men, where he first fell, General Mora, in passing, aimed a blow with his sword to despatch him — Travis rallied his failing strength, struck up the descending weapon, and ran his assailant through the body. This was poor Travis' last effort. Both fell and expired on the spot. The battle now became a complete *melee*. Every man fought "for his own hand," with gun-butts, swords, pistols and knives, as best he could. The handful of Americans, not 150 effective men, retreated to such cover as they had, and continued the battle, until *only one man*, a little weakly body, named Warner, was left alive. He, and he only, asked for quarter. He was spared by the soldiery; but on being conducted to Santa Anna, he ordered him to be shot, which was promptly done. So that not *one white man*, of that devoted band, was left to tell the tale.

Crockett, the kind hearted, brave DAVID CROCKETT, and a few of the devoted friends who entered the Fort with him, were found lying together, with 21 of the slain enemy around them. Bowie is said to have fired through the door of his room, from his sick bed. He was found dead and mutilated where he had lain. The body of Travis, too, was pierced with many bayonet stabs. The despicable Col. Cos, fleshed his dastard sword in the dead body. Indeed, Joe says, the soldiers continued to stab the fallen Americans, until all possibility of life was extinct. Capt. Baragan was the only Mexican officer who showed any disposition to spare the Americans. He saved Joe, and interceded for poor Warner, but in vain. There were several Negroes and some Mexican women in the Fort. They were all spared. One only of the Negroes was killed — a woman — who was found lying dead between two guns. Joe supposes she ran out in her fright, and was killed by a chance shot. Lieut. Dickenson's child was not killed, as was first reported. The mother and child were both spared and sent home. The wife of Dr. Aldridge [Alsbury] and her sister, Miss Navarro, were also spared and restored to their father, who lives in Bejar.

After the fight, when they were searching the houses, an officer called out in English "are there any negroes here?" Joe then emerged from his concealment, and said, "Yes, here's one." Immediately two soldiers attempted to despatch him — one by discharging his piece at him, and the other by a thrust of the bayonet. He escaped with a scratch only from the steel, and one buck shot in his side, which, however, did little damage. He was saved by the intervention of Captain Baragan, who beat off the soldier with his sword.

The work of death being completed, the Mexicans were formed in hollow square, and Santa Anna addressed them in a very animated manner. They responded to it with loud vivas. Joe described him as a light built, slender man, rather tall — sharp, but handsome and animated features, dressed very plainly; somewhat "*like a Methodist preacher,*" to use the negro's own words. Joe was taken into Bejar, and detained several days. He was shown a grand review of the army after the battle, and was told there were 8,000 troops under arms. He supposes there were that many. But those acquainted with the ground on which he says they formed, think that not half of that number could be formed there. Santa Anna took much notice of him, and questioned him about Texas and the state of the army. — Among other things, he asked if there were many soldiers from the United States in the army, and if more were expected? On being answered in the affirmative, he sneeringly said he had men enough to *march to the city of Washington if he chose.*

The slain were collected in a pile and burnt.[8]

This is yet another version of Joe's account, and it is probably the most well known. It is attributed to William Fairfax

Gray, who had been associated with the *Fredericksburg Arena*. This account is interesting since there are a few key elements of it that are traditionally attributed to Joe, such as the description of the Mexican soldiers as coming over the wall "like sheep" and the description of Crockett and a few friends lying dead with twenty-one of the enemy around them. After a closer reading of this account, however, it is likely that these details were taken from Dickinson's account in the *Telegraph and Texas Register* (Account #2.1). Of interest is the fact that Joe describes other blacks in the fort and a black woman as having been killed during the battle.

Gray also stated in his letter that he heard Joe interrogated in the presence of the Cabinet [the Texan Cabinet], and described the experience as an "interesting treat." He described Joe as having "…related the affair as far as known to him, with much modesty, apparent candor, and remarkable distinctness for one of his class."[9] (For other accounts by or attributed see #2.3, 2.4, and 4.13.)

2.7
Juan Nepomuceno Almonte, June 23 - 27, 1836
From Almonte's journal published in the *New York Herald*

[Feb.] *Tuesday* 23 - At 7 ½ A.M. the army was put in march - To the Potranca 1 ½ leagues - to the Creek of Leon or Del Medio, 3 ½ leagues - To Bexar 3 leagues, in all 8 leagues. At half a league from Bexar the division halted on the hills of Alazan at 12 ½ o'clock. General Sesma arrived at 7 A.M. and did not advance to reconnoiter because he expected an advance of the enemy which was about to be made according to accounts given by a spy of the enemy who was caught. There was water, though little, in a stream of Las Lomas del Alazan. At 2 the army took up their march, the President and his staff in the van. The enemy, as soon as the march of the division was seen, hoisted the tri-colored flag with two stars, designed to represent Coahuila and Texas. The President with all his staff advanced to Campo Santo (burying ground.) The enemy lowered the flag and fled, and possession was taken of Bexar without firing a shot. At 3 P.M. the enemy filed off to the fort of Alamo, where there was __ pieces of artillery; among them one 18 pounder: It appeared they had 130 men; during the afternoon 4 grenades were fired at them. The firing was suspended in order to receive a messenger, who brought a dispatch the contents of which appears in No. 1, and the answer which was given will be found in No. 2 [accounts #1.3 and 1.4]. I conversed with the bearer who was Jameson (G.B.) and he informed me of the bad state they were in at the Alamo, and manifested a wish that some honorable conditions should be proposed for a surrender. Another messenger afterwards came, (Martin) late a clerk in a house in New Orleans. He stated to me what Mr. Travis said, "that if I wished to speak with him, he would receive me with much pleasure." I answered that it did not become the Mexican Government to make any propositions through me, and that I had only permission to hear such as might be made on the part of the rebels. After these contestations night came on, and there was no more firing. In the night another small battery was made up the river near the house of Veremenda. I lodged in the house of Nixon, (Major) with Urriza and Marcil Aguirre. An inventory of the effects taken was made; many curious papers were found. One Smith, carpenter and cabinet maker they say was the owner of the effects. I did not sleep all night, having to attend to the enemy and the property, the charge of which was entrusted to me; its value was about $3000.

Wednesday, 24th. - Very early this morning a new battery was commenced on the bank of the river, about 350 yards from the Alamo. It was finished in the afternoon, and a brisk fire was kept up from it until the 18 pounder and another piece was dismounted. The President reconnoitered on horseback, passing within musket shot of the fort. According to a spy, four of the enemy were killed. At evening the music struck up, and went to entertain the enemy with *it* and some *grenades*. In the night, according to the statement of a spy, 30 men arrived at the fort from Gonzales.

Thursday, 25th. - The firing from our batteries was commenced early. The General in Chief, with the battalion de Cazadores, crossed the river and posted themselves in the Alamo - that is to say, in the houses near the fort. A new fortification was commenced by us near the house of McMullen. In the random firing the enemy wounded 4 of the Cazadores de Matamoras battalion, and 2 of the battalion of Jimenes, and killed one corporal and a soldier of the battalion of Matamoros. Our fire ceased in the afternoon. In the night two batteries were erected by us on the other side of the river in the Alameda of the Alamo - the battalion of Matamoros was also posted there, and the cavalry was posted on the hills to the east of the enemy, and in the road from Gonzales at the Casa Mata Antigua. At half past eleven at night we retired. The enemy, in the night, burnt the straw and wooden houses in their vicinity, but did not attempt to set fire with their guns to those in our rear. A strong north wind commenced at nine at night.

Friday, 26th. - The northern wind continued very strong; the thermometer fell to 39°, and during the rest of the day remained at 60°. At daylight there was a slight skirmish between the enemy and a small party of the division of the east, under the command of General Sesma. During the day the firing from out cannon was continued. The enemy did not reply, except now and then. At night the enemy burnt the small houses near the parapet of the battalion of San Luis, on the other side of the river. Some sentinels were advanced. In the course of the day the enemy sallied out for wood and water, and were opposed by our marksmen. The norther wind continues.

Saturday 27th. - The northern wind was strong at day break, and continued all the night. Thermometer at 39°. Lieutenant Manuel Menchacho was sent with a party of men for the corn, cattle, and hogs at the Ranchos (small farms) of Seguin and Flores. It was determined to cut off the water from the enemy on the side next to the old mill. There was little firing from either side during the day. The enemy worked hard to repair some entrenchments. In the afternoon the President was observed by the enemy and fired at. In the night a courier extraordinary was dispatched to the city of Mexico, informing the Government of the taking of Bexar, and also to Gen'ls Urrea, Filisola, Cos & Vital Fernandez. No private letters were sent.

Sunday, 28th. - The weather abated somewhat. Thermometer at 40° at 7 A.M. News were received that a reinforcement to the enemy was coming by the road from La Bahia, in number 200. It was not true. The cannonading was continued.

Monday, 29th. - The weather changed - thermometer at 55°; in the night it commenced blowing hard from the west. In the afternoon the battalion of Allende took post at the east of the Alamo. The President reconnoitered. One of our soldiers was killed in the night. The wind changed to the north at midnight. About that time Gen. Sesma left the camp with the cavalry of Dolores and the infantry of Allende to meet the enemy coming from La Bahia or Goliad to the aid of the Alamo. Gen'l Castrillon on guard.

March [Tuesday] 1st. - The wind subsided, but the weather continued cold - thermometer at 36° in the morning - day clear. Early in the morning Gen. Sesma wrote from the Mission de la Espador that there was no such enemy, and that he reconnoitered as far as the Tinaja, without finding any traces of them. The cavalry returned to camp, and the infantry to this city. At 12 o'clock the President went out to reconnoiter the mill site to the north west of the Alamo. Lieut. Col. Ampudia was commissioned to construct more trenches. - In the afternoon the enemy fired two 12 pound shots at the house of the President, one of which struck the house, and the other passed it. Nothing more of consequence occurred. Night cold - Thermometer 34° Fahrenheit, and 1° Reaumur.

Wednesday, 2d. - Commenced clear and pleasant - thermometer 34° - no wind. An Aid of Col. Duque arrived with despatches from Arroyo Hondo, dated 1st inst.; in reply, he was ordered to leave the river Medina, and arrive the next day at 12 or 1 o'clock. Gen. J. Ramirez came to breakfast with the President. Information was received that there was corn at the farm of Sequin [Seguin], and Lieut. Menchaca was sent with a party for it. The President discovered, in the afternoon, a covered road within pistol shot of the Alamo, and posted the battalion of Jimenes there. At 5 A.M. Bringas went out to meet Gaona.

Thursday, 3d. - Commenced clear, at 40°, without wind. The enemy fired a few cannon and musket shots at the city. I wrote to Mexico and to my sister, directed them to send their letters to Bexar, and that before 3 months the campaign would be ended. The General-in-Chief went out to reconnoiter. A battery was erected on the north of the Alamo within musket shot. Official despatches were received from Gen. Urrea, announcing that he had routed the colonists at San Patricio - killing 16 and taking 21 prisoners. The bells were rung. The battalion of Zapadores, Aldama, and Toluca arrived. The enemy attempted a sally in the night at the Sugar Mill, but were repulsed by our advance.

Friday, 4th. - The day commenced windy, but not cold - thermometer 42°. Commenced firing very early, which the enemy did not return. In the afternoon one or two shots were fired by them. A meeting of Generals and Colonels was held, at which Generals Cos, Sesma, and Castrillon were present; (Generals Amador and Ventura Mora did not attend - the former having been suspended, and the latter being in active commission.) Also present, Colonels Francisco Duque, battalion of Toluca - Orisñuela, battalion of Aldama - Romero, battalion of Matamoros - Amat, battalion of Zapadores, and the Major of battalion of San Luis. - The Colonels of battalion of Jimenes and San Luis did not attend, being engaged in actual commission I was also called. After a long conference, Cos, Castrillon, Orisñuela, and Romero were of the opinion that the Alamo should be assaulted - first opening a breach with the two cannon of __ and the two mortars, and that they should wait the arrival of the two 12

Col. Juan Nepomuceno Almonte. His journal of the
Alamo siege was published in the *N.Y. Herald.*

From Ann Fears Crawford, *The Eagle—The Autobiography of Santa Anna.*
(Courtesy of the Institute of Texan Cultures)

pounders expected on Monday the 7th. The President, Gen. Ramirez, and I were of opinion that the 12 pounders should not be waited for, but the assault made. - Colonels Duque and Amat, and the Major of the San Luis battalion did not give any definite opinion about either of the two modes of assault proposed. In this state things remained - the General not making any definite resolution. In the night the north parapet was advanced towards the enemy through the water course. A Lieutenant of Engineers conducted the entrenchment. A messenger was despatched to Urrea.

Saturday, March 5th. - The day commenced very moderate - thermometer 50° - weather clear. A brisk fire was commenced from our north battery against the enemy, which was not answered, except now and then. At mid-day the thermometer rose to 68°. - The President determined to make the assault; and it was agreed that the four columns of attack were to be commanded by Generals Cos, Duque, Romero, and Morales, and second in command, Generals Castrillon, Amador, and Miñon. For this purpose the points of attack were examined by the commanding officers, and they came to the conclusion that they should muster at 12 o'clock tonight, and at 4 o'clock to morrow morning (Sunday, 6th,) the attack should be made.

Sunday, 6th. - At 5 A.M. the columns were posted at their respective stations, and at half past 5 the attack or assault was made, and continued until 6 A.M.: when the enemy attempted in vain to fly, but they were overtaken and *put to the sword, and only five women, one Mexican soldier (prisoner,) and a black slave escaped from instant death.* On the part of the enemy the result was, 250 killed, and 17 pieces of artillery - a flag; muskets and fire-arms taken. Our loss was 60 soldiers and 5 officers killed, and 198 soldiers and 25 officers wounded - 2 of the latter General officers. The battalion of Toluca lost 98 men between the wounded and killed. *I was robbed by our soldiers.*[10]

Juan N. Almonte (1803-1869) was born in Necupétaro, Michoacán, Mexico. He took part in the siege and battle of the Alamo as a colonel on the staff of Gen. Santa Anna. Almonte was taken prisoner by the Texan army after the defeat of the Mexican army at San Jacinto on April 21, 1836. His private journal was discovered on the battlefield and was confiscated by Anson Jones. It was sent to the *New York Herald* via Galveston Island on May 22, 1836. One month later it was published by that paper in several installments. The *Herald*'s initial article states that the journal was seen and examined by Mr. Childress [George C. Childress, see Joe's account #2.4] who had been in New York City and then left for Washington D.C. a few days before the journal was published. The paper also states that on June 28 the original was sent on to

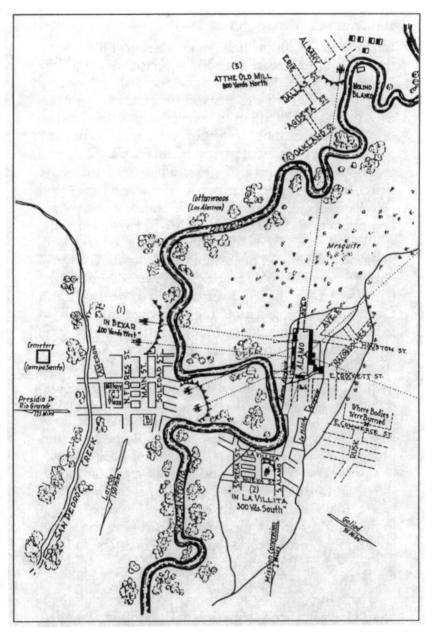

San Antonio de Bexar—The Alamo Battlefield
(Courtesy of the Archives Division—Texas State Library)

Washington D.C. to the president. An interesting editorial remark regarding the Alamo that appeared in the *Herald* on June 27 states, "It will be observed that Almonte's account differs very essentially from what was received at the time through the Texas Papers." The whereabouts of the original journal remains unknown at this time.[11] (For another account by or attributed to Almonte see #2.10.)

2.8
David Crockett, Early Summer 1836
From the book *Col. Crockett's Exploits and Adventures in Texas, Written by Himself*

I write this on the nineteenth of February, 1836, at San Antonio. We are all in high spirits, though we are rather short of provisions for men who have appetites that could digest anything but oppression; but no matter, we have a prospect of soon getting our bellies full of fighting, and that is victuals and drink to a true patriot any day. We had a little sort of convivial party last evening: Just about a dozen of us set to work most patriotically to see whether we could not get rid of that curse of the land, whisky, and we made considerable progress.

This morning I saw a caravan of about fifty mules passing by Bexar and bound for Santa Fé. They were loaded with different articles to such a degree that it was astonishing how they could travel at all, and they were nearly worn out by their labors. They were without bridle or halter, and yet proceeded with perfect regularity in a single line, and the owners of the caravan rode their mustangs with their enormous spurs, weighing at least a pound apiece, with rowels an inch and a half in length, and lever bits of the harshest description, able to break the jaws of their animals under a very gentle pressure. The men were dressed in the costume of Mexicans. Colonel Travis sent a guard to see that they were not laden with munitions of war for the enemy. I went out with the party.

Finding that the caravan contained nothing intended for the enemy, we assisted the owners to replace the heavy burdens on the backs of the patient but dejected mules and allowed them to pursue their weary and lonely way. For full two hours we could see them slowly winding along the narrow path, a faint line that ran like a thread through the extended prairie, and finally they were whittled down to the little end of nothing in the distance and were blotted out from the horizon.

February 22 — The Mexicans, about sixteen hundred strong, with their president, Santa Anna, at their head, aided by Generals Almonte, Cos, Sesma, and Castrillon, are within two leagues of Bexar. General Cos, it seems, has already forgot his parole of honor and is come back to retrieve the credit he lost in this place in December last. If he is captured a second time, I don't think he can have the impudence to ask to go at large again without giving better bail than on the former occasion. Some of the scouts came in and bring reports that Santa Anna has been endeavoring to excite the Indians to hostilities against the Texans, but so far without effect. The Comanches in particular entertain such hatred for the Mexicans and at the same time hold them in such contempt that they would rather turn their tomahawks against them and drive them from the land than lend a helping hand. We are up and doing and as lively as Dutch cheese in the dog days. Two hunters left town this afternoon for the purpose of reconnoitering.

February 23 — Early this morning the enemy came in sight, marching in regular order and displaying their strength to the greatest advantage in order to strike us with terror. But that was no go; they'll find that they have to do with men who will never lay down their arms as long as they can stand on their legs. We held a short council of war and finding that we should be completely surrounded and overwhelmed by numbers if we remained in the town, we concluded to withdraw to the fortress of Alamo and defend it to the last extremity. We accordingly filed off in good order, having some days before placed all the surplus provisions, arms, and ammunition in the fortress. We have had a large national flag made; it is composed of thirteen stripes, red and white alternately, on a blue ground with a large white star of five points in the center, and between the points the letters TEXAS. As soon as all our little band, about one hundred and fifty in number, had entered and secured the fortress in the best possible manner, we set about raising our flag on the battlements; on which occasion there was no one more active than my young friend, the Bee hunter. He had been all along sprightly, cheerful, and spirited, but now, notwithstanding the control that he usually maintained over himself, it was with difficulty that he kept his enthusiasm within bounds. As soon as we commenced raising the flag he bursts forth, in a clear, full tone of voice, that made the blood tingle in the veins of all who heard him: —

"Up with your banner, Freedom,
Thy champions cling to thee;
The'll follow where'er you lead 'em,
To death, or victory; —
Up with your banner, Freedom.

Tyrants and slaves are rushing
To tread thee in the dust;
Their blood will soon be gushing,
And stain our knives with rust;—
But not thy banner Freedom.

While stars and strips are flying,
Our blood we'll freely shed;
No groan will 'scape the dying,
Seeing thee o'er his head;—
Up with your banner, Freedom."

This song was followed by three cheers from all within the fortress, and the drums and trumpets commenced playing. The enemy marched into Bexar and took possession of the town, a blood-red flag flying at their head, to indicate that we need not expect quarters if we should fall into their clutches. In the afternoon a messenger was sent from the enemy to Colonel Travis, demanding an unconditional and absolute surrender of the garrison, threatening to put every man to the sword in case of refusal. The only answer he received was a cannon shot, so the messenger left us with a flea in his ear, and the Mexicans commenced firing grenades at us, but without doing any mischief. At night Colonel Travis sent an express to Colonel Fanning at Goliad, about three or four days' march from this place, to let him know we are besieged. The old pirate volunteered to go on this expedition and accordingly left the fort after nightfall.

February 24 — Very early this morning the enemy commenced a new battery on the banks of the river about three hundred and fifty yards from the fort, and by afternoon they amused themselves by firing at us from that quarter. Our Indian scout came in this evening, and with him a reinforcement of thirty men from Gonzales, who are just in the nick of time to reap a harvest of glory, but there is some prospect of sweating blood before we gather it in. An accident happened to my friend Thimblerig this afternoon. He was intent on his eternal game of thimbles, in a somewhat exposed position, while the enemy were bombarding us from the new redoubt. A three-ounce ball glanced from the parapet and struck him on the breast, inflicting a painful, but not dangerous wound. I extracted the ball, which was of lead, and recommended to him to drill a hole through it, and carry it for a watch seal. "No," he replied, with energy, "may I be shot six times if I do: that would be making a bauble for an idle boast. No, Colonel, lead is getting scarce, and I'll lend it out at compound interest. Curse the thimbles!" he muttered, and went his way, and I saw no more of him that evening.

February 25 — The firing commenced early this morning, but the Mexicans are poor engineers, for we haven't lost a single man, and our outworks have sustained no injury. Our sharpshooters have brought down a considerable number of stragglers at a long shot. I got up before the peep of day, hearing an occasional discharge of a rifle just over the place where I was sleeping, and I was somewhat amazed to see Thimblerig mounted alone on the battlement, no one being on duty at the time but the sentries. "What are you doing there?" says I. "Paying my debts," says he, "interest and all." "And how do you make out?" says I. "I've nearly got through," says he; "stop a moment, Colonel, and I'll close the account." He clapped his rifle to his shoulder and blazed away, then jumped down from his perch and said: "That account's settled; them chaps will let me play out my game in quiet next time." I looked over the wall and saw four Mexicans lying dead on the plain. I asked him to explain what he meant by paying his debts, and he told me that he had run the grapeshot into four rifle balls and that he had taken an early stand to have a chance of picking off straggles. "Now, Colonel, let's go take our bitters," said he, and so we did. The enemy have been busy during the night and have thrown up two batteries on the opposite side of the river. The battalion of Matamoras is posted there, and cavalry occupy the hills to the east and on the road to Gonzales. They are determined to surround us and cut us off from reinforcement or the possibility of escape by a sortie. Well, there's one thing they cannot prevent: We'll still go ahead and sell our lives at a high price.

February 26 — Colonel Bowie has been taken sick from overexertion and exposure. He did not leave his bed to-day until twelve o'clock. He is worth a dozen common men in a situation like ours. The Bee hunter keeps the whole garrison in good heart with his songs and his jests, and his daring and determined spirit. He is about the quickest on the trigger, and the best rifle shot we have in the fort. I have already seen him bring down eleven of the enemy, and at such a distance that we all thought it would be a waste of ammunition to attempt it. His gun is first rate, quite equal to my Betsey, though she has not quite as many trinkets about her. This day a small party sallied out of the fort for wood and water, and had a slight skirmish with three times their number from the division under General Sesma. The Bee hunter headed them, and beat the enemy off, after killing three. On opening his Bible at night, of which he always reads a portion before going to rest, he found a musket ball in the middle of it. "See here, Colonel," said he, "how they have treated the valued present of my dear little Kate of Nacogdoches." "It has saved your life," said I. "True," replied he, more seriously than usual, "and I am not the first sinner whose life has been saved by this book." He prepared for bed, and before retiring he prayed, and returned thanks for his providential escape; and I heard the name of Catherine mingled in his prayer.

February 27 — The cannonading began early this morning, and ten bombs were thrown into the fort, but fortunately exploded without doing any mischief. So far it has been a sort of tempest in a teapot, not unlike a pitched battle in the Hall of Congress, where the parties array their forces, make fearful demonstrations on both sides, then fire away with loud-sounding speeches, which contain about as much meaning as the report of a howitzer charged with a blank cartridge. Provisions are becoming scarce, and the enemy are endeavoring to cut off our water. If they attempt to stop our grog in that manner, let them look out, for we shall become too wrathy for our shirts to hold us. We are not prepared to submit to an excise of that nature, and they'll find it out. This discovery has created considerable excitement in the fort.

February 28 — Last night our hunters brought in some corn and hogs and had a brush with a scout from the enemy beyond gunshot of the fort. They put the scout to flight and got in without injury. They bring accounts that the settlers are flying in all quarters, in dismay, leaving their possessions to the mercy of the ruthless invader, who is literally engaged in a war of extermination more brutal than the untutored savage of the desert could be guilty of. Slaughter is indiscriminate, sparing neither sex, age, nor condition. Buildings have been burnt down, farms laid waste, and Santa Anna appears determined to verify his threat and convert the blooming paradise into a howling wilderness. For just one fair crack at that rascal even at a hundred yards distance I would bargain to break my Betsey and never pull trigger again. My name's not Crockett if I wouldn't get glory enough to appease my stomach for the remainder of my life. The scouts report that a settler by the name of Johnson, flying with his wife and three little children, when they reached the Colorado, left his family on the shore, and waded into the river to see whether it would be safe to ford with his wagon. When about the middle of the river he was seized by an alligator, and after a struggle, was dragged under the water, and perished. The helpless woman and her babes were discovered, gazing in agony on the spot, by other fugitives, who happily passed that way, and relieved them. Those who fight the battles experience but a small part of the privation, suffering, and anguish that follow in the train of ruthless war. The cannonading continued at intervals throughout the day, and all hands were kept up to their work. The enemy, somewhat emboldened, draws nigher to the fort. So much the better. There was a move in General Sesma's division toward evening.

February 29 — Before Daybreak we saw General Sesma leave his camp with a large body of cavalry and infantry and move off in the direction of Goliad. We think that he must have received news of Colonel Fanning's coming to our relief. We are all in high spirits at the prospect of being able to give the rascals a fair shake on the plain. This business of being shut up makes a man wolfish. I had a little sport this morning before breakfast. The enemy had planted a piece of ordnance within gunshot of the fort during the night, and the first thing in the morning they commenced a brisk cannonade pointblank against the spot where I was snoring. I turned out pretty smart and mounted the rampart. The gun was charged again, a fellow stepped forth to touch her off, but before he could apply the match I let him have it, and he keeled over. A second stepped up, snatched the match from the hand of the dying man, but Thimblerig, who had followed me, handed me his rifle, and the next instant the Mexican was stretched on the earth beside the first. A third came up to the cannon, my companion handed me another gun, and I fixed him off in a like manner. A fourth, then a fifth, seized the match, who both met with the same fate, and then the whole party gave it up as a bad job and hurried off to the camp leaving the cannon ready charged where they had planted it. I came down, took my bitters, and went to breakfast. Thimblerig told me that the place from which I had been firing was one of the snuggest stands in the whole fort, for he never failed picking off two or three stragglers before breakfast when perched up there.

And I recollect now having seen him there, ever since he was wounded, the first thing in the morning and the last at night — and at time thoughtlessly playing at his eternal game.

March 1 — The enemy's forces have been increasing in numbers daily, notwithstanding they have already lost about three hundred men in the several assaults they have made upon us. I neglected to mention in the proper place that when the enemy came in sight we had but three bushels of corn in the garrison but have since found eighty bushels in a deserted house. Colonel Bowie's illness still continues, but he manages to crawl from his bed every day, that his comrades may see him. His presence alone is a tower of strength — the enemy becomes more daring as his numbers increase.

March 2 — This day the delegates meet in general convention at the town of Washington to frame our Declaration of Independence. That the sacred instrument may never be trampled on by the children of those who have freely shed their blood to establish it is the sincere wish of David Crockett. Universal independence is an almighty idea, far too extensive for some brains to comprehend. It is a beautiful seed that germinates rapidly, and brings forth a large and vigorous tree, but like the deadly Upas, we sometimes find the smaller plants wither and die in its shades. Its blooming branches spread far and wide, offering a perch of safety to all alike, but even among its protecting branches was find the eagle, the kite, and the owl preying upon the helpless dove and sparrow. Beneath its shades myriads congregate in goodly fellowship; but the lamb and the fawn find but frail security from the lion and the jackal, though the tree of independence waves over them. Some imagine independence to be a natural charter, to exercise without restraint, and to their fullest extent, all the energies, both physical and mental, with which they have been endowed; and for their individual aggrandizement alone, without regard to the rights of others, provided they extend to all the same privilege and freedom of action. Such independence is the worst of tyranny.

March 3 — We have given over all hopes of receiving assistance from Goliad or Refugio. Colonel Travis harangued the garrison and concluded by exhorting them, in case the enemy should carry the fort, to fight to the last gasp and render their victory even more serious to them than to us. This was followed by three cheers.

March 4 — Shells have been falling into the fort like hail during the day, but without effect. About dusk in the evening, we observed a man running toward the fort, pursued by about half a dozen Mexican cavalry. The bee hunter immediately knew him to be the old pirate who had gone to Goliad, and calling to the two hunters, he sallied out of the fort to the relief of the old man, who was hard pressed. I followed close after. Before we reached the spot the Mexicans were close on the heel of the old man, who stopped suddenly, turned upon his pursuers, discharged his rifle, and one of the enemy fell from his horse. The chase was renewed, but finding that he would be overtaken and cut to pieces, he now turned again and, to the amazement of the enemy, became the assailant in his turn. He clubbed his gun and dashed among them like a wounded tiger, and they fled like sparrows. By this time we reached the spot and in the ardor of the moment followed some distance before we saw that our retreat to the fort was cut off by another detachment of cavalry. Nothing was to be done but to fight our way through. We were all of the same mind. "Go ahead!" cried I, and they shouted, "Go ahead, Colonel!" We dashed among them, and a bloody conflict ensued. They were about twenty in number, and they stood their ground. After the fight had continued about five minutes, a detachment was seen issuing from the fort to our relief, and the Mexicans scampered off, leaving eight of their comrades upon the field. But we did not escape unscathed, for both the pirate and the bee hunter were mortally wounded, and I received a saber cut across the forehead. The old man died, without speaking, as soon as we entered the fort. We bore my young friend to his bed, dressed his wounds, and I watched beside him. He lay without complaint or manifesting pain until about midnight, when he spoke, and I asked him if he wanted anything. "Nothing," he replied, but drew a sigh that seemed to rend his heart as he added, "Poor Kate of Nacogdoches!" His eyes were filled with tears as he continued, "Her words were prophetic, Colonel," and then he sang in a low voice that resembled the sweet notes of his own devoted Kate:

> But toom cam' the saddle, all bluidy to see,
> And hame ca' the steed, but hame never cam' he.

He spoke no more and, a few minutes after died.
Poor Kate, who will tell this to thee!

March 5 — Pop, pop, pop! Bom, bom, bom! throughout the day. No time for memorandums now. Go ahead! Liberty and independence forever![12]

The simplest way to begin a brief explanation of this account is to say that it was not written by Crockett. It was not included in the original version of this book for that reason. In retrospect I felt that it should be included since it has served as an eyewitness account of the Alamo in the past. Since there are other accounts that clearly are phoney, or at least suspect, there is enough reason to include this one.

This account of the Alamo siege appeared in *Col. Crockett's Exploits and Adventures in Texas, Written by Himself,* published in the early summer of 1836. It was written by Richard Penn Smith (1799-1854) at the suggestion of E.L. Carey of the Philadelphia publishers E.L. Carey and A. Hart. Carey and Hart had a load of copies of the ghostwritten *Account of Colonel Crockett's Tour to the North and Down East* (1835) that they could not sell. Carey felt that if Smith could concoct an *autobiographical* account of Crockett's adventures in Texas, it not only would sell itself but move the older books as well. Carey's instinct proved correct. Smith wrote the book in a matter of days, supplying the printer, in the morning, with new material he had written the night before. The books did sell, and the account quickly became a part of Alamo lore.

The book is written in the form of a *journal* or *diary* supposedly kept by Crockett on his way to and at the Alamo. The survival of this diary is explained by it having been appropriated by Mexican General Manuel Castrillón in the aftermath of the Alamo battle. It is later found after the Mexican army's defeat at San Jacinto by a Charles T. Beale. In some tellings it is found on Castrillón's body after the battle. The implication is that the diary is so valuable that Castrillón would not have parted with it even after six weeks of having found it, and while unsuccessfully fighting for his life.

This "Crockett" account has been incorporated into a number books on Crockett and the Alamo down through the years, most notably Constance Rourke's *Davy Crockett* (1934), and Virgil E. Baugh's *Rendezvous at the Alamo* (1960). Both authors rely more on the diary for Crockett's journey through Texas than on the events at the Alamo. Also, both rely on it for substantial parts of their books while expressing some doubt about its authorship. Rourke stated that "…'Exploits' as a whole seems to have a partial basis in fact," and "[Crockett] could hardly have enjoyed all the magnificent adventures attributed to him between its covers, even though any one of them is plausible."[13]

Baugh wrote that "Whether the 'autobiography' [of which *Exploits and Adventures* was a part] was written by Crockett in collaboration with someone or exclusively by him with only editorial corrections by some other hand is unimportant. What is important is that the authentic picture of the man shines forth from its pages unmistakable, unique, identifiable, as it never has from any biography of the man yet written."[14]

The Crockett diary also has appeared in books of eyewitness accounts of American history and the history of the American West to represent the Alamo battle. In these cases the account appears in edited form, leaving out the more colorful interaction between Crockett and his companions. As in the case of Rourke and Baugh, the editors of the eyewitness books used the account while expressing some doubt as to its authenticity. In Henry Steele Commager and Allan Nevins' *Heritage of America* (1939 and 1949) the editors state, "The authenticity of this autobiographical fragment is open to doubt, but its accuracy as a picture of the siege is accepted." This book later appeared as *Witness to America* (1999) edited by Stephen Ambrose and Douglas Brinkley, including post World War II accounts up to those of the present day. The Alamo entry remained the same. In David Colbert's *Eyewitness to the American West* (1998), the editor stated, "This last testament has been both quoted and disputed by historians since it first appeared, but it is considered faithful to the facts and is irresistibly colorful."[15]

These examples only serve to show the irresistible pull of an account as long as it conveys the idea of an "eyewitness" account, especially if it has a famous name attached to it.[16]

2.9
Unidentified Witness, July 9, 1836
From an article by an unidentified reporter in the *Morning Courier and New York Enquirer*

After the Mexicans had got possession of the Alamo, the fighting had ceased, and it was clear day light, *six* Americans were discovered near the wall yet unconquered, and who were instantly surrounded and ordered by Gen. Castrillon to surrender, and who did so under a promise of his protection, finding resistance any longer in vain — indeed, perfect madness. Castrillon was brave and not cruel, and disposed to save them. He marched them up to that part of the fort where stood "His Excellency," surrounded by his murderous crew, his sycophantic officers. DAVID CROCKETT was one of the six. The steady, fearless step, and undaunted tread, together with the bold demeanor of this hardy veteran — "his firmness and noble bearing," to give the words of the narrator, had a most powerful effect on himself and Castrillon. Nothing daunted, he marched up boldly in front of Santa Anna, looked him steadfastly in the face, while Castrillon addressed "His Excellency," "Sir here are *six* prisoners I have taken alive; how shall I dispose of them?" Santa Anna looked at Castrillon fiercely, flew into a most violent rage, and replied, "Have I not told you before how to dispose of them? Why do you bring them to *me*?" At the same time his brave officers drew and plunged their swords into the bosoms of their defenseless prisoners!! So anxious and intent were these blood-thirsty cowards to gratify the malignity of this inveterate tyrant, that Castrillon barely escaped being run through in the scuffle, himself. Castrillon rushed from the scene, apparently horror-struck — sought his quarters and did not leave them for some days, and hardly ever spoke to Santa Anna after. This was the fate of poor Crockett, and in which there can be no mistake. Who the five others were, I have not been able to learn. Three other wounded prisoners were discovered and brought before "His Excellency," and were ordered to be instantly shot. There are certain reasons why the name of the narrator of these events should not be made known. I will only repeat that he was an *eye-witness.*[17]

The first known appearance of this letter was in the *Morning Courier and New York Enquirer* on July 9, 1836, and then it made its way southwest in various newspapers. It also appeared in the *Richmond Enquirer* on July 15 and in the *Frankfort (Kentucky) Commonwealth* on July 27. Not only is the reporter of this story anonymous but so is the alleged witness. The witness is often described as a Mexican officer, but there is really nothing in the letter that indicated this. His identification as a Mexican officer most likely results from the assumption that only one of the Mexican officers would have been in a position to have witnessed the executions after the Alamo battle.

The description of David Crockett as one of the executed prisoners is important since this is one of the first if not *the* first to single out Crockett as one of these victims. There had been earlier newspaper articles that described the whole Alamo garrison as having been executed after they had surrendered, with Crockett being named as one of the slain. There also were articles that described Crockett and others as having attempted to surrender but were told that there was to be no mercy for them and so they continued fighting until all were killed. Somehow these tales grew into the story of Crockett having been executed. This letter eventually became one of the corner stones of evidence used to put forth the theory that Crockett did not die in combat at the Alamo.

Although the reporter of this account is unidentified, he was very probably William H. Attree. Attree had written for the *Courier and Enquirer* as well as the *Star* and was also the police reporter for one of New York City's newest penny papers the *New York Transcript*. He traveled to Texas in early March 1836 armed with a letter of introduction to David G. Burnett from the *Transcript* editor Billings Hayward.[18]

There is no concrete proof that Attree was originator of this letter, but the letter is attributed to a correspondent of the *Courier and Enquirer*. Attree had written for that paper, and since he was in Texas at the time, it is very likely that he was responsible for it. If this is so, it is necessary to evaluate the letter's reliability in reference to Attree's background.

Before traveling to Texas, Attree had spent five months traveling around the United States trying to raise volunteers for Texas. Apparently he was enthused enough with Texas to leave New York and go there himself "with the land boomers," as one author has put it.[19] This description may not be just a colorful exaggeration since Attree's editor at the *Courier and Enquirer* was James W. Webb, who was involved heavily in Texas land speculation with Samuel Swartwout, the Collector of the Port of New York, and others. There is evidence that once in Texas, Attree became a despatch rider for the Texan army, probably under Thomas Jefferson Green. Green himself was intensely interested in raising volunteers for the Texan army since a coveted rank of brigadier general went along with raising a certain number of men. Green embarked on a vigorous recruiting drive in the U.S. fueled by the emotional impact of the Alamo's fall. Recognizing the propaganda value of the "big names" at the Alamo, he recruited for a company in David Crockett's district in Tennessee and also attempted to raise a company around James Bowie's brother Rezin as commander.[20]

Attree was known in New York for his flamboyant style and sometimes outrageous stories.[21] With his colorful pen and his New York newspaper connections, he would have been invaluable to someone like Green as well as the land speculators. Nothing would have raised sentiment more for Texas than the story of helpless prisoners being executed by Santa Anna after the Alamo battle, especially if one of those prisoners was the popular Crockett. This story would have served the dual purpose of raising volunteers for Texas and helping to keep Santa Anna a prisoner of the Texans, thus providing security for the land speculators.

Did this unidentified witness really exist? If he did exist, did he give his story directly to Attree? If so, is the story true? Does the story contain journalistic license excusable in the noble cause of battling a tyrannical Santa Anna? The answers to all of these questions remain unknown at this time.

2.10
Juan N. Almonte, September 7, 1836
From a letter by George M. Dolson to his brother printed in the *Detroit Democratic Free Press*

...on the morning the Alamo was captured, between the hours of five and six o'clock, General Castrillon, who fell at the battle of St. Jacinto, entered the back room of the Alamo, and there found Crockett and five other Americans, who had defended it until defense was useless; they appeared very much agitated when the Mexican soldiers undertook to rush in after their General, but the humane General ordered his men to keep out, and, placing his hand on his breast, said "here is a hand and a heart to protect you; come with me to the General-in-Chief, and you shall be saved." Such redeeming traits, while they ennoble in our estimation this worthy officer, yet serve to show in a more heinous light the damning atrocities of the chief. The brave but unfortunate men were marched to the tent of Santa Anna. Colonel Crockett was in the rear, had his arms folded, and appeared bold as the lion as he passed my informant (Almonte.) Santa Anna's interpreter knew Colonel Crockett and said to my informant, the one behind is the famous Crockett. When brought in the presence of Santa Anna, Castrillon said to him, "Santa Anna the august, I deliver up to you six brave prisoners of war." Santa Anna replied, "who has given you orders to take prisoners, I do not want to see those men living - shoot them." As the monster uttered these words each officer turned his face the other way, and the hell hounds of the tyrant dispatched the six in his presence, and within six feet of his person....[22]

This letter, like the previous one, originated on Galveston Island, and it has become one of the important pieces of evidence in supporting the theory that David Crockett was one of those executed after the Alamo battle. It is more accurately described and is more popularly known as the "Dolson account."

The account is attributed to Col. Almonte, but even that is subject to debate. It comes to us in the form of a letter written by George M. Dolson to his brother, which appeared in the *Detroit Democratic Free Press* six months after the Alamo's fall. The original of this letter has never been located. The scenario by which this account allegedly was obtained is somewhat contrived. According to Dolson's letter, a secret meeting was convened for no other purpose than determining Crockett's fate at the Alamo. Those present at this alleged meeting were Colonel James Morgan, the commander of Galveston Island where the Mexican army prisoners of war were being held, a Mexican officer, who is later identified, by Dolson, as Almonte, and Dolson himself acting as interpreter.

Besides the fact that Almonte was educated in the U.S., could speak English, and would not have needed an interpreter, he was not even on Galveston Island at the time this interview allegedly took place. In addition, Col. Morgan, who supposedly took the trouble of setting up this interview to elicit this information, never bothered to set anything down in writing about it.

What would have been the reason for trying to establish that Crockett was brutally executed after being taken prisoner? Dolson gives an answer later on in the letter.

Such an act [the executions] I consider murder of the blackest kind. Do you think that he [Santa Anna] can be released? No - exhaust all the mines of Mexico, but it will not release him. The combined powers of Europe cannot release him, for before they can come to his release, Texas will have released him of his existence, but I coincide with the secretary of war, as to the disposal to be made of him, that is to try him as a felon. Strict justice demands it and reason sanctions it.[23]

The purpose of this letter like the preceding one is to incite popular feeling against Santa Anna and to prevent his release from Texas. This becomes significant when Dolson, later on in his letter, boasts,

The enlistment roll of Capt. A. B. Tweetzer's [Alonzo Bowman Sweitzer] company of volunteers, from Cincinnati, will always show that George M. Dolson is orderly sergeant of that company.[24]

Sweitzer's company was not recruited by Thomas Jefferson Green, but Sweitzer enrolled the company in Green's brigade when the company was mustered into service on May 18, 1836. Dolson's letter, like the one by the correspondent of the *Courier and Enquirer*, could have only helped Green's recruitment drive.

Dolson's sentiments concerning the fate of Santa Anna closely resemble those of Samuel Swartwout, the Collector of the Port of New York. It should be remembered that Swartwout's speculations in Texas land relied on the incarceration of Santa Anna until all possibility of Mexico reconquering Texas could be removed. Swartwout had so much riding on Santa Anna's continued captivity and was so incensed by the possibility of his release that he even called for the death of David G. Burnet, Texas's first president.[25]

Col. Morgan was involved heavily in the land speculation business with Swartwout. It would have been in the best financial interests of both of these men and many others if Santa Anna remained a prisoner of the Texans. It is possible that this account may have originated from motives other than the strict desire to obtain information about the Alamo battle. (For the account from Almonte's Journal see: #2.7.)

George M. Dolson's grave, Oakwood Cemetary, Austin, Texas.

Photo by Cynthia Wolf

Chapter Three

19TH CENTURY

And behold, a great wind came across the wilderness,
and struck the four corners of the house,
and it fell upon the young people, and they are dead,
and I alone have escaped to tell you.

— Job I:19

3.1
Antonio Lopez de Santa Anna, 1837
From his *Manifesto que de sus Operaciones en la
Campaña de Tejas Dirige a sus Conciudadanos*

Béxar was held by the enemy and it was necessary to open the door
to our future operations by taking it. It would have been easy enough to
have surprised it, because those occupying it did not have the faintest
news of the march of our army. I entrusted, therefore, the operation to
one of our generals, who with a detachment of cavalry, part of the dragoons mounted on infantry officers' horses, should have fallen on Béxar
in the early morning of February 23, 1836. My orders were concise and
definite. I was most surprised, therefore, to find the said general a quarter of a league from Béxar at ten o'clock of that day, awaiting new orders.
This, perhaps, was the result of inevitable circumstances; and, although
the city was captured, the surprise that I had ordered to be carried out
would have saved the time consumed and the blood shed later in the taking of the Alamo.

Having taken Béxar and the proceeds of the small booty having been sold by the commissary department to meet its immediate needs, all of which I communicated to the government ... the enemy fortified itself in the Alamo, overlooking the city. A siege of a few days would have caused its surrender, but it was not fit that the entire army should be detained before an irregular fortification hardly worthy of the name. Neither could its capture be dispensed with, for bad as it was, it was well equipped with artillery, had a double wall, and defenders who, it must be admitted, were very courageous and caused much damage to Béxar. Lastly, to leave a part of the army to lay siege to it, the rest continuing on its march, was to leave our retreat, in case of a reverse, if not entirely cut off, at least exposed, and to be unable to help those besieging it, who could be reinforced only from the main body of the advancing army. This would leave to the enemy a rallying point, although it might be only for a few days. An assault would infuse our soldiers with that enthusiasm of the first triumph that would make them superior in the future to those of the enemy. It was not my judgment alone that moved me to decide upon it, but the general opinion expressed in a council of war, made up of generals, that I called even though the discussions which such councils give rise to have not always seemed to me appropriate. Before undertaking the assault and after the reply given to Travis who commanded the enemy fortification, I still wanted to try a generous measure, characteristic of Mexican kindness, and I offered life to the defenders who would surrender their arms and retire under oath not to take them up again against Mexico. Colonel Don Juan Nepomuceno Almonte, through whom this generous offer was made, transmitted to me their reply which stated that they would let us know if they accepted and if not, they would renew the fire at a given hour. They decided on the latter course and their decision irrevocably sealed their fate.

On the night of the fifth of March, four columns having been made ready for the assault under the command of their respective officers, they moved forward in the best order and with the greatest silence, but the imprudent huzzas of one of them awakened the sleeping vigilance of the defenders of the fort and their artillery fire caused such disorder among our columns that it was necessary to make use of the reserves. The Alamo was taken, this victory that was so much and so justly celebrated at the time, costing us seventy dead and about three hundred wounded, a loss that was also later judged to be avoidable and charged, after the disaster of San Jacinto, to my incompetence and precipitation. I do not know of a way in which any fortification, defended by artillery, can be carried by assault without the personal losses of the attacking party being greater than those of the enemy, against whose walls and fortifications the brave assailants can present only their bare breasts. It is easy enough, from a desk in a peaceful office, to pile up charges against a general out on the field but this cannot prove anything more than the praiseworthy desire of making war less disastrous. But its nature being such, a general has no power over its immutable laws. Let us weep at the tomb of the brave Mexicans who died at the Alamo defending the honor and the rights of their country. They won a lasting claim to fame and the country can never forget their heroic names.[1]

This account appeared as part of a pamphlet written by Santa Anna as an explanation for his actions during the Texan campaign. Like a variety of such pamphlets written by a number of participants, it justifies the actions of its author and shifts blame to others for the disastrous campaign. (For other accounts by or attributed to Santa Anna see #1.9, 1.11. 1.15, 4.31, and 4.33.)

3.2
Ramón Martínez Caro, 1837
From his *Verdadera Idea de la Primera Campaña de Tejas y Sucesos Ocurridos Después de la accion de San Jacinto*

His Excellency finally reached the Río Grande. There he found the brigade of General Ramírez y Sesma which he ordered to proceed to San Antonio de Béxar. The general-in-chief, his staff, and the 50 mounted men of his escort followed a few days later. We overtook the brigade before it reached Béxar, about two days' journey from that place, and His Excellency took over the command in order to enter the city, which he did on the 26th of February, without encountering any resistance on the part of the Americans. According to the citizens of the place, the enemy, which numbered 156, took refuge in the so-called fortress of the Alamo* the moment they saw our troops approaching. On the following day, His

---

* A mere corral and nothing more, built about 550 paces from the town, on the opposite side of the San Antonio River. The town is named after the river. Many of the walls of the fort are of adobe.

Excellency placed a battery of two cannons and a mortar within 600 paces of the fort and began a bombardment, taking possession at the same time of several small isolated houses that were to the left. These were nearer to the enemy's position and were occupied by our troops who suffered the loss of several killed and wounded in the operation. Around the fortress there were ditches which were used by the enemy to fire upon our troops, while our soldiers, in order to carry out their orders to fire, were obliged to abandon the protection that the walls afforded them, and suffered the loss of one or two men, either killed or at least wounded, in each attempt to advance. During one of our charges at night, His Excellency ordered Colonel Juan Bringas to cross a small bridge with five or six men. He had no sooner started to carry out his instructions than the enemy opened fire upon this group and killed one man. In trying to recross the bridge the colonel fell into the water and saved himself only by a stroke of good luck.

On the 29th or 30th, His Excellency sent Colonel Bringas to meet the brigade of General Gaona with instructions for him to send, by forced marches, the picked companies of his brigade. These arrived in Béxar on the 4th of March. The following day the orders for the assault which was to take place on the 6th were issued.

It has already been stated that when we entered Béxar we were assured by the citizens that there were only 156 Americans. In the time intervening between our entrance into the city and the day set for the assault, the enemy received two small reinforcements from Gonzáles that succeeded in breaking through our lines and entering the fort. The first of these consisted of four men who gained the fort one night, and the second was a party of twenty-five who introduced themselves in the day-time. Two messengers succeeded in leaving the fort, one of whom was the Mexican, Seguín. The entry of these reinforcements and the departure of the messengers were witnessed by the whole army and need no particular proof.* At the time of the assault, therefore, the enemy's force consisted of 183 men.

Early in the morning of the 6th the four attacking columns as well as the reserve took up their respective positions as assigned by the general order of the 5th, a copy of which was transmitted to the supreme government. From this it will be seen that our force numbered 1400 men in

---

* It is to be kept in mind that their reinforcement succeeded in entering the fort and the messengers in leaving it through no lack of vigilance, for 600 men, cavalry, and infantry surrounded it.

all. At daybreak and at the agreed signal our whole force moved forward to the attack. The first charge was met with a deadly fire of shot and shell from the enemy, the brave colonel of the Toluca Battalion, Francisco Duque, being among the first who fell wounded. His column wavered as a result of his fall while the other three columns were held in check on the other fronts. His excellency, seeing the charge waver, gave orders for the reserve to advance.

The brave General Juan Valentín Amador, General Pedro Ampudia, Colonel Esteban Mora, and Lieutenant-Colonel Marcial Aguirre succeeded in gaining a foothold on the north side where the strife was bitterest, which encouraged the soldiers in their advance and resulted in their capture of the enemy's artillery on that side. The enemy immediately took refuge in the inside rooms of the fortress, the walls of which had been previously bored to enable them to fire through the holes. Generals Amador and Ampudia trained the guns upon the interior of the fort to demolish it as the only means of putting an end to the strife.

On the opposite side, where there was another entrance to the enemy's stronghold, the resistance was equally stubborn, but Colonels Juan Morales and José Miñón, commanding the attacking column, succeeded in overcoming it. Though the bravery and intrepidity of the troops was general, we shall always deplore the costly sacrifice of the 400 men who fell in the attack. Three hundred were left dead on the field and more than a hundred of the wounded died afterwards as a result of the lack of proper medical attention and medical facilities in spite of the fact that their injuries were not serious. This is a well-known fact, as stated before, which made the fate of those who lingered in pain and suffering without the proper comfort or relief. The enemy died to a man and its loss may be said to have been 183 men, the sum total of their force. Six women who were captured were set at liberty.* Among the 183 killed there were five who were discovered by General Castrillón hiding after the assault. He took them immediately to the presence of His Excellency who had come up by this time. When he presented the prisoners, he was severely reprimanded for not having killed them on the spot, after which

---

*   In the report made on that date to the supreme government by His Excellency it is stated that more than 600 of the enemy were killed. I myself wrote that report and must now confess that I put down that number at the command of His Excellency. In stating the truth now, I must say that only 183 men were killed. I call upon the whole army to witness my statement.

he turned his back upon Castrillón while the soldiers stepped out of their ranks and set upon the prisoners until they were all killed.*[2]

---

* We all witnessed this outrage which humanity condemns but which was committed as described. This is a cruel truth, but I cannot omit it. More cruel falsehoods have been promulgated against my character.

Ramón Martínez Caro was the civilian secretary of Santa Anna during the Texan campaign. He was captured at the Battle of San Jacinto and remained a very traumatized hostage of the Texan army along with Santa Anna. His story of the Texan campaign and the Alamo battle was published as a pamphlet after his return to Mexico in 1837.

3.3
Pedro de Amupdia, February 21, 1837
As a certification written on June 22, 1836, and published in the newspaper *El Mosquito Mexicano* in February of 1837

I certify: that the captain with the rank of lieutenant colonel, attached to the corps of Engineers, don José Enrique de la Peña, in the assault made on the fort of the Alamo functioned as adjutant of the señor colonel, commander of one of the columns, don Francisco Duque, and that in the strength of the fray he crossed through the fires [gunfire] to inform that the aforementioned chief was wounded, with the object that his second, the general don Manuel Fernández Castrillón, to replace him, as had been earlier commanded. This young man with valor clambered up, in my sight, on the palisade that formed part of the enclosed area and in the interior did his duty as good officer....

Pedro Ampudia (?-1869) was born in Cuba and was the commander of the Mexican artillery at the battle of the Alamo. His certification and the two following describe the action of José Enrique de la Peña, who served as an aide to Colonel Francisco Duque during the Mexican Army First Division's march into Texas. There also is a similar certification of praise for de la Peña written by General Juan José Urrea. It is not included here since Urrea was not at the Alamo battle, and his letter merely voices his agreement with the others. It is unlikely that these four officers spontaneously would write certifications praising de la Peña, or any other soldier for that matter. They probably were solicited by de la Peña to help advance his career after the Texas campaign. Following the campaign de la Peña engaged in a war of words in the newspapers with General Vicente Filisola, regarding Filisola's handling of the campaign after the Mexican defeat at San Jacinto. De la Peña published these certifications in the newspaper *El Mosquito Mexicano* in February of 1837 to defend his own actions during their exchange.[3] (For accounts by or attributed to de la Peña see accounts 4.30 and 4.35.)

3.4

Francisco Duque, February 21, 1837

As a certification written on July 11, 1836, and published in the newspaper *El Mosquito Mexicano* in February of 1837

I certify: that in the section of the first brigade that I was commanding at Béjar composed of the battalions of Zapadores, Aldama and mine [Toluca]; the lieutenant colonel of army don José Enrique de la Peña discharged the functions of command major with uncommon zeal and liveliness. I equally certify: that having been named to command the second attack column in the assault on the Alamo, on receiving the final orders of the general in chief, I recall that although Peña was assigned to the reserve column, I had in him the greatest confidence and desired that he accompany me. His Excellency acceded to my request and Peña confirmed the advantageous concept that I had formed of him. He advanced with the enthusiasm that is his characteristic and with much calmness at the head of the column; and when I was wounded in the proximity of the enemy parapets, he was the only one of my aides of whom I was able to arrange to call the field officer who was named to succeed me. Peña then without being daunted by the danger, went to the other end of the enemy line, to find the general don Manuel Fernandez Castrillón, who came up from the rear guard of the reserve column, and he was timely in communicating the notice that I was out of the combat. It would be necessary to have seen the lively fire of cannon, of rifle and of musket that was made across the front, that Peña crossed a second time, in order to appreciate the merit that he earned in this expedition's record and I am not able to say enough about this valiant officer.

Francisco Duque (1792-1854) was the colonel of the Toluca battalion and led one of the attack columns during the battle of the Alamo. He was wounded outside the walls during the attack, and de la Peña rushed to inform General Castrillón of the fact. Duque's certification was one of those published by de la Peña in *El Mosquito Mexicano* in February of 1837.

3.5
Augustin Amat, February 21, 1837
As a certification written on August 17, 1836, and published in the newspaper *El Mosquito Mexicano* in February of 1837

I certify: that the lieutenant colonel of the army, captain don José Enrique de la Peña, command major of the force that the senor colonel Duque was commanding at Bejar whose commission was confirmed with the liveliness and zeal that was so known in this officer: that in the assault made on the fort of the Alamo the 6th of March of the present year he was one of the most outstanding in the column commanded by the colonel cited, crossing the front twice in that lethal fire, to communicate an important order, and I know for certain the efforts he made being inside, of regularizing the attack and saving the victims hurt in those cases of confusion...

Augustin Amat was the commander of the Zapadores battalion (combat engineers) of the Mexican force at the Alamo battle. His certification was published by de la Peña along with the previous ones.

3.6
Ben, 1838
According to Chester Newell in his
History of the Revolution in Texas

"I," says a highly respectable officer of the General's Staff, "had repeated conversations with Ben relative to the fall of the Alamo. He knew but little. He stated that Santa Anna and Almonte occupied the same house in the town of Bexar, and that he cooked for both; that, on the night previous to the storming of the fort, Santa Anna ordered him to have coffee ready for them all night, that both he and Almonte were conversing constantly, and did not go to bed; that they went out about midnight, and about two or three o'clock returned together to the house; that Santa Anna ordered coffee immediately, threatening to run him through the body if it was not instantly brought; that he served them with coffee; that Santa Anna appeared agitated and that Almonte remarked 'it would cost them much;' that the reply was, 'it was of no importance what the cost was, that it must be done.'

'After drinking coffee,' says Ben, 'they went out, and soon I saw rockets ascending in different directions, and shortly after I heard musketry and cannon, and by the flashes I could distinguish large bodies of Mexican troops under the walls of the Alamo. I was looking out of a window in the town, about five hundred yards from the Alamo, commanding a view of it. The report of the cannon, rifles and musketry, was tremendous. It shortly died away, day broke upon the scene, and Santa Anna and Almonte returned, when the latter remarked, that 'another such victory would ruin them.' They then directed me to go with them, to the fort, and point out the bodies of Bowie and Travis - Whom I had before known - which I did. The sight was most horrid."[4]

Ben is somewhat of an enigmatic witness. He is described as having been a steward on board several American vessels and having accompanied Almonte from New York to Vera Cruz and then to Bexar. It is still difficult to understand how or why he would have been able to identify Travis and Bowie. Ben's account comes to us third hand. Ben tells a "highly respectable officer" who in turn tells Chester Newell who publishes the story in his book *A History of the Revolution in Texas - particularly of the War of 1835 & '36.* In the foreword to his book Newell reports that he received "...much important information from repeated conversations with several men distinguished in the war of '35-'36." He names Sam Houston in addition to General Lamar, General F. Huston, Colonel Poe, Colonel Ward, Colonel Neil [sic], and Captain Shackleford. Any one of these may have been the officer who provided the information on Ben.[5] (For another account by or attributed to Ben see #3.7.)

3.7

Santa Anna's Servant, 1840

According to Col. Edward Stiff in his *Texan Emigrant*

The assault took place on the night of the 7th [*sic*], and some circumstances attending it were narrated to me by a gentleman formerly an officer in the Texan army, which he had obtained from Santa Anna's servant, who after the battle of San Jacinto was cook for Gen. Houston. The statements of this servant were generally relied on by those who knew him, and he contradicted in the most positive terms the oft repeated rumor that the dead bodies of the Americans were burnt. On the night of the 7th [*sic*], Santa Anna ordered this servant to prepare and keep refreshments ready all night, and he stated that Santa Anna appeared cast down and discontented, and did not retire to rest at all. That accompanied by his private Secretary the General went out about 11 o'clock and did not return until 3 in the morning; that he served them with coffee of which Santa Anna took but little, and seemed much excited, and observed, to Almonte, that if the garrison could be induced to surrender, he would be content; for said he, if they will not, I well know, that every man before the dawn of day must, unprepared, meet his God. But what more can I do; my summonses, said he, are treated with disdain; it appears to me the only alternative presented is to assault the garrison; we cannot delay longer here wasting the resources of the nation and any termination of the affair will relieve me of a load of anxiety. He further stated that at 4 o'clock Santa Anna and other officers left the house, and very soon a tremendous discharge of cannon told that the work of death was began; he saw rockets in awful brilliancy blazing through the darkness of the night, and the walls and grounds of the Alamo reflected the light so that from a window he could plainly perceive columns of Mexican troops around the fort and ascending the walls on ladders, and that the whole interior of the Alamo was perfectly illuminated, as he supposed, by the firing of the Americans within, and that the old servant feelingly remarked that he liked master Santa Anna, but that when he heard the thunders of the artillery and saw blazing rockets gleaming through the air, he thought of Master George Washington and old Virginia, and prayed to God that the Americans might whip.

Before day light the firing had ceased and every thing was again wrapped in silence and gloom, when Santa Anna and his staff returned, one of them, remarking that the victory had cost more than it was worth and that many such would ruin them. At day light this servant who had

seen Col. Crockett at the city of Washington many years ago, and perhaps Col. Travis and Bowie, was taken to the fort to designate their
bodies; he done so, and found no less than 16 dead Mexicans around the
corpse of Colonel Crockett and one across it with the huge knife of Davy
buried in the Mexican's bosom to the hilt. He stated that these three bodies were interred in the same grave separate from all the rest, and that he
heard the Mexican officers say that their own loss was about 1200 men.[6]

This account that comes to us via Edward Stiff in his book
The Texan Emigrant is obviously a variation of that of Ben's.
Stiff also repeated the same story seven years later in his *A New
History of Texas.* This version does not refer to Ben by name, but
it does describe a very early interview with Susanna Dickinson
in which she provided information that she was accompanied
from Bexar by Santa Anna's servant. It states, "...with this
infant and Col. Travis' black man she [Dickinson] was escorted
to the Texan head quarters, then at Gonzales on the
Guadalope [*sic*] River, Santa Anna sending his own servant to
assist her safe."[7] In Newell's book Ben is directed to point out
the bodies of Bowie and Travis because it is explained that he
had known them before. In Stiff's version Ben designates the
bodies because he had seen Crockett in Washington years
before "...and perhaps Col. Travis and Bowie...."[8] If the
account in the Stiff book is accurate, then it adds more evidence to the debate regarding Crockett's death. However, it is
more likely that Stiff may have confused Ben's account with
one of those of Joe. (For another account by or attributed to
Ben see #3.6.)

3.8
Unidentified Mexican Army Sources, 1848
As reported and published by General Vicente Filisola in his
Memorias Para la Historia de la Guerra de Tejas published by R.
Rafael

The day of the twenty-fourth [February] was spent in reconnoitering
the fortifications of the Alamo and the river crossings in order to prepare
the operations that were to be taken in sequence until they overcome
the colonists, adventurers or bandits that under such a mask had come
from the United States to harass a friendly nation that had no way

offended them, which group now found itself shut up in the quarters of the Alamo. With this purpose in mind during the night two batteries were set up, and the next day, the twenty-fifth, at dawn they opened fire on the enemy parapets, which did likewise in the direction of our batteries.

The commander in chief, with the companies of chasseurs [cazadores] from Jimenez and Matamoros crossed the river and took up a position in the houses and huts to the south of the Alamo about half a rifle shot's distance from the enemy parapets. At the same time our men were digging a trench near Mr. Mullen's house. In these operations, with the fierce fire from the enemy, we had one corporal and a chasseur from Matamoras killed, and four wounded, and two more wounded of those from Jimenez. Our fire ceased in the afternoon with the conclusion of the movements that had been decided upon for the moment by the commander in chief. The latter, wishing to step up the action of the taking of the Alamo, that same day issued the following order to General Gaona, commander of the first infantry brigade.

During the night two trenches were constructed adjoining the houses located in the cottonwood grove of the Alamo for the infantry. The Matamoros battalion was established in them for their defense, and the cavalry posted itself on the hills to the east of the fort on the road to the town of Gonzáles and in the vicinity of the former Casa Mata. This operation was completed at eleven thirty at night, and during that time the enemy burned the hay and the wooden houses that were near them, or within their reach; a brisk norther blew up. The Alamo from then on was surrounded by our troops, with only the north side open.

On the twenty-sixth the norther continued to blow strongly, and in the morning there was a small skirmish between some of the enemy that ventured outside the walls and the advance sentries of the eastern line under the command of General Ramirez y Cesma [Sesma]. Our artillery fire continued, and it was answered only by a shot now and then from their guns. During the night they burned some other straw huts that were built against the walls and tried to obtain water and some wood. They were prevented from doing so by our advance sharpshooters.

On the twenty-seventh there was some fire from both sides, and Lieutenant Menchaca of the presidio guard was dispatched with a party to the ranches of Seguin and Flores to obtain corn, cattle and hog. An attempt was made to cut off the water to the rebels on the side of the old Mill, but that was not possible. It was noted that they were working incessantly on opening up a ditch on the inside of the parapet with the intention of enlarging it and giving more resistance against our artillery.

However, this operation was more harmful than useful to them. Since they had no walkway it was necessary for them on the day of the assault to stand up on it in order to fire with their guns, and thus they presented an immense target for our fire. In the afternoon the enemy became aware of the presidio group as they reconnoitered the points of the line, and they opened fire upon it. During the night the government was advised of the capture of the city in the terms that are included here. That same day General Gaona in Charco de la Peña received the order of the twenty-fifth to advance with the three battalions mentioned there, and these were immediately put on forced march to Béxar.

Since the supplies that had been brought from Rio Grande by the first division were about to be exhausted, the commander in chief sent the following communication to General Filisola who was with the reguard of the army.

"Most Excellent Sir: In a separate note Your Excellency will see the state of the first division facing the enemy and the need that there is for Your Excellency to order that the army brigades march with all haste since up to this time they are moving very slowly.

Your Excellency will give orders to the quartermaster general to gather together all supplies and set out on the march, avoiding delays that would be prejudicial to the service of the nation since these troops are very short on supplies.

Your Excellency will also have sent forward under escort and with forced marches the payroll with the commissary, for there is urgent need for money.

With the money Your Excellency will also arrange to send two packs of salt since there is not a single grain here, and it is greatly needed.

I charge Your Excellency to work efficiently and diligently, which is your wont to do, so that these orders may be carried out as all of them are urgent.

God and liberty. General headquarters in Béxar, February 27, 1836. Antonio López de Santa Anna. His Excellency General Don Vicente Filisola, second in command of the army of operations."

All these orders were carried out, but it was not possible for the brigades, provisions, etc., to move faster than had been designated for them in the itinerary that was laid out beforehand for the reasons that we have set forth. Also, only at the places that had been indicated for them in the itinerary was there water for the men and animals, and it was not possible to double the days' marches without having all the troops and cargoes scattered.

On the twenty-eighth news was received that two hundred men from Goliad were due to arrive to aid those against the Alamo, and the cannon fire continued almost all day long. On the twenty-ninth the Jiménez battalion was ordered to establish itself to the right of the cavalry, or to the left of the road that runs from the town of González, in order to surround and enclose even more of the Alamo. During the night General Cesma [Sesma] moved in, leaving the field covered, with the approval of the commander in chief.... He [Sesma] marched with a detachment of the Jiménez battalion and another from the Dolores regiment in the direction of Goliad expecting to meet up with the reinforcements that he had been told were coming to the aid of that place. However, since he had met no one and had had no news whatsoever concerning the troops, he returned to his post the next day, and the Jiménez battalion was again a part of general headquarters.

With our troops now in possession of the city of Béxar the commander in chief began to put into action his commands beginning on the night of the fifth of March to undertake the siege and capture of the Alamo if it were possible to surprise the enemy that were garrisoned there. To this end the general ordered that four attack columns commanded by their respective leaders—these all of unquestioned loyalty—should leave the city in greatest silence and order the operations to begin that same night.

But such was the enthusiasm and excitement of those brave men to meet up with the enemies of the name and the government of their country, that it degenerated into a sad and overwhelming lack of discretion of the sort that is never committed with impunity on such occasions. One of the columns began to shout "Long live the Republic" in a loud voice. This cry immediately resounded in the air and awakened the drowsy vigilance of the Texans. Thus warned of the approach of our army, they prepared to make a desperate defense and began to train their artillery in such manner that their fire shortly played terrible havoc in our ranks.

Although the bravery and daring of our soldiers hastened to fill in the ranks, after a long while they began to become disorganized and perhaps would have retreated if General Santa Anna who was watching had not ordered the reserves into action. With their support confidence and order were restored to our men, and the siege was begun. The enemy against whom it was directed strove to repel this attack with vigorous resistance and fire from all their arms. They were convinced that they had no other choice than to perish if only they could overcome us.

Thus, although the Alamo fell, this triumph cost the Mexican army more than seventy men dead and three hundred wounded.[9]

Vicente Filisola (1789-1850) was a native of Italy and the second in command of the Mexican force invading Texas in

General Vicente Filisola wrote two descriptions of the Alamo battle based on the eyewitness observations of others.

From *Remember Goliad* by Clarence Wharton (Courtesy of the Center for American History, University of Texas at Austin)

1836. He was not a witness to events at the Alamo, nor was he in San Antonio de Bexar at the time of the battle. He arrived in San Antonio on March 9, 1836. In 1848 and 1849 Filisola published two distinct works on the Texas campaign, both in two volumes, and both with the same title, *Memorias Para la Historia de la Guerra de Tejas.* In both works he wrote accounts of the battle based on information given to him by witnesses whom he did not identify. Since he was in San Antonio only three days after the battle, it is likely that his witnesses were those who took part in the siege and battle of the Alamo. This first description comes from his book published by R. Rafael in 1848-49.[10]

3.9
Unidentified Mexican Army Sources, 1849
As reported and published by General Vicente Filisola in his *Memorias Para la Historia de la Guerra de Tejas*, published by Ignacio Cumplido

In the staff meeting held for this purpose on the afternoon of March 5 several of the officers and leaders were of the opinion that they should have waited to have in hand the 12 caliber pieces that were supposed to arrive on the 7th or 8th. However, since the commander in chief's mind was made up, and the other officers were of the same opinion, it was agreed, and there were distributed to the participating members of the staff copies of the following plan of attack:

[Here Filisola inserts the attack orders of March 5, 1836, issued by Juan Valentine Amador. See account #1.14.]

On that same evening about nightfall it was reported that Travis Barnet [William Barret Travis], commander of the enemy garrison, through the intermediary of a woman, proposed to the general in chief that they would surrender arms and fort with everybody in it with the only condition of saving his life and that of all his comrades in arms. However, the answer had come back that they should surrender unconditionally, without guarantees, not even of life itself since there should be no guarantees for traitors. With this reply it is clear that all were determined to lose their existence, selling it as dearly as possible. Consequently they were to exercise vigilance in order not to be surprised at any time of the day or night.

The Mexican troops, at 4:00 A.M. on the 6th, were in their places as had been indicated in the instructions set forth. The artillery, as is gathered from the same instructions, was to remain inactive since they were not scheduled for anything, nor was it impossible in the darkness, and also according to the plans for the troops, to attack on four sides. There could be no artillery fire without blowing their comrades to bits. Thus the enemy enjoyed the advantage of not enduring the artillery fire throughout the whole time of the attack.

Their own artillery was ready and alert so that when the fatal trumpet sounded, there was no doubt that the ultimate scene was at hand—conquer or die. And if there had been any doubt, they were promptly disillusioned by the reckless shouting and *vivas* by the attacking columns as soon as they were seen. They were hit by a hail of shrapnel and bullets that the besieged men let loose on them. The attackers at the first sound of the trumpet were all on their feet at their respective posts with their arms at the ready.

The three columns that attacked on the West, North and East drew back or hesitated a little at the first fire from the enemy, but the example and the efforts of the leaders and officer soon caused them to resume the attack. They did so although the columns of the West and the East found no means of getting on top of the flat roofs of the small rooms, whose walls formed the enclosure, by means of a move to the right and the left simultaneously and unorganized, both swung to the North so that the three columns almost merged into a single mass. Whereupon, with their officers leading them on, they redoubled their efforts to mount the parapet or top of the wall of that front line. They went over finally with General Juan V. Amador being one of the first to reach the goal.

At the same time, to the South Colonels José Vicente Miñón and Juan Morales with their columns skillfully took advantage offered by some small jacales with walls of stone and mud which were next to the angle corresponding to the West. By a daring move they seized the cannon which was placed on a platform, as were all the others in the enclosure. They made their way into the fortified area of the quarters, assisting the efforts of General Amador. He had made use of the enemy's own artillery and turned them towards the doors of the small inner rooms in which the rebels had taken cover. From there they opened fire on the troops who were coming down from the parapet to the patio or plaza of the aforesaid enclosure so that all were finally killed by shrapnel, bullets and bayonets. Our losses were great and deplorable. Colonel Francisco Duque was one of the first who fell gravely wounded; from the ground where he lay prostrate, trampled upon by his own subordinates, he continued encouraging the attack. The assault, according to the manner in which it was first set up along the four sides of the enclosure, was very poorly planned and unmilitary. Our own men, in addition to the gunfire from the enemy had to suffer all that from our men themselves from the opposite sides. Since they attacked in a closed column, all the shots, the direction of which was turned somewhat downward, aimed the bullets towards the backs of those ahead of them. Thus it was that most of our dead and wounded that we suffered were caused by this misfortune. It may be said that not a fourth of them were the result of enemy fire. The way their cannon were positioned they were not alongside the wall, nor could they aim their fire against our men once they were surrounded by the wall itself. Nor could they use their rifles thus because the parapet did not have a banquette on the inner side. Consequently it was necessary in order for them to take the offensive to mount the parapet, where as is easily understood they could not remain for a single second without being killed.

Here is a list of our dead and wounded which was made up by General Juan de Andrade according to the accounts from the various corps.

| | Officers | | Troops | | |
Corps	Dead	Wounded	Dead	Wounded	Total
Sappers	1	3	2	21	27
Jiménez	1	3	8	22	34
Matamoros	—	2	7	35	44
Aldama	2	5	9	46	62
San Luis	2	—	7	37	46
Toluca	2	5	18	69	94
Dolores	—	—	1	3	4
Totals	8	18	52	233	311

A large number of wounded died because of poor care and lack of beds, surgical instruments, etc.

All of the enemy perished with only one old woman and a Negro slave left alive. The soldiers spared them out of compassion and because it was supposed that only by force had they been kept in such danger. Of the enemy dead there were 150 volunteers, 32 people of the Town of Gonzales who under cover of darkness joined the group two days before the attack on the fort, and some twenty people and tradesmen of the city of Béxar itself.

From the manner in which the attack was laid out our losses should have been greater than they were if the pieces of the enemy had [sic] could have been placed in the wall or enclosure. But the rooms of the latter of the inner part would not permit it, and those that were in the right location could fire only to the front. In addition the enemy did not have enough trained men to man the guns because good artillerymen cannot be just jumped up, as is done with rebellions. Furthermore, the instinct of the troops as they attacked, moving to the right and to the left on the North side and the movement made by Miñón and Morales with their column on the West corner of the South side which they attacked, left without a target all the guns that the enemy had located on the other three sides.

In short, be that as it may, the place fell to the possession of the Mexicans, and its defenders were all killed. It is most regrettable that after the first moments of the heat of the battle there should have been atrocious acts unworthy of the valor and resolve with which that operation was carried out, which forthwith left it with an indelible mark for history. These acts were denounced immediately by all who were disgusted upon witnessing them, and afterwards by the entire army who surely were not moved by any such feelings. They heard this with the horror and repugnance in keeping with the bravery and generosity of the Mexicans who can agree only with noble and generous actions. There were deeds that we refrain from relating because of the sorrow that the account of the events would cause us, and which with all good will and the honor of the republic we would wish had never existed. This is like others that preceded these while that poor imitation of a blockade or siege lasted. Although of a different sort and purely personal, they did not fail to scandalize and to cost a number of lives and wounded of the most inspired soldiers of the army.

In our opinion all that bloodshed of our soldiers as well as of our enemies was useless, having as its only objective an inconsiderate, childish and culpable vanity so that it might be proclaimed that Béxar had been reconquered by force of arms and that in the attack many men had died on both sides. As we have already stated, the defenders of the Alamo were ready to surrender with only the condition that their lives should be saved.

But let us suppose that such an arrangement had not existed, what would those wretched men do or hope for with more than 5,000 men surrounding them with no means of resistance nor any means of escape by retreat, nor that any friendly force that might have caused the Mexicans to raise the siege to save them, without food to keep them alive in that indefensible location? Even though there had been more than enough of what we had indicated that they lacked, by merely placing twenty artillery pieces properly, that poor wall could not have withstood one hour of cannon fire without being reduced to rubble with the poor quarters inside.

How much more glorious would have been the good name of Mexico if instead of so much blood and so many dead, the lives of the unbridled and ungrateful enemies of the Alamo, as well as Refugio, Goliad, and Guadalupe Victoria had been saved and the men sent to Mexico to engage in public works that would have in some degree indemnified the expenses that they had caused! And how great would not have been the fame of that same general in chief when without the loss of a single soldier and without any remorse whatsoever over the blood spilled later in San Jacinto, if he had brought back to his country that vast territory that the ungrateful protegés were trying to usurp.

Those were the consequences of the executions of the Alamo, of Refugio, Goliad, and Guadalupe Victoria. The rebels saw that with such conduct and design there could be no hope for a peaceful understanding and that they had no other way but to conquer, die or abandon the fruits and labors of their fondest dreams that they may have thought to be forever.[11]

This second description of the Alamo battle was related by Filisola in the book published by Ignacio Cumplido in 1849. As with the previous account, Filisola only reported events that were related to him by others.

3.10
John Sutherland, 1854
From his land claim for service in the Texas Revolution

On morning of commencement of siege, I was sent out by Col. Travis with John W. Smith to reconnoiter the enemy whom Col. had learned was in neighborhood of San Antonio. We found the enemy about 1-1/2 miles from the town, and in running to give the warning my horse fell, pitching me over his head and falling on my thighs - so injured my right knee and left arm as to render me unfit for the duties of the fort.

Being still able to ride, the Colonel sent me as above stated to Gonzales to urge the settlers to send him supplies and relief. A few days afterward, Genl. Sam Houston came to Gonzales, and on the same day we received the news that a friendly Mexican sent by Col. Navarro of the fall of the Alamo.[12]

John Sutherland (1792-1867) was born in Danville, Virginia. He emigrated to Texas from Alabama in 1835. Sutherland's tale has long been an established part of the Alamo story. It provides the dramatic opening scenes of the siege. His account is given here as it appeared in its earliest stage, as a petition for land based on his service in the Texas Revolution. The story continued to resurface in expanded and embellished forms for the next eighty years. Recent investigation into the Sutherland account by Austin researcher Thomas Ricks Lindley has revealed that there is plenty to doubt about it. Among the information that Lindley has brought out is the fact that there is no documentation which places Sutherland in San Antonio at the beginning of the Alamo siege on February 23, 1836, and that Sutherland had made a claim for land earlier than 1854 based on his service in the revolution in which he made no mention of the scene described above.[13] (For another account by or attributed to Sutherland see #3.37.)

3.11
Juan Nepomuceno Seguin, 1858
From his memoirs

On the 22d of February, at 2 o'clock P.M., General Santa Anna took possession of the city, with over 4000 men, and in the mean time we fell back on the Alamo.

On the 28th, the enemy commenced the bombardment, meanwhile we met in a Council of War, and taking into consideration our perilous situation, it was resolved by a majority of the council, that I should leave the fort, and proceed with a communication to Colonel Fannin, requesting him to come to our assistance. I left the Alamo on the night of the council; on the following day I met, at the Ranch of San Bartolo, on the Cibolo, Captain Desac [DeSauque], who, by orders of Fannin, had foraged on my ranch, carrying off a great number of beeves, corn, &c. Desac informed me that Fannin could not delay more than two days his arrival at the Cibolo, on his way to render assistance to the defenders of the Alamo. I therefore determined to wait for him. I sent Fannin, by express, the communication from Travis, informing him at the same time of the critical position of the defenders of the Alamo. Fannin answered me, through Lieutenant Finley, that he had advanced as far as "Rancho Nuevo," but, being informed of the movements of General Urrea, he had countermarched to Goliad, to defend that place; adding, that he could not respond to Travis' call, their respective commands being separate, and depending upon General Houston, then at Gonzales, with whom he advised me to communicate. I lost no time in repairing to Gonzales, and reported myself to the General, informing him of the purport of my mission. He commanded me to wait at Gonzales for further orders. General Houston ordered Captain Salvador Flores with 25 men of my company to the lower ranchos on the San Antonio river, to protect the inhabitants from the depredations of the Indians.

Afterwards, I was ordered to take possession, with the balance of my company, of the "Perra," distant about four miles on the road to San Antonio, with instructions to report every evening at head-quarters. Thus my company was forming the vanguard of the Texan army, on the road to San Antonio.

On the 6th of March, I received orders to go to San Antonio with my company and a party of American citizens, carrying, on the horses, provisions for the defenders of the Alamo.

Arrived at the Cibolo, and not hearing the signal gun which was to be discharged every fifteen minutes, as long as the place held out, we retraced our steps to convey to the General-in-Chief the sad tidings. A new party was sent out, which soon came back, having met with Anselmo Vergara and Andres Barcena, both soldiers of my company, whom I had left for purposes of observation in the vicinity of San Antonio; they brought the intelligence of the fall of the Alamo. Their report was so circumstantial as to preclude any doubts about that disastrous event.[14]

Juan N. Seguin (1806-1890) was born in Texas and was a member of one of the most influential families in the San Antonio area. At the outbreak of the Texas Revolution, the Seguins threw in their lot with the Texans against Santa Anna. Seguin was the highest ranking officer of the Alamo garrison to leave during the siege. He later led one of the Texan companies

Juan Nepomuceno Seguin, the highest ranking officer to leave the Alamo during the seige. He later claimed to have buried the remains of some of the Alamo dead beneath the altar of the San Fernando Cathedral.

From Dudley G. Wooten, *A Comprehensive History of Texas* (Dallas: Wm. G. Scarff, 1898) (Courtesy of the Institute of Texan Cultures) at the Battle of San Jacinto. From 1838 to 1840 Seguin served in the Texas Senate. In 1841 he was elected the mayor of San Antonio. While mayor, Seguin came into conflict with newer residents of Texas who had recently emigrated from the United States. In 1842 he was compelled to leave Texas for Mexico where, whether by force or by choice, he aided in a Mexican military incursion into Texas. It his said that his memoirs were written as a response to those who claimed that he had betrayed Texas. Seguin was later able to return to Texas and served in the politics of San Antonio.[15] (For other accounts by or attributed to Seguin see #3.30 and 3.32.)

3.12
Francisco Esparza, August 26, 1859
From his deposition in a land grant petition on behalf of the heirs of Gregorio Esparza

After the fall of the Alamo I applied and obtained permission from General Cos to take the body of my brother (Gregorio Esparza) and bury it. I proceeded to the Alamo and found the dead body of my brother in one of the rooms of the Alamo, he had received a ball in his breast and a stab from a sword in his side. I, in company with two of my brothers, took his body and we proceeded and interred it [in] the burying ground on the west side of the San Pedro Creek, where it still lies. My brother at the taking of Béxar was under the command of Colonel Juan Seguin and Captain Don Manuel Flores and a member of their company. I was in service at the time of the storming of Béxar [in December of 1835]. The company to which I belonged, the local Presidial Company of Béxar, and the soldiers of the company of the Alamo were under the capitulation of General Cos [and were] allowed to remain in Béxar with their families. I remained with my family, as I was born here and had always lived here. When Santa Anna arrived here in February 1836, he gave orders that all those who were the local soldiers at the capitulation of General Cos should hold themselves in readiness to join the army for active service, but he never called us away from our homes. I remained here when Santa Anna's army went into the interior of Texas and I am now fifty-four years of age and have lived here ever since and done and performed all the duties of a good citizen, as all my neighbors can testify. I mention these facts to show the reason why permission was given me to bury the body of my brother.[16]

Francisco Esparza was the brother of Alamo defender Gregorio Esparza. Francisco was a member of the Presidial Company of Bexar and technically was in the service of the Mexican army during the battle of the Alamo. He was not, however, called to take part in the assault on the Alamo. His account was in the form of a deposition made before Samuel S. Smith, Clerk of the Bexar County Court.

3.13
Candelario Villanueva, August 26, 1859
**From his deposition in a land grant petition
on behalf of the heirs of Gregorio Esparza**

I remained at Béxar and when Santa Anna's troops were entering the town I started with Colonel Seguin for the Alamo, when we were on the way Colonel Seguin sent me back to lock his house up; whilst performing that duty Santa Anna's soldiers got between me and the Alamo and I had to remain in the town during the siege and assault of the Alamo. After the fall of the Alamo I went there and among the dead bodies of those lying inside of the rooms I recognized the body of Gregorio Esparza; I also saw the dead bodies of Antonio Fuentes, Toribio Losoya, Guadalupe Rodriguez and other Mexicans who had fallen in the defense of the Alamo, as also the bodies of Colonel Travis, Bowie, Crockett and other Americans that I had previously known. I saw Francisco Esparza and his brothers take the body of Gregorio Esparza and carry it off towards the campo santo for interment; the bodies of the Americans were laid in a pile and burnt. I remained in Béxar until the return of Captain Seguin and his companions after the battle of San Jacinto when I rejoined his company.[17]

Candelario Villanueva was the husband of the celebrated Madam Candelaria. He gave his account as a deposition in the same proceedings before Samuel S. Smith, Clerk of the Bexar County Court, for the heirs of Gregorio Esparza.

3.14
Fernando Urriza, 1859
**According to Nicholas Labadie in his "San Jacinto
Campaign" published in the *Texas Almanac***

And as regards the slaughter of the Alamo, Castrion was opposed to putting the men to death. One night, past midnight, when Santa Anna and

Castrion were planning an assault, Santa Anna declared that none should survive. It was then inevitable that the fort could hold out but little longer, and Castrion was persuading the commander to spare the lives of the men. Santa Anna was holding in his hand the leg of a chicken which he was eating, and holding it up, he said: "What are the lives of soldiers more than of so many chickens? I tell you, the Alamo must fall, and my orders must be obeyed at all hazards. If our soldiers are driven back, the next line in their rear must force those before them forward, and compel them to scale the walls, cost what it may." I was then acting as Santa Anna's secretary, and ranked as Colonel. My name is Urissa. After eating, Santa Anna directed me to write out his orders, to the effect that all the companies should be brought out early, declaring that he would take his breakfast in the fort the next morning. His orders were dispatched and I retired. I soon after heard the opening fire. By day-break our soldiers had made a breach, and I understood the garrison had all been killed. At about eight o'clock I went into the fort, and saw Santa Anna walking to and fro. As I bowed, he said to me, pointing to the dead: "These are the chickens. Much blood has been shed; but the battle is over: it was but a small affair." As I was surveying the dreadful scene before us, I observed Castrion coming out of one of the quarters, leading a venerable-looking old man by the hand; he was tall, his face was red, and he stooped forward as he walked. The President stopped abruptly, when Castrion, leaving his prisoner, advanced some four or five paces towards us, and with his graceful bow, said: "My General, I have spared the life of this venerable old man, and taken him prisoner." Raising his head, Santa Anna replied. "What right have you to disobey my orders? I want no prisoners," and waving his hand to a file of soldiers, he said, "Soldiers, shoot that man," and almost instantly he fell, pierced with a volley of balls. Castrion turned aside with tears in his eyes, and my heart was too full to speak. So there was not a man left. Even a cat that was soon after seen running through the fort, was shot, as the soldiers exclaimed: "It is not a cat, but an American." [In response to the question of "What was that old man's name?" asked by Nicholas Labadie, Urriza replied] I believe they called him *Coket.*[18]

Fernando Urriza was a colonel in the Mexican army and was wounded on April 20, the day before the Battle of San Jacinto. There is no evidence that the account attributed to him actually originated with him. Instead it comes to us second hand from Nicholas Labadie (1801-1867), a self-styled doctor who published his account of the Texas Revolution in the *Texas Almanac* in 1859. Labadie's account of the Alamo is questionable since it was related from memory twenty-three years after the fact by a man who was not actually a witness to the event related. In addition Labadie suffered the shock of losing two of his children due to illness during the Texas Revolution; he lapsed into a coma for a week following the campaign due to sickness and lack of food; and then he suffered the trauma of discovering that he had lost his hearing upon regaining consciousness. Any reminiscences of his regarding events of that time must be judged in light of these facts.[19]

3.15
Francisco Antonio Ruiz, 1860
As published in the *Texas Almanac*

On the 23d day of February, 1836, (2 o'clock P.M.,) Gen. Santa Anna entered the city of San Antonio with a part of his army. This he effected without any resistance, the forces under the command of Travis, Bowie, and Crockett having on the same day, at 8 o'clock in the morning, learned that the Mexican army was on the banks of the Medina river, they concentrated in the fortress of the Alamo.

In the evening they commenced to exchange fire with guns, and from the 23d of February to the 6th of March (in which the storming was made by Santa Anna) the roar of artillery and volleys of musketry were constantly heard.

On the 6th of March, at 3 o'clock P.M. [A.M.] Gen. Santa Anna at the head of 4,000 men advanced against the Alamo. The infantry, artillery, and cavalry had formed about 1000 vrs from the walls of said fortress. The Mexican army charged and were twice repulsed by the deadly fire of Travis' artillery, which resembled a constant thunder. At the third charge the Toluca battalion commenced to scale the walls and suffered severely. Out of 800 men, 130 were only left alive.

When the Mexican army had succeeded in entering the walls, I, with the Political Chief, (Gefe politico,) Don Ramon Musquiz, and other members of the Corporation, accompanied the Curate, Don Refugio de la Garza, who, by Santa Anna's orders, had assembled during the night at a temporary fortification erected in Portrero street, with the object of attending the wounded, etc. As soon as the storming commenced, we crossed the bridge on Commerce street with this object in view, and about 100 yards from the same a party of Mexican dragoons fired upon us and compelled us to fall back on the river and place we occupied before. Half an hour had elapsed when Santa Anna sent one of his aid-de-camps with an order for us to come before him. He directed me to call on some of the neighbors to come up with carts to carry the dead to the Cemetery, and also to accompany him as he was desirous to have Col. Travis, Bowie, and Crockett shown to him.

On the north battery of the fortress lay the lifeless body of Col. Travis on the gun-carriage, shot *only* in the forehead. Toward the west, and in the small fort opposite the city, we found the body of Col. Crockett. Col. Bowie was found dead in his bed, in one of the rooms of the south side.

Santa Anna, after all the Mexicans were taken out, ordered wood to be brought to burn the bodies of the Texians. He sent a company of dragoons with me to bring wood and dry branches from the neighboring forest. About 3 o'clock in the afternoon they commenced laying the wood and dry branches, upon which a file of dead bodies was placed; more wood was piled on them, and another file brought, and in this manner they were all arranged in layers. Kindling wood was distributed through the pile, and about 5 o'clock in the evening it was lighted.

The dead Mexicans of Santa Anna were taken to the graveyard, but not having sufficient room for them, I ordered some of them to be thrown in the river, which was done on the same day.

Santa Anna's loss was estimated at 1600 men. These were the flower of his army.

The gallantry of the few Texians who defended the Alamo was really wondered at by the Mexican army. Even the Generals were astonished at their vigorous resistance, and how dearly victory had been bought.

The Generals who, under Santa Anna, participated in the storming of the Alamo, were Juan Amador, Castrillon, Ramirez, Sesma, and Andrade.

The men burn[ed] numbered 182. I was an eye-witness, for as *Alcalde* of San Antonio, I was with some of the neighbors collecting the dead bodies and placing them on the funeral pyre.[20]

Francisco Antonio Ruiz was the alcalde of San Antonio de Bexar at the time of the Alamo battle. No original of his account is known to exist. It was translated into English by J.A. Quintero. Ruiz's estimation of Santa Anna's losses are unrealistically high, and his description of throwing bodies into the San Antonio River seems questionable; however, some later accounts tend to corroborate this. The "small fort opposite the city" in which Crockett's body was found is confusing, but the description could be that of the area directly outside of the front (the west) of the Alamo chapel. This courtyard was opposite a small section of San Antonio known as La Villita, situated on the same side of the San Antonio River as the Alamo. La Villita may have been mistranslated or misinterpreted as "the city." If this is so, the location of Crockett's body would tend to be corroborated by a later account by Susanna Hannig.[21] (See account #3.18.)

3.16
Brigidio Guerrero, January 4, 1861
From a land grant petition

Your petitioner further represents and affirms on oath that far from leaving the country to avoid participation in struggle, far from refusing to participate in the war, he was one of those who entered the Alamo under Colonel Travis in February 1836, that he was one of the defenders of that place, that he remained there up to the last moment and that, after the storming of the place by the Mexican army, he saw that there was no hope left, he had the good fortune of saving his life by concealing himself, he and perhaps one other man an American being the only survivors of that awful butchery....[22]

Brigidio Guerrero made his statement in the form of a petition for a land grant entitled to those residents of Texas at the time of the Texas Revolution who did not side with Mexico. He was twenty-six years old at the time of the Alamo battle. He is mentioned in a number of the accounts by Enrique Esparza, but he has always been somewhat of an enigmatic character regarding the battle of the Alamo.[23]

3.17
Louis (Moses) Rose, 1873
According to William P. Zuber in his "Escape from the Alamo"

About two hours before sunset, on the third day of March, 1836, the bombardment suddenly ceased, and the enemy withdrew an unusual distance. Taking advantage of that opportunity, Colonel Travis paraded all of his effective men in a single file, and taking his position in front of the center, he stood for some moments apparently speechless from emotion.

Then, nerving himself for the occasion, he addressed them substantially as follows:

"My brave companions: Stern necessity compels me to employ the few moments afforded by this probably brief cessation of conflict in making known to you the most interesting, yet most solemn, melancholy and unwelcome fact that perishing humanity can realize. But how shall I find language to prepare you for its reception? I cannot do so. All that I can say to this purpose is, be prepared for the worst. I must come to the point. Our fate is sealed. Within a very few days - perhaps a very few hours - we must all be in eternity. This is our destiny and we cannot avoid it. This is our certain doom.

I have deceived you long by the promise of help. But I crave your pardon, hoping that after hearing my explanation you will not only regard my conduct as pardonable, but heartily sympathize with me in my extreme necessity. In deceiving you, I also deceived myself, having been first deceived by others.

I have continually received the strongest assurances of help from home. Every letter from the Council and every one that I have seen from individuals at home has teemed with assurances that our people were ready, willing and anxious to come to our relief; and that within a very short time we might confidently expect recruits enough to repel any force that would be brought against us. These assurances I received as facts. They inspired me with the greatest confidence that our little band would be made the nucleus of an army of sufficient magnitude to repel our foes and to enforce peace on our own terms. In the honest and simple confidence of my heart, I have transmitted to you these promises of help and my confident hopes of success. But the promised help has not come and our hopes are not to be realized.

I have evidently confided too much in the promises of our friends. But let us not be in haste to censure them. The enemy has invaded our territory much earlier than we anticipated; and their present approach is a matter of surprise. Our friends were evidently not informed of our perilous condition in time to save us. Doubtless they would have been here by the time they expected any considerable force of the enemy. When they find a Mexican army in their midst, I hope they will show themselves true to their cause.

My calls on Colonel Fannin remain unanswered and my messengers have not returned. The probabilities are that his whole command has fallen into the hands of the enemy, or been cut to pieces, and that our couriers have been cut off.

I trust that I have now explained my conduct to your satisfaction and that you do not censure me for my course. I must again refer to the assurances of help from home. They are what deceived me, and they caused me to deceive you. Relying upon those assurances, I determined to remain within these walls until the promised help should arrive, stoutly resisting all assaults from without. Upon the same reliance, I retained you here, regarding the increasing forces of our assailants with contempt till they out-numbered us more than twenty to one, and escape became impossible. For the same reason, I scorned their demand of a surrender at discretion and defied their threat to put every one of us to the sword if the fort should be taken by storm.

I must now speak of our present situation. Here we are surrounded by an army that could almost eat us for breakfast, from whose arms our lives are for the present protected by these stone walls. We have no hope for help, for no force that we could have reasonably expected could cut its way through the strongest ranks of these Mexicans. We dare not surrender; for should we do so, that black flag now waving in our sight, as well as the merciless character of our enemies, admonishes us of what would be our doom. We can not cut our way out through the enemy's ranks; for, in attempting that, we should all be slain in less than ten minutes. Nothing remains, then, but to stay within this fort and fight to the last moment. In this case we must sooner or later all be slain; for I am sure that Santa Anna is determined to storm the fort and take it, even at the greatest cost of the lives of his own men.

Then we must die! Our speedy dissolution is a fixed and inevitable fact. Our business is not to make a fruitless effort to save our lives, but to choose the manner of our death. But three modes are presented to us. Let us choose that by which we may best serve our country. Shall we surrender and be deliberately shot without taking the life of a single enemy? Shall we try to cut our way out through the Mexican ranks and be butchered before we can kill twenty of our adversaries? I am opposed to either method; for in either case we could but lose our lives without benefiting our friends at home - our fathers and mothers, our brothers and sisters, our wives and little ones. The Mexican army is strong enough to march through the country and exterminate its inhabitants, and our countrymen are not able to oppose them in open field. My choice, then, is to remain in this fort, to resist every assault, and to sell our lives as dearly as possible.

Then let us band together as brothers and vow to die together. Let us resolve to withstand our adversaries to the last; and at each advance to kill as many of them as possible. And when at last they shall storm our fortress, let us kill them as they come! Kill them as they scale our walls! Kill them as they leap within! Kill them as they raise their weapons and as they use them! Kill them as they kill our companions! And continue as long as one of us shall remain alive!

By this policy I trust that we shall so weaken our enemies that our countrymen at home can meet them on fair terms, cut them up, expel them from the country, and thus establish their own independence and secure prosperity and happiness to our families and our country. And be assured our memory will be gratefully cherished by posterity till all history shall be erased and all noble deeds shall be forgotten.

But I leave every man to his own choice. Should any man prefer to surrender and be tied and shot; or to attempt an escape through the Mexican ranks and be killed before he can run a hundred yards, he is at liberty to do so.

My choice is to stay in this fort and die for my country, fighting as long as breath shall remain in my body. This I will do, even if you leave me alone. Do as you think best - but no man can die with me without affording me comfort in the moment of death."

Colonel Travis then drew his sword and with its point traced a line upon the ground extending from the right to the left of the file. Then, resuming his position in front of the center, he said, "I now want every man who is determined to stay here and die with me to come across this line. Who will be the first? March!"

The first respondent was Tapley Holland, who leaped the line at a bound, exclaiming, "I am ready to die for my country!" His example was instantly followed by every man in the file, with the exception of Rose. Manifest enthusiasm was universal and tremendous. Every sick man that could walk arose from his bunk and tottered across the line. Colonel Bowie, who could not leave his bed, said, "Boys, I am not able to go to you, but I wish some of you would be so kind as to remove my cot over there." Four men instantly ran to the cot and, each lifting a corner, carried it across the line. Then every sick man that could not walk made the same request and had his bunk removed in the like manner.

Rose, too was deeply affected, but differently from his companions. He stood till every man but himself had crossed the line. A consciousness of the real situation overpowered him. He sank upon the ground, covered his face, and yielded to his own reflections. For a time he was unconscious of what was transpiring around him. A bright idea came to his relief: He spoke the Mexican dialect very fluently, and, could he once get safely out of the fort, he might easily pass for a Mexican and effect an escape. Thus encouraged, he suddenly roused as if from sleep. He looked over the area of the fort; every sick man's berth was at its wonted place; every effective soldier was at his post as if waiting orders; he felt as if dreaming.

He directed a searching glance at the cot of Colonel Bowie. There lay his gallant friend. Colonel David Crockett was leaning over the cot, conversing with its occupant in an undertone. After a few seconds Bowie looked at Rose and said: "You seem not to be willing to die with us, Rose!" "No," said Rose, "I am not prepared to die and shall not do so if I can avoid it." Then Crockett also looked at him and said, "You may as well conclude to die with us, old man, for escape is impossible."

Rose made no reply, but looked up at the top of the wall. "I have often done worse than to climb that wall," thought he. Suiting the action to the thought, he sprang up, seized his wallet of unwashed clothes, and ascended the wall. Standing on its top, he looked down within to take a last view of his dying friends. They were all now in motion, but what they were doing he heeded not. Overpowered by his feelings, he looked away and saw them no more.

Looking down without, he was amazed at the scene of death that met his gaze. From the wall to a considerable distance beyond, the ground was literally covered with slaughtered Mexicans and pools of blood.

He viewed this horrid scene but a moment. He threw down his wallet and leaped after it; he alighted on his feet, but the momentum of the spring threw him sprawling upon his stomach in a puddle of blood. After several seconds he recovered his breath, arose and picked up his wallet; it had fallen open and several garments had rolled out upon the blood. He hurriedly thrust them back, without trying to cleanse them of the coagulated blood which adhered to them. Then, throwing the wallet across his shoulders, he walked rapidly away.

He took the road which led down the river, around the bend to the ford and through the town by the church. He waded the river at the ford and passed through the town. He saw no person in town, but the doors were all closed and San Antonio appeared as a deserted city.

After passing through town, he turned down the river. A stillness as of death prevailed. When he had gone about a quarter of a mile below the town, his ears were saluted by the thunder of the bombardment which was then renewed. That thunder continued to remind him that his friends were true to their cause by a continuous roar with but slight intervals until a little before sunrise on the morning of the sixth, when it ceased and he heard it no more.[24]

This account does not come to us directly from Louis Rose but from William Physich Zuber (1820-1913), who was born in Georgia and moved with his family to Texas in 1830. Zuber's tale of Travis's line and Rose's escape from the Alamo is undoubtedly the most famous one associated with the battle and also one of the most controversial. It is treated as the height of drama in an already dramatic story, and no telling of the Alamo is complete without some mention of the tale. Unfortunately, there is plenty to question in it. The story actually comes to us third hand. Rose allegedly made his way to the home of Zuber's parents after his escape and related the story to them, not to William Zuber himself. Zuber's mother supposedly related the tale to him over a period of thirty years. He did not set the story down in writing until 1871 and then only after he had experienced "...a phenomenal refreshment of my memory" after reading about early events in Texas history in the *Texas Almanac*.[25]

Zuber came under a great deal of pressure from skeptics and critics following the publication of his story. Finally, in 1877, he admitted that he had made up Travis's elaborate speech but stuck to the story that he based it on information supplied by Rose. He also confessed that he "threw in" one paragraph which he felt was characteristic of Travis and without which the story would be deficient. Some historians feel that there is a great deal in what Zuber left unsaid and that his "thrown in" paragraph is the one in which Travis draws his line.[26] In addition there is no documentation showing that Louis Rose had been a member of the Alamo garrison. He never corroborated the story, having died twenty-three years prior to the publication of Zuber's tale. Yet there still may have been some connection between Rose and the Alamo, since it is said that in later life Rose was sometimes asked why he did not remain at the Alamo. His alleged reply to this question was said to be "By God, I wasn't ready to die." It is never said that he mentioned Travis's speech and the whole line drawing

William P. Zuber reported several tales of the Alamo
battle including the famous story of Travis and the line.

(Courtesy of the Daughters of the Republic of Texas Library at the Alamo)

story.[27] It is possible that Rose may have been a member of the Alamo garrison whose presence there never made it into any contemporary documentation. However, a new investigation of the story indicates that Rose's connection to the Alamo may have been in an abortive attempt by a group of volunteers to reinforce the besieged garrison. Whether or not the story of the line and Rose's alleged escape originated with Rose himself or through the fertile imagination of William P. Zuber remains to be seen.[28] (For other accounts reported by Zuber see #3.24 and 4.4.)

3.18
Susanna Hannig (Dickinson), 1875
According to James M. Morphis in *The History of Texas from its First Discovery and Settlement*

On February 23d, 1836, Santa Anna, having captured the pickets sent out by Col. Travis to guard the post from surprise, charged into San Antonio with his troops, variously estimated at from six to ten thousand, only a few moments after the bells of the city rang the alarm.

Capt. Dickinson galloped up to our dwelling and hurriedly exclaimed: "The Mexicans are upon us, give me the babe, and jump up behind me." I did so, and as the Mexicans already occupied Commerce street, we galloped across the river at the ford south of it, and entered the fort at the southern gate, when the enemy commenced firing shot and shell into the fort, but with little or no effect, only wounding one horse.

There were eighteen guns mounted on the fortifications, and these, with our riflemen, repulsed with great slaughter two assaults made upon them before the final one.

I knew Colonels Crockett, Bowie and Travis well. Col. Crockett was a performer on the violin, and often during the siege took it up and played his favorite tunes.

I heard him say several times during the eleven days of the siege: "I think we had better march out and die in the open air. I don't like to be hemmed up."

There were provisions and forage enough in the fort to have subsisted men and horses for a month longer.

A few days before the final assault three Texans entered the fort during the night and inspired us with sanguine hopes of speedy relief, and thus animated the men to contend to the last.

A Mexican woman deserted us one night, and going over to the enemy informed them of our very inferior numbers, which Col. Travis said made them confident of success and emboldened them to make the final assault, which they did at early dawn on the morning of the 6th of March.

Under the cover of darkness they approached the fortifications, and planting their scaling ladders against our walls just as light was approaching, they climbed up to the tops of our walls and jumped down within, many of them to immediate death.

As fast as the front ranks were slain, they were filled up again by fresh troops.

The Mexicans numbered several thousands while there were only one hundred and eighty-two Texans.

The struggle lasted more than two hours when my husband rushed into the church where I was with my child, and exclaimed: "Great God, Sue, the Mexicans are inside our walls! All is lost! If they spare you, save my child."

Then, with a parting kiss, he drew his sword and plunged into the strife, then raging in different portions of the fortifications.

Soon after he left me, three unarmed gunners who abandoned their then useless guns came into the church where I was, and were shot down by my side. One of them was from Nacogdoches and named Walker. He spoke to me several times during the siege about his wife and four children with anxious tenderness. I saw four Mexicans toss him up in the air (as you would a bundle of fodder) with their bayonets, and then shoot him. At this moment a Mexican officer came into the room, and, addressing me in English, asked: "Are you Mrs. Dickinson?" I answered "Yes." Then said he, "If you wish to save your life, follow me." I followed him, and although shot at and wounded, was spared.

As we passed through the enclosed ground in front of the church, I saw heaps of dead and dying. The Texans on an average killed between eight and nine Mexicans each - 182 Texans and 1,600 Mexicans were killed.

I recognized Col. Crockett lying dead and mutilated between the church and the two story barrack building, and even remember seeing his peculiar cap lying by his side.

Col. Bowie was sick in bed and not expected to live, but as the victorious Mexicans entered his room, he killed two of them with his pistols before they pierced him through with their sabres.

Cols. Travis and Bonham were killed while working the cannon, the body of the former lay on top of the church. In the evening the Mexicans brought wood from the neighboring forest and burned the bodies of all the Texans, but their own dead they buried in the city cemetery across the San Pedro.[29]

This version of Susanna Hannig's account appeared in the book *The History of Texas from Its First Discovery and Settlement* by James M. Morphis (1826-1900). Morphis was born in North Carolina and moved to Texas in 1846. He was elected mayor of Marshall, Texas in 1851 and unsuccessfully ran for the U.S. Senate in 1859. After serving in the Confederate army he worked as a traveling correspondent for the Galveston *Civilian* and the *Telegraph and Texas Register*.[30] (For other accounts by or attributed to Dickinson see #2.1, 2.5, 3.20, 3.22, 3.28, 3.29, and 4.22.)

3.19

Juana Navarro Alsbury, 1876

According to John S. Ford in his memoirs

When the news of Santa Anna's approach, at the head of a considerable force, was verified in San Antonio, Dr. Alsbury proceeded to the Brazos River to procure means to remove his family, expecting to return before Santa Anna could reach the city. He failed to do so; and his wife went into the Alamo where her protector was, when the Mexican troops were near by. She was accompanied by her younger sister, Gertrudis. Col. Bowie was very sick of typhoid fever. For that reason he thought it prudent to be removed from the part of the building occupied by Mrs. Alsbury. A couple of soldiers carried him away. On leaving he said: "Sister, do not be afraid. I leave you with Col. Travis; Col. Crockett, and other friends. They are gentlemen, and will treat you kindly." He had himself brought back two or three times to see and talk with her. Their last interview took place three or four days before the fall of the Alamo. She never saw him again, either alive or dead.

She says she does not know who nursed him, after he left the quarters she occupied, and expresses no disbelief in the statement of Madam Candelaria. "There were people in the Alamo I did not see."

Mrs. Alsbury and her sister were in a building not far from where the residence of Col. Sam Maverick was afterwards erected. It was considered quite a safe locality. They saw very little of the fighting. While the final struggle was progressing she peeped out, and saw the surging columns of Santa Anna assaulting the Alamo on every side, as she believed. She could hear the noise of the conflict - the roar of the artillery, the rattle of the small arms - the shouts of the combatants, the groans of the dying, and the moans of the wounded. The firing approximated where she was, and she realized the fact that, the brave Texians had been overwhelmed by numbers. She asked her sister to go to the door, and request the Mexican soldiers not to fire into the room, as it contained women only. Señorita Gertrudis opened the door, she was greeted in offensive language by the soldiers. Her shawl was torn from her shoulders, and she rushed back into the room. During this period Mrs. Alsbury was standing with her one-year-old son strained to her bosom, supposing he would be motherless soon. The soldiers then demanded of Señorita Gertrudis: "Your money and your husband." She replied: "I have neither money nor husband." About this time a sick man ran up to Mrs. Alsbury, and attempted to protect her. The soldiers bayoneted him at her side. She thinks his name was Mitchell.

After this tragic event a young Mexican, hotly pursued by soldiers, seized her by the arm, and endeavored to keep her between himself and his assailants. His grasp was broken, and four or five bayonets plunged into his body, and as nearly as many balls went through his lifeless corpse. The soldiers broke open her trunk and took her money and clothes; also the watches of Col. Travis and other officers.

A Mexican officer appeared on the scene. He excitedly inquired "How did you come here?" "What are you doing here any how?" "Where is the entrance to the fort?" He made her pass out of the room over a cannon standing near by the door. He told her to remain there, and he would have her sent to President Santa Anna. Another officer came up, and asked: "What are you doing here?" She replied: "An officer ordered us to remain here, and he would have us sent to the President." - "President! the devil. Don't you see they are about to fire that cannon? Leave." They were moving when they heard a voice calling - "Sister." "To my great relief Don Manuel Perez came to us. He said: 'Don't you know your own brother-in-law?' I answered: 'I am so excited and distressed that I scarcely know anything.'" Don Manuel placed them in charge of a colored woman belonging to Col. Bowie, and the party reached the house of Don Angel Navarro in safety.

Mrs. Alsbury says to the best of her remembrance she heard firing at the Alamo, till twelve o'clock that day.[31]

Juana Navarro de Alsbury (1808-1888) was the daughter of Concepcion Cervantes and José Angel Navarro II, and the niece of Vice-Governor Juan Martin Veramendi and his wife, the in-laws of James Bowie. In January of 1836 she married a Texan soldier, Dr. Horace Alsbury. Dr. Alsbury had been sent away from San Antonio de Bexar on a scouting mission before Santa Anna's army arrived. Juana Alsbury entered the Alamo with Alejo Perez, her infant son by a previous marriage, and her younger sister Gertrudis Navarro, probably under the protection of Bowie. Alsbury gave her story to John Salmon Ford (1815-1897). It appears in his memoirs and was referred to for his *Origin and Fall of the Alamo.*[32] (For another account by or attributed to Alsbury see #3.39.)

3.20
Susanna Hannig (Dickinson), September 23, 1876
From an official testimony

The Mexicans came unexpectedly into San Antonio & witness & her husband & a child retreated into the Fort. The enemy began throwing bombs into Fort, but no one hurt till the last day, i.e. the assault except one horse killed. Had provisions enough to last the besieged 30 days. Among the besieged were 50 or 60 wounded men from Cos' fight. About 18 cannon (she believes) were mounted on parapet & in service all the time. The enemy gradually approached by means of earth-works thrown up. Besieged were looking for reinforcements which never arrived. The only outsiders who succeeded in coming into Fort were 3 of our spys who entered 3 days before the assault & were all killed.

Dr. Horace Alsbury (bro. of Perry Alsbury of S.A.) retreated into the Fort for protection with his Mexican wife & sister-in-law. He left, unknown to witness, & the two women escaped to the enemy & betrayed our situation about 2 days before the assault.

On the morning of 6th Mch, about daylight enemy threw up a signal rocket & advanced & were repulsed. They rallied & made 2d assault with scaling ladders, first thrown up on E. side of Fort. Terrible fight ensued. Witness retired into a room of the old church & saw no part of fight - though she could distinctly hear it. After the fall she was approached by a Col. (?) Black (an Englishman and officer in the Mexican service) who sheltered her from Mexican injury & took her in a hurry to Mr. Musquiz, a merchant in town, where she staid [sic] till next day, where she was conducted before Santa Anna who threatened to take her to Mexico with her child; when Almonte, his nephew, addressing his English, pleaded, pleaded for witness, saying he had been educated in N.O. & had experienced great kindness from Americans. Witness was then permitted to depart to her home in Gonzales. Col. Travis commanded the Fort.

The only man witness saw killed was a man named Walker from Nacidoches [sic], who was bayonetted & shot. She knew John Garnet from Gonzales, who she is certain was killed though she did not see it. After her [unintelligible] to Musquiz's she expressed a wish to visit the scene of carnage, but was informed by the people of the house that it would not be permitted as the enemy was then burning the dead bodies and in conformation thereof, she was shown a smoke in the direction of the Alamo. She knew Col. Bowie & saw him in the Fort, both before & after his death. He was sick before & during the fight, and had even been expected to die.-

Col. Crockett was one of the 3 men who came into the Fort during the siege & before the assault. He was killed, she believes.

A Negro man named Joe, was in the Fort, & was the slave & body-servant of Col. Travis. After the fall of the Alamo, Jo [sic] was forced by the Mexicans at the point of the bayonet to point out to them the bodies of Col. Travis & Col. Crockett among the heaps of dead. Jo [sic] was the only Negro in the Fort. The witness's infant was the only child in the fort. The witness & the two Mexican women already mentioned were the only women in the Fort.[33]

This account of Susanna Hannig is related second hand. It was given as a part of some official testimony forty years after the Alamo battle. It was probably given as part of an attempt by the state of Texas to determine exactly who the defenders of the Alamo were. It is part of the State Adjutant General's papers at the Texas State Archives.[34] (For other accounts by or attributed to Dickinson see #2.1, 2.5, 3.18, 3.22, 3.23, 3.28, 3.29, and 4.22.)

3.21

Manuel Loranca, June 23, 1878

From an article originally in the Corpus Christi *Free Press* and reprinted in the *San Antonio Express*

About nine in the morning, the President Santa Anna arrived and joined with his escort and staff, the column which was now in the vicinity of San Antonio. We marched upon the place and were received by the fort with one or two cannon shots; those in the Alamo raising a red flag.

Santa Anna then ordered a parley to be sounded, which was answered by the chiefs of the Alamo, and the President commissioned the Mexican Colonel Batres to confer with Bowie and Travis, both Colonels of the Texan forces holding the Alamo. This was on the 26th of February, 1836.

The President Santa Anna proposed to Travis and Bowie that they should surrender at discretion, with no other guarantee than that their lives should be spared. The said Texan chiefs answered and proposed to surrender the fort on being allowed to march out with their arms and go join their government (as they had permitted the Mexican forces under Generals Cos and Filisola when they capitulated to the Texans at the Mission de la Espada and were allowed to march out with their arms, munitions of war, provisions, etc., and join the Mexican army then in the field against Texas), and if this was not willingly conceded to them, they would willingly take all the chances of war.

The bombardment was effectually commenced on the 27th of the same month. During this time the Mexican forces were joined by several bodies of infantry, making about four thousand men.

On the 4th of March the President Santa Anna called a council of war to consider the mode of assault of the Alamo, and they decided to make the assault on the 6th, at daybreak, in the following manner: On the north, Col. Don Juan Baptisto Morales with the Battalion "Firmas," of San Luis Potosi; on the west, Col. Don Mariano Salas, with the Battalion of Aldama; on the south, Col. Jose Vincente Minon, with the Battalion of Infantry; on the east, a squadron of Lancers, flanked by a ditch, to cut off the retreat at the time of the assault. These Lancers were commanded by Gen. Don Joaquin Ramires y Sesma.

The assault took place at 3:30 A.M. on the 6th, and was so sudden that the fort had only time to discharge four of the eighteen cannon which it had.

The Fort Alamo had only one entrance, which was on the south; and the approach was made winding to impede the entrance of the cavalry. The Mexican infantry, with ladders, were lying down at musket-shot distance, awaiting the signal of assault, which was to be given from a fort about a cannon-shot to the east of the Alamo, where the President Santa Anna was with the music of the regiment of Dolores and his staff to direct the movements. In the act of assault a confusion occurred, occasioned by darkness, in which the Mexican troops opened fire on each other. A culverin, or 16 pound howitzer, fired from the fort, swept off a whole company of the Battalion Aldama, which made the attack on the point toward San Antonio.

After that we all entered the Alamo, and the first thing we saw on entering a room at the right was the corpses of Bowie and Travis. Then we passed to the corridor which served the Texans as quarters, and here found all refugees which were left. President Santa Anna immediately ordered that they should be shot, which was accordingly done, excepting only a negro and a woman having a little boy about a year old. She was said to be Travis' cook.

Sixty-two Texans who sallied from the east side of the fort, were received by the Lancers and all killed. Only one of these made resistance; a very active man, armed with a double barrel gun and a single-barrel pistol, with which he killed a corporal of the Lancers named Eugenio. These were all killed by the lance, except one, who ensconced himself under a bush and it was necessary to shoot him.

There in front of the fosse were gathered the bodies of all those who died by the lance, and those killed in the fort, making a total to two-hundred and eighty-three persons, including a Mexican found among them, who, it appears, had come from La Bahia (Goliad) with dispatches; and here they were ordered to be burned, there being no room in the *campo santo* or burying ground, it being all taken up with the bodies of upwards of four hundred Mexicans, who were killed in the assault.[35]

This account is attributed to Manuel Loranca, described as a second sergeant of the Mexican army whose regiment was the vanguard of the division under General Ramirez y Sesma as it marched north towards Saltillo, Mexico in 1835. It is from an article in the *San Antonio Express* but originated in the Corpus Christi *Free Press*. It is the only mention of Sergeant Loranca in any Alamo account. The following appeared as an introduction to the account's publication in the *San Antonio Express*:

> The following narrative, written for the Corpus Christi *Free Press* by an ex-sergeant in the last Mexican expedition under Santa Anna, is full of thrilling interest. It might be appropriately termed a "knapsack sketch." We are assured that the writer (ex-sergeant Manuel Loranca) has his original discharge from the expedition, and, if needed, can be sent to us. We are indebted to D.M. Hastings, Esq., Corpus Christi, who kindly made the translation.- Ed, *Free Press*.[36]

This account was used by Walter Lord for his book *A Time to Stand*, but it has been virtually ignored by others in the telling of the Alamo story. Perhaps the description of sixty-two Texans sallying out from the walls of the Alamo during the battle only to be cut down by the Mexican lancers did not really fit the traditional view of the story. It flew in the face of the idea that every Alamo defender willingly chose to stand and fight to the death for every inch of Alamo ground. However, Loranca's statement may be verified by others. (See accounts #1.15, 2.2, 2.7, and 3.28.) This is no reflection on the defenders of the Alamo since once the Mexican soldiers had begun to pour into the walls, the Alamo lost whatever strategic value it had as a fortress. At that point it did not make much difference whether the defenders jumped from the walls into or out of the Alamo.[37]

3.22
Mrs. J.W. Hannig [Susanna Dickinson], 1878
According to Charles Evers in an
unidentified Ohio newspaper

She expressed her wish to see Frank Mayo, whom she heard was playing "Davy Crockett" in Texas. She was, of course, well acquainted with Crockett and saw the noble manhood and devotion of himself and comrades through all those eventful 13 days preceding the final, bloody culmination. Her husband, Lieutenant Dickinson, acted during the siege as a sort of nurse and doctor among the men, and she often aided him in caring for the sick and wounded. She was then a young woman and had a child one or two years old, which some writers have stated was killed in his father's arms. This statement, she says, is incorrect, as well as the story that some of the Texans begged for quarter. She says that only one man, named Wolff, asked for quarter, but was instantly killed. The wretched man had two little boys, aged 11 and 12 years. The little fellows came to Mrs. Dickinson's room, where the Mexicans killed them, and a man named Walker, and carried the boys bodies out on their bayonets.

The room had become dark with smoke and to this circumstance, and the intervention of the Mexican colonel, Almonte, who was educated in New Orleans, and could speak English, and who drove the bloodthirsty Mexicans from her room, she feels indebted for her life. She was shot through the leg between the knee and ankle, but her little child was unhurt. The last she ever saw of her husband he rushed into the room and said, "My dear wife, they are coming over the wall, we are all lost!" He embraced her and the babe, saying "May God spare you both!" then drew his sword and went out. His body when found was riddled with bullets, and later burned by the inhuman victors with the rest of the slain.

Mrs. Dickinson's escape was almost as thrilling as her capture. Santa Anna tried to persuade her to go to Mexico and take the child. He seemed fearful of the effect of her horrible story among the Texans, and he seemed also afraid to murder her. She states that when she came to her right mind and the reality of her situation stared her in the face, she broke down with grief and for several days her emotion was beyond control.

Finally, under the persuasion of Almonte, Santa Anna, at her own earnest solicitation, consented to send her under escort to her friends in the direction of Goliad. When out of the camp a few miles the cowardly Mexican cavalry deserted her, probably fearing the vengeance of Deaf Smith and his scouts. She made her way through the prairie on a pony, carrying the child, scarcely knowing where she was going as the country was entirely wild, when to her great fright a human being raised his head from the tall grass and spoke to her. It was the negro, Ben, Colonel Travis' servant. He had escaped from the Mexicans and was nearly frightened to death lest the mounted woman might prove to be a Mexican who would recapture him. Ben was overjoyed to find Mrs. Dickinson and trudged along beside the pony, but would take to the tall grass every time any suspicious circumstances occurred. While on the journey they saw two horsemen in the distance. Ben took to the grass and urged Mrs. Dickinson to do so, saying they were Comanches, but she refused to turn aside, declaring she would as soon perish one way as another. As the horsemen approached Ben discovered that they rode with martingales and again he became wild with joy knowing they were white men. It proved to be Deaf Smith and Captain Carnes of the scouts. General Houston had heard the cannonade and sent his scouts to reconnoiter and report. She told me that General Houston wept like a child as he held her hand and heard the terrible fate of the brave defenders of the Alamo.[38]

This account by Susanna Hannig comes to us second hand from Charles W. Evers, who published his interview with her in an unidentified Ohio newspaper circa 1878. The story was repeated in the *San Antonio Express* in 1929 after a copy of the original was retrieved from "a dusty attic." This account mentions Ben, but apparently there was some confusion with Ben taking on the role of Joe.[39] Hannig's description of the deaths she witnessed continued to change. This time it included two young boys, sons of a soldier named Wolff [Anthony Wolf].[40] (For other accounts by or attributed to Dickinson see #2.1, 2.5, 3.18, 3.20, 3.23, 3.28, 3.29, and 4.22.)

3.23

Susan J. Hannig (Susanna Dickinson), April 28, 1881
According to an article in the *San Antonio Express*

After a long absence, indeed, after the lapse of forty five years, Mrs. Hannig yesterday returned to the old scene. She is a Tennesseean by birth, is now sixty-six years of age, and when the Alamo fell lost her husband, Capt. Dickinson. Just before the Mexicans arrived, headed by Santa Anna, she was, together with her child, at the Musquiz house, near Main plaza. The enemy appeared first in [unintelligible] early in the morning in the southwestern suburbs of the city. Their forces were from ten to thirteen thousand strong. As soon as they were announced to be coming, her husband rode up to the door of her abode and called to her to seize her child and take refuge in the Alamo. She mounted the bare back of the horse he rode, behind his saddle, and holding her child between her left arm and breast, soon reached the old church. An apartment was assigned her, while her husband turned away, after an embrace and a kiss, and an eternal adieu, to meet his obligations to his fellowmen and his country. By this time the Mexican bugles were sounding the charge of battle, and the cannon's roar was heard to reverberate throughout the valley of the San Antonio. But about one hundred and sixty sound persons were in the

Alamo, and when the enemy appeared, overwhelmingly, upon the environs of the city to the west, and where the International depot now stands, the Noble Travis called up his men, drew a line with his sword and said: "My soldiers, I am going to meet the fate that becomes me. Those who will stand by me, let them remain but those who desire to go, let them go - and who crosses the line that I have drawn, *shall* go!" The scene is represented by Mrs. Hannig to have been grand - in that its location was above the results and influences of ordinary sentiment and patriotism, and bore the plain tige of that divinity of principle which characterizes the acts of the truly noble and brave.

The heroes defied the Mexicans, though the former were but a handful and the aztec horde came on like the swoop of a whirlwind. Organized into divisions, they came in the form of a semi-circle that extended from the northeast to southwest, but the strongest attack was from about where the military plaza is and from a direction of the Villita. Three times they were repulsed, and the two cannon, planted high upon the ramparts, carried dismay with their belches of fire and lead. There was indeed a resolution to battle till the end. And that fated end came, and brought with it horrors of which even the vivid conception of Crockett could not have dreamed. Mrs. Hannig says there was no second story to the Alamo at that time - it was all one floor. She can give but little of the struggle, as she was in a little dark room in the rear of the building. The party yesterday entered this apartment, and even with a candle could scarcely see each other's faces. The old lady recognized almost every stone, however, and the arch overhead, and the corners she said, with tears in her eyes, came back as vividly to memory as though her experiences of yore had been but yesterday. She showed the reporter where her couch had stood, and the window through which she peeped to see the blood of noble men seeping into the ground, and the bodies of heroes lying cold in death. It was in this room that she saw the last man fall, and he was a man named Walker, who had often fired the cannon at the enemy. Wounded, he rushed into the room and took refuge in a corner opposite her own. By this time the Alamo had fallen and the hordes of Santa Anna were pouring over its ramparts, through its trenches and its vaults. The barbarous hordes followed the fated Walker, and, as Mrs. Hannig describes the scene, "they shot him first, and then they stuck their bayonets into his body and raised him up like a farmer does a bundle of fodder with his pitchfork when he loads his wagon." Then she says they dropped the body. They were all bloody, and crimson springs crossed the yard. The old lady says she doesn't know how it all happened, yet tells a great deal. What became of her husband Al Marion [Almeron] Dickinson, she cannotnnotnnot but saw him last when he went from her pres ence with gun in hand to die for his country. She says that for a while she feared for her own fate, but soon was assured by an English colonel in the Mexican army that the Mexicans were not come to kill women but to fight men. Through the intervention of Almonte she was permitted to leave the city on a horse and carry her child with her. Before she left, however, she was conveyed back to the Musquiz place, her home before the time that she was a widow, and the terrible fate which met the followers of Travis, Bowie and Crockett came on. After leaving on the horse, she proceeded a short distance beyond the Salado, when she met with Travis's servant, who had escaped from the guard and was lurking in the brush. The servant recognized her and followed after her. It may be here remarked incidentally, that there were in the Alamo at its fall about seventy five men who had been wounded in the fight with Cos, and they were all killed, outright, in spite of their pleadings. The servant of Travis followed her for some time, and when about fifteen miles distant three men were observed approaching. The heart of the woman did not quail, but the servant feared Indians. Said she, under these circumstances: "This is a bald prairie, and if it is an enemy we must meet them face to face." But the apprehensions of the party were assuaged when it was discovered that the dreaded forms were Deaf Smith, Robert E Handy and Capt. Karnes, sent out by Sam Houston to ascertain the condition of the garrison of the Alamo. It was a meeting of friends, and soon Mrs. Dickinson, now Mrs. Hannig, reached Gonzales. Her subsequent history would require too much space to be given.

The review of the Alamo was truly interesting, and the reporter could not keep pace with her recitals of experiences there in the long ago. It was asked whether the men who defended the Alamo were drunk, as some have published, when the fight came on, covertly to defeat the effect of the noblest of human contests for liberty. Mrs. Hannig declared that any such assertion would be an insult to common patriotism, and condemned it. She had never seen either Travis, Crockett or Bowie under any liquored influence, and deprecated any impression of such nature as might come abroad. At the time of the fatal encounter, all were ready for the fray, and all prepared to die for the nationality of the republic of Texas.[41]

This is yet another version of the Alamo attributed to Susanna Hannig, which was inspired by an emotional visit to the Alamo by Hannig and a party of others. One of the party was a reporter from the *San Antonio Express*. The account is given in his words in a dramatic and probably heavily edited style.[42] (For other accounts by or attributed to Dickinson see #2.1, 2.5, 3.18, 3.20, 3.22, 3.28, 3.29, and 4.22.)

3.24

Apolinario (Polin) Saldigna, March 1, 1882
According to William P. Zuber in
an article in the *Houston Daily Post*

After the fort (the celebrated church of the Alamo at San Antonio) had been stormed and all of its defenders had been reported to have been slain, and when the Mexican assailants had been recalled from within the walls, Santa Anna and his staff entered the fortress. Polin, being a fifer, and therefore a privileged person, and possibly more so because of his tender years, by permission, entered with them. He desired to see all that was to be seen, and for this purpose he kept himself near his general in chief. Santa Anna had ordered that no corpses should be disturbed till after he had looked upon them all, and seen how every man had fallen. He had employed three or four citizens of San Antonio to enter with him, and to point out the bodies of several distinguished Texans.

The principal corpses that Santa Anna desired to see were those of Colonel W. Barret Travis, Colonel James Bowie, and another man whose name Polin could not remember, but which, by his description, must have been Crockett.

On entering the fort, the eyes of the conqueror were greeted by a scene which Polin could not very well describe. The bodies of the Texans lay as they had fallen, and many of them were covered by the bodies of the Mexicans who had fallen upon them. The close of the struggle seemed to have been a hand-to-hand engagement, and the number of dead Mexicans exceeded that of Texans. The ground was covered by the bodies of the slain. Santa Anna and his suite for a long time wandered from one apartment of the fortress to another, stepping over and on the dead, seemingly enjoying this scene of human butchery.

After a general reconnoitering of the premises, the Dictator came upon the body of Colonel Travis. After viewing the form and features a few moments, Santa Anna thrust his sword through the dead man's body and turned away. He was then conducted to the remains of the man (Crockett) whose name Polin could not remember. This man lay with his face upward, and his body was covered by those of many Mexicans who had fallen upon him, His face was florid like that of a living person, and he looked like a healthy man asleep. Santa Anna viewed him for a few moments, thrust his sword through his breast and turned away.

The one who had come to point out certain bodies made a long but unsuccessful search for that of Colonel Bowie, and reported to Santa Anna that it was not to be found.

Then a detail of Mexican soldiers came into the fort. They were commanded by two officers, a captain and a junior officer whose title Polin could not explain, but whom I shall, for convenience, call Lieutenant. They were both quite young men, very fair, very handsome, and so nearly alike in complexion, form, size, and features, that Polin judged them to be brothers, the captain being apparently a little older that the other. Polin did not remember to have seen them before, was confident that he never saw them afterward, and did not learn their names.

After the entry of the detail, Santa Anna and his suite retired, but the two officers and their men remained within. The two kept themselves close together, side by side. Polin was desirous to know what was to be done, and remained with the detail and to enable himself to see all that was to be seen, he kept near the two officers, never losing sight of them.

As soon as the Dictator and his suite had retired, the squad began to take up the dead Texans, and to bring them together, and to lay them in a pile, but before thus depositing them, the Mexicans rifled the pockets, and in many cases stripped the bodies of all clothing.

The two officers took a stand about the center of the arena. The first corpse was brought and laid as the captain directed. This formed a nucleus for a pile. The bodies were brought successively each by four men, and dropped near the captain's feet. In imitation of his general, the captain viewed the body of each dead Texan for a few moments, and thrust his sword through it, after which the mutilated corpse was cast upon the heap at another motion of the captain's sword.

When all the Texans had been thrown on the pile, four soldiers walked around it, each carrying a pan of camphene, that was poured upon the bodies for a funeral pyre. This process was continued until all the bodies were thoroughly wetted....

While the fluid was being thrown upon the pile, four soldiers brought a cot, on which lay a sick man, and set it down by the captain and one of them remarked, "Here, captain, is a man that is not dead." "Why is he not dead?" asked the captain. "We found him in a room by himself," said the soldier. "He seems to be very sick, and I suppose he was not able to fight, and was placed there by his companions, to be in a safe place and out of the way." The captain gave the sick man a searching look and said, "I think I have seen this man before." The lieutenant replied, "I think I have too," and, stooping down, he examined his features closely. Then raising himself, he addressed the captain, "He is no other than the infamous Colonel Bowie."

The captain then also stopped, gazed intently upon the sick man's face, assumed an erect position, and confirmed the conviction of the young lieutenant.

The captain looked fiercely upon the sick man and said: "How is it, Bowie, you have been found hidden in a room by yourself and have not died fighting, like your companions?" To which Bowie replied in good Castilian: "I should certainly have done so, but you see I am sick and cannot get off this cot." "Ah, Bowie," said the Captain, "you have come to a *fearful* end - and well do you deserve it. As an immigrant to Mexico you have taken an oath before God to support the Mexican Government; but you are now violating that oath by fighting against that government which you have been sworn to defend. But this perjury, common to all your rebellious countrymen, is not your only offense. You have married a respectable Mexican lady and are fighting against her countrymen. Thus you have not only perjured yourself, but you have also betrayed your own family."

"I did," said Bowie, "take an oath to support the Constitution of Mexico, and in defense of that Constitution I am now fighting. You took the same oath when you accepted your commission in the army and you are now violating that oath and betraying the trust of your countrymen, by fighting under a faithless tyrant for the destruction of that Constitution and for the ruin of your people's liberties. The perjury and treachery are not *mine*, but *yours*."

The captain indignantly ordered Bowie to shut his mouth. "I shall never shut my mouth for your like," said Bowie, "while I have a tongue to speak." "I will soon relieve you of that," said the captain.

Then he caused four of his minions to hold the sick man, while a fifth, with a sharp knife, split his mouth, cut off his tongue, and threw it upon the pile of dead men. Then, in obedience to motion of the captain's sword, the four soldiers who held him, lifted the writhing body of the mutilated, bleeding, tortured invalid from his cot, and pitched him alive upon the funeral pile.

At that moment a match was touched to the bodies. The combustible fluid instantly sent up a flame to an amazing height. The sudden generation of a great heat drove all the soldiers back to the wall. The officers, pale as corpses, stood gazing at the immense columns of fire, and trembled from head to foot as if they would break asunder at every joint. Polin stood between them and saw and heard the lieutenant whisper, in a faltering and broken articulation, "It takes him up - to God."

Polin believed that the lieutenant alluded to the ascension, upon the wings of that flame, of Bowie's soul to that God who would surely award due vengeance to his fiendish murderers.

Not being able to fully comprehend the great combustibility of the camphene, Polin also believed that the sudden elevation of that great pillar of fire was an indication of God's hot displeasure toward those torturing murderers. He further believed that the two officers were of the same opinion and thus he accounted for their agitation. And he thought the same idea pervaded the whole detail, as every man appeared to be greatly frightened.

For the time Polin stood amazed, expecting each moment that the earth would open a chasm through which every man in the fort would drop into perdition. Terrified by this conviction, he left the fort as speedily as possible.

On a subsequent day Polin visited the fort again. It was then cleansed and it seemed to be a comfortable place. In the main area he saw the one relic of the great victory - a pile of charred fragments of human bones.[43]

This ghastly tale of the mutilation and death of James Bowie is attributed to a young Mexican fifer, Apolinario Saldigna. Of course there is no verification of this unlikely tale, and it appears to come strictly from the lurid imagination of William P. Zuber as an article in the *Houston Daily Post* of March 1, 1882.[44] (For other accounts reported by Zuber see #3.17 and 4.4.)

3.25
Francisco Becerra, April 1882
According to John S. Ford in an article in the *Texas Mute Ranger*

Col. Mora was ordered to take the advance, and when near San Antonio to move to the right, cross the river, and take possession of the Mission of Concepcion. Santa Anna feared the Texians might abandon the Alamo, and occupy Concepcion. He considered the latter place more defensible by a small force than the Alamo.

When the head of the column reached the cemetery a cannon shot was fired. Skirmishers were deployed, and pushed into town. They reported having encountered no resistance. The men laid on their arms during the night; and we fired one shot which was answered by the Texians. Col. Mora was directed to take position north and east of the Alamo to prevent escape from the fort.

When the army arrived many inhabitants fled from the city, leaving every thing behind them; most of them went to the country. This was late in February. Gen. Santa Anna's army numbered about four thousand. He determined to take the Alamo by storm, but concluded to await the arrival of Gen. Tolza with two thousand men. Santa Anna made the preparatory arrangements during the interval. The first movement was made by the battalion Matamoros which crossed the river and took possession of some houses situated below the Alamo. Their mission was to collect timbers to build a bridge over the San Antonio river. They were in charge of Gen. Castrillon. The Texians fired on them. Gen. Santa Anna and Gen. Minon went to the spot. During these operations an incident occurred not connected with military operation, which will be referred to in another place.

The next two companies were sent to make a reconnaissance. They went within range of the deadly rifles; thirty were killed within a few minutes. Gen. Castrillon requested Gen. Santa Anna to withdraw them, if he wished to save any of their lives; the order was given. The main body of the army was still on the south side of the river, but the battalion Matamoros was still under fire. The Texians kept up a steady fire all day, with little effect. That night the battalion Matamoros was sent to reinforce Col. Mora, and to more effectually cover the approaches north and east of the Alamo. They were replaced by Col. Romero's command. A small work was commenced above the Alamo. The next day the battalion Matamoros was sent to reoccupy position in front of the Alamo. Various movements were made in succession, brisk skirmish fighting occurred, the Texians were invested, and losses were inflicted on the Mexican army. When the small work was finished and inspected it did not suit the commanding general. He ordered another to be constructed nearer the Alamo, under supervision of Gen. Amador. The working party took advantage of the night to commence. The Texians discovered them, and kept up a heavy fire on them all night. They completed the little fort in due time. Fire was opened from it upon the Alamo.

On the third day of March Gen. Tolza arrived. The greatest activity prevailed in every department. The plan of assault was formed, and communicated to the commanders of corps, and others, on the fifth. On the same day ammunition, scaling ladders, etc., were distributed. Every thing was made ready for the storming. During the night the troops were placed in position. About three o'clock on the morning of the sixth the battalion Matamoros was marched to a point near the river, and above the Alamo. At their rear were two thousand men under Gen. Cos. Gen. Castrillon commanded this portion of the army. Gen. Tolza's command held the ground below the Alamo. Gen. Santa Anna spent the night in the work near the Alamo. The troops were to march to the attack when the bugler at headquarters sounded the advance. The order delivered by Santa Anna to the commanders was to move in silence, and not to fire a single shot until the trenches of the enemy had been reached. The Mexican troops little thought of the terrible ordeal through which they were about to pass.

On the morning of March 6, 1836, at four o'clock, the bugle sounded the advance from the small work near the Alamo. The troops under Gen. Castrillon moved in silence. They reached the fort, planted scaling-ladders, and commenced ascending; some mounted on the shoulders of others; a terrific fire belched from the interior; men fell from the scaling-ladders by the score, many pierced through the head by balls, others fell by clubbed guns. The dead and the wounded covered the ground. After half an hour of fierce conflict, after the sacrifice of many lives, the column under Gen. Castrillon succeeded in making a lodgement in the upper part of the Alamo. It was a sort of outwork. I think it is now used as a lot, or a courtyard. This seeming advantage was a mere prelude to the desperate struggle which ensued. The doors of the Alamo building were barricaded by bags of sand as high as the neck of a man, the windows also. On the top of the roofs of the different apartments were rows of sand bags to cover the besieged.

Our troops, inspired by success, continued the attack with energy and boldness. The Texians fought like devils. It was at short range - muzzle to muzzle - hand to hand - musket and rifle - bayonet and Bowie knife - all were mingled in confusion. Here a squad of Mexicans, there a Texian or two. The crash of firearms, the shouts of defiance, the cries of the dying and the wounded, made a din almost infernal. The Texians defended desperately every inch of the fort - overpowered by numbers, they would be forced to abandon a room; they would rally in the next, and defend it until further resistance became impossible.

Gen. Tolza's command forced an entrance at the door of the church building. He met the same determined resistance without and within. He won by force of numbers, and at a great cost of life.

There was a long room on the ground floor - it was darkened. Here the fight was bloody. It proved to be the hospital. The sick and the wounded fired from their beds and pallets. A detachment of which I had command had captured a piece of artillery. It was placed near the door of the hospital, doubly charged with grape and canister, and fired twice. We entered and found the corpses of fifteen Texians. On the outside we afterwards found forty-two dead Mexicans.

On the top of the church building I saw eleven Texians. They had some small pieces of artillery, and were firing on the cavalry, and on those engaged in making the escalade. Their ammunition was exhausted, and they were loading with pieces of iron and nails. The captured piece was placed in a position to reach them, doubly charged, and fired with so much effect, that they ceased working their pieces.

In the main building, on the ground floor, I saw a man lying on a bed - he was evidently sick. I retired, without molesting him, notwithstanding the order of Gen. Santa Anna to give no quarter to the Texians. A sergeant of artillery entered before I had finally left the room - he leveled his piece at the prostrate man; the latter raised his hand and shot the sergeant through the head with a pistol. A soldier of the Toluca regiment came in, aimed his gun at the invalid, and was killed in a similar manner. I then fired and killed the Texian. I took his two empty pistols, and found his rifle standing by his bed. It seemed he was too weak to use it.

In another room I saw a man sitting on the floor among feathers. A bugler, who was with me, raised his gun. The gentleman said to him in Spanish: - "Don't kill me - I have plenty of money." He pulled out a pocketbook, also a large roll of bank bills, and handed the latter to the bugler. We divided the money.

While this was occurring another Texian made his appearance. He had been lying on the floor, as if resting. When he arose I asked: - "How many is there of you?" He replied: - "Only two."

The gentleman, who spoke Spanish, asked for Gen. Cos, and said he would like to see him. Just then Gen. Amador came in. He asked why the orders of the President had not been executed, and the two Texians killed. In answer the bugler exhibited his roll of bank bills, and they were taken from him immediately by the general. In a few moments Gen. Cos, Gen. Almonte, and Gen. Tolza, entered the room. As soon as Gen. Cos saw the gentleman who spoke Spanish he rushed to him, and embraced him. He told the other generals it was Travis, that on a former occasion he had treated him like a brother, had loaned him money, etc. He also said the other man was Col. Crockett. He entreated the other generals to go with him to Gen. Santa Anna, and join with him in a request to save the lives of the two Texians. The generals and the Texians left together to find Santa Anna. The bugler and myself followed them. They encountered the commander-in-chief in the court yard, with Gen. Castrillon. Gen. Cos said to him: - "Mr. President, you have here two prisoners - in the name of the Republic of Mexico I supplicate you to guarantee the lives of both." Santa Anna was very much enraged. He said: - "Gentleman generals, my order was to kill every man in the Alamo." He turned, and said: - "Soldiers, kill them." A soldier was standing near Travis, and presented his gun at him. Travis seized the bayonet, and depressed the muzzle of the piece to the floor, and it was not fired. While this was taking place the soldiers standing around opened fire. A shot struck Travis in the back. He then stood erect, folding his arms, and looked calmly, unflinchingly, upon his assailants. He was finally killed by a ball passing through his neck. Crockett stood in a similar position. They died undaunted like heroes.

The firing was brisk for a time. It came from all sides. Gen. Santa Anna, and most of the officers ran. Gen. Castrillon squatted down - so did I. In this affair eight Mexican soldiers were killed, and wounded, by their comrades.

I did not know the names of two Texians, only as given by Gen. Cos. The gentleman he called Crockett had a coat with capes to it.

The Alamo, as had been stated, was entered at daylight - the fighting did not cease till nine o'clock

Gen. Santa Anna directed Col. Mora to send out his cavalry to bring in wood. He ordered that they should make prisoners of all the inhabitants they might meet, and force them to pack wood to the Alamo. In this manner a large quantity of wood was collected. A large pile was raised. It consisted of layers of wood and layers of corpses of Texians. It was set on fire. The bodies of those brave men, who fell fighting that morning, as men have seldom fought, were reduced to ashes before the sun had set. It was a melancholy spectacle.

There was an order to gather our own dead and wounded. It was a fearful sight. Our lifeless soldiers covered the grounds surrounding the Alamo. They were heaped inside of the fortress. Blood and brains covered the earth, and the floors, and had spattered the walls. The ghostly faces of our comrades met our gaze, and we removed them with despondent hearts. Our loss in front of the Alamo was represented at two thousand killed, and more than three hundred wounded. The killed were generally struck on the head. The wounds were in the neck, or shoulder, seldom below that. The firing of the besieged was fearfully precise. When a Texas rifle was leveled on a Mexican he was considered as good as dead. All this indicated the dauntless bravery and the cool self possession of the men who were engaged in a hopeless conflict with an enemy numbering more than twenty to one; They inflicted on us a loss ten times greater than they sustained. The victory of the Alamo was dearly bought. Indeed, the price in the end was well nigh the ruin of Mexico.

During the evening we buried our dead. These were sad duties which each company performed for its fallen members. How many never again responded at roll call! It was a day of bitter strife, of sadness, and sorrow. A triumph which bore bitter fruits.

Our wounded were placed in houses, and properly cared for.[45]

Francisco Becerra was born in Guanajuato, Mexico in 1810. He is described as a first sergeant in the division of Gen. Ramirez y Sesma during the Mexican army's march to Texas in 1835. The account of Sergeant Becerra is one of the more controversial accounts of the Alamo battle. It originally appeared as part of the John S. Ford papers. The account itself was given as a talk before an audience at the Austin Public Library in 1875, but it did not appear in print until April of 1882 when it was published in an obscure journal, the *Texas Mute Ranger*.[46] Becerra served as a living source for one of the first major studies of the Alamo battle when Reuben M. Potter (1802-1890) consulted him for his "Fall of the Alamo" in 1860. He later served John S. Ford in a similar capacity.

Becerra's account has been described by Walter Lord as "Probably the least reliable of all the Mexican accounts." Dan Kilgore attributed Lord's evaluation to the "lurid passages and high number of Mexican casualties listed."[47] This alone may be reason enough to question the account, but the manner in which the account was given creates more doubt. John S. Ford related that Becerra's "Recollections...were prepared from copious notes, which had been read to Sergeant Becerra in Spanish and English — he spoke both languages — and he endorsed them as a true version of the affair."[48] In other words Becerra's account is not a spontaneous first person recollection. Someone else, most likely Ford, prepared an account, read it to Becerra, and Becerra agreed with the details. This method of questioning or interviewing a witness is recognized by experts to be very susceptible to suggestion. This is the method used by investigators when their desire is to "squeeze" some bits of information out of a witness. It provides considerably less accurate information than a "free" report.[49]

Becerra's account has served as evidence to the execution death of Crockett. This one adds the unique twist of having Travis found with Crockett and both executed together. Ford later wrote that Becerra "...admitted he did not know them [Travis and Crockett] personally and might be mistaken as to their identity."[50]

3.26
Bettie, 1882
According to John S. Ford in his book *The Fall of the Alamo*

On the morning of March 6, 1836, she was in the kitchen [of the Alamo] with a colored man, named Charlie; after the resistance of the defenders had ceased a detachment of Mexican soldiers entered the kitchen, Charlie attempted to secrete himself, was found and dragged out. The officer in charge of the men was very small. A soldier made a bayonet thrust at Charlie. The colored gentleman seized the little officer and held him before his own body as a shield - at the same time he backed into a corner. The soldier made many attempts to bayonet Charlie, and in every instance he skillfully covered himself with the diminutive officer. This lasted for several minutes. The soldiers began to relish the joke, and were laughing. The officer did not feel comfortable. He finally called for a parley. He promised to save Charlie's life, on condition that his precious little person should be safely deposited on the floor. Charlie acceded, and the treaty was faithfully observed.[51]

The little known account of Bettie comes to us third hand. Bettie allegedly gave her story to William Neale (1807-1896), a one-time mayor of Brownsville, Texas, who then told John S. Ford. Ford included the account in the same article as Becerra's in the *Texas Mute Ranger*. According to Ford, Neale told him that Becerra's account had omitted an incident. He told Ford that at the time the Mexican army had pulled back to Matamoras, after the Battle of San Jacinto, he was living in the state of Tamaulipas near the mouth of the Rio Grande. Neale stated that a black slave woman who claimed to be the former cook of James Bowie arrived with the Mexican army. She was hired by Neale and remained with him for one to two years. During that time she often spoke of the Alamo battle. When Texan war ships cruised near the mouth of the Rio Grande, Bettie became frightened that she would be carried back to Texas in slavery, and she disappeared into Monterrey. Sergeant Becerra supposedly said he remembered this affair, but "it had escaped his memory."[52]

3.27
Unidentified man, 1882
According to John S. Ford in his book *The Fall of the Alamo*

[He] insisted that he escaped being killed at the storming of the Alamo. He claimed to have hid himself among some pack saddles and rubbish, that the Mexicans overlooked him, and he finally slipped out of the fort.[53]

This account also comes to us third hand from John S. Ford via William Neale. This man is described as being a German by birth who lived in Matamoras for several years and gave lessons in fencing. He was said to be an expert swordsman.[54]

3.28
Mrs. S. A. Hannig (Susanna Dickinson), undated
From a document in the Adjutant General's Miscellaneous Papers, Texas State Archives

On the evening previous to the massacre, Col. Travis asked the command that if any desired to escape, now was the time, to let it be known, & to step out of the ranks. But one stepped out. His name to the best of my recollection was Ross. The next morning he was missing - During the final engagement one Milton, jumped over the ramparts & was killed -

Col Almonte (Mexican) told me that the man who had deserted the evening before had also been killed & that if I wished to satisfy myself of the fact that I could see the body, still lying there, which I declined.[55]

This statement appears as a short typescript note in the Adjutant General's Miscellaneous Papers in the Texas State Library archives. Since Susanna Dickinson's last name was "Hannig" from 1857 to her death in 1883, this statement may have been given at any time between those years. However, her reference to Travis giving the men a choice and the mention of a man named "Ross" suggest that her statement was given sometime after William P. Zuber broke his famous "line" story. The inclusion of Hannig's statement at this point simply reflects the latest point in time it could have been given if it is indeed authentic.[56] (For other accounts by or attributed to Dickinson see #2.1, 2.5, 3.18, 3.20, 3.22, 3.23, 3.29, and 4.22.)

3.29
Susanna Hannig (Dickinson), 1884
According to Andrew Jackson Sowell in his book *Rangers and Pioneers of Texas*

Mrs. Dickinson related one touching incident that she witnessed while the Mexicans were storming the walls. When the storming part advanced, she had retired to the inner room of the fort, and sat there, pale and trembling, with her baby hugged close to her breast, while the conflict was raging, almost deafened by the cannon shots which shook the walls around her. While there, Albert [Galba] Fuqua, of Gonzales, a boy of about seventeen years of age, came where she was with both jaws broken by a bullet. He looked pale and haggard, with the blood flowing from his mouth. He made several attempts to tell her something, but she was unable to understand him. He then held his jaws together with his hands and tried to communicate with her, but was unable to do so. He then shook his head and went back on the walls where the fight was still raging.[57]

This account of Susanna Dickinson is reported by Andrew Jackson Sowell in his book *Rangers and Pioneers of Texas*. Sowell probably learned this story from his uncle of the same name who heard the story directly from Dickinson. Sowell reports that his uncle Andrew "...was just preparing to start [for San Antonio] when Mrs. Dickinson arrived with the fearful news [of the fall of the Alamo]. Galba Fuqua was a young resident of

Theodore Gentilz's *Fall of the Alamo* depicting approximately
3/4 of the Mission/Fortress on the morning of the battle.

(Courtesy of the Daughters of the Republic of Texas at the Alamo)

Photo of the Alamo ca. 1880s, from the same vantage point as the Gentilz
painting. Accounts of the battle from the late 19th century focused on
the familiar roofed-over chapel rather than the entire fortress.

(Courtesy of the Daughters of the Republic of Texas at the Alamo) the town of Gonzales who died at the Alamo.[58] (For other accounts by or attributed to Dickinson see #2.1, 2.5, 3.18, 3.20, 3.22, 3.23, 3.28, and 4.22.)

3.30
Juan N. Seguin, March 28, 1889
From a letter to Hamilton Bee

The remains of those who died in the Alamo were burned by order of General Santa Anna, and the few fragments I ordered deposited in an urn. I ordered a sepulcher opened in San Antonio's cathedral next to the altar, that is, in front of the two railings but very near the steps.[59]

This statement is from a letter written by Seguin to Hamilton P. Bee (1822-1897) in response to an inquiry by Bee of March 9 of that year. The information given by Seguin does not specifically concern itself with the Alamo battle, and it is not suggested that Seguin actually witnessed the burning of the Texan bodies. However, since he did claim to bury the remains of the defenders within the San Fernando cathedral one year after the battle, it seems fitting that this letter be included.[60] (For other accounts by or attributed to Seguin see #3.11 and 3.31.)

3.31
Felix Nuñez, June 30, 1889
According to George W. Noel in an article in the *San Antonio Express*

After the army invested San Antonio and the Americans had retreated to the Alamo, Santa Anna ordered the Americans to surrender. The summons was answered by those of the Alamo by the discharge of a cannon, whereupon Santa Anna caused a blood-red flag to be hoisted from the Cathedral of San Fernando on the west side of the Main plaza, which at that time was in plain view of the Alamo. Simultaneously all the bugles sounded a charge all along the lines of both cavalry and infantry, but this charge was repulsed by the Americans with heavy loss to us. Whereupon the President ordered "sapas" (subterranean houses) to be dug on the north, south and east of the Alamo, which were strongly garrisoned with troops, for the double purpose of preventing re-inforcements from entering the Alamo and to cut the Americans off from water.

This completed the cordon of troops which was drawn around the doomed Alamo. And right here let me state that no ingress or egress could have been accomplished from the time our army regularly besieged the Alamo, and there was none, with the single exception of Don Juan Seguin and his company, who were permitted to leave. They were let go from the fact that they were Mexicans and we did not wish to harm them.

There was no Capt. John W. Smith and company, nor no one else ever cut their way through our lines and entered the Alamo, because they would have been cut to pieces in the attempt, for the main object of Santa Anna was to keep the garrison from receiving reinforcements. And, moreover, there is but one Captain John W. Smith mentioned about San Antonio and he was mayor of the city at the time of the desperate fight with the Comanche chiefs on the east side of the Main plaza. If he had been in the Alamo he would have been killed, and therefore could not have been mayor of San Antonio afterwards.

The second and third day of the siege resulted with very little variance from the first, to-wit: With heavy losses to our army. This so exasperated Santa Anna that he said, to use his own language, that he was losing the flower of his army, and to see the Alamo still hold out he became terribly enraged, and it was at this time that he made the fatal promise, which he so scrupulously carried out, that he would burn the last one of them when taken whether dead or alive. He immediately called a council of all his officers and proposed another attack on the Alamo in the evening of the third day's siege with his entire force. His cry was: "On to the Alamo." This was met with the cry by the officers and men that: "On to the Alamo was on to death."

A large majority of the officers were in favor of waiting until they could get more heavy cannon and perhaps by that time the garrison would be starved out and surrender and further bloodshed be avoided. But Santa Anna, with his usual impetuosity, swore that he would take the fort the next day or die in the attempt. So on Wednesday, the 6th day of March, and the fourth day of the siege, was the time fixed for the final assault.

Each and everything pertaining to the final assault underwent the personal supervision of General Santa Anna, to the end that it would be successful. Three of his most experienced officers were selected to assist him in commanding the assaulting parties. General Vincente Filisola, his second in command, with a thousand picked men took charge of the assault on the east of the Alamo. General Castrillon, with a like number, was placed on the south side. General Ramirez Sesma was to have taken command on the west side next to the river, but seeing that President Santa Anna was determined to make the final assault the next day feigned sickness, the evening before, and was put under arrest and started back to the capital. This part of the command then devolved on Gen. Woll, so there was no General Sesma in command of any portion of the army at the fall of the Alamo, nor afterwards. The troops on the north and northwest, 1,500 in number, were commanded by General Santa Anna in person. This made 4,500 men who participated in the engagement. In addition to this, there was a fatigue party well supplied with ladders, crowbars and axes for the purpose of making breaches in the walls, or at any other vulnerable point.

The infantry were formed nearest the Alamo, as we made the least noise. The cavalry was formed around on the outside of the infantry, with special orders from all of the commanders to cut down every one who dared to turn back.

Everything being in readiness just at dawn of the day on the 6th of March, and the fourth day of the siege, all the bugles sounded a charge from all points. At this time our cannon had battered down nearly all the walls that enclosed the church, consequently all the Americans had taken refuge inside the church, and the front door of the main entrance fronting to the west was open. Just out side of this door Col. Travis was working his cannon. The division of our army on the west was the first to open fire. They fired from the bed of the river near where the opera house now stands. The first fire from the cannon of the Alamo passed over our heads and did no harm; but as the troops were advancing the second one opened a lane in our lines at least fifty feet broad. Our troops rallied and returned a terrible fire of cannon and small arms. After this the cannonading from the Alamo was heard no more. It is evident that this discharge killed Travis, for then the front door was closed and no more Americans were seen outside. By this time the court yard, the doors, the windows, roof and all around the doomed Alamo became one reeking mass of armed humanity. Each one of us vied with the other for the honor of entering the Alamo first. Just at sunrise a lone marksman appeared on top of the church and fired. A colonel was struck in the neck by this shot and died at sundown. This the officer took as an evidence that the Americans had opened a hole in the roof themselves. This proved to be true, for almost in the next moment another American appeared on top of the roof with a little boy in his arms, apparently about three years old, and attempted to jump off, but they were immediately riddled with bullets and both fell lifeless to the ground. With this the troops pressed on, receiving a deadly fire from the top of the roof, when it was discovered that the Americans had constructed a curious kind of ladder, or gangway, of long poles tied together with ropes and filled up on the top with sticks and dirt. This reached from the floor on the inside of the church to over the top edge of the wall, to the ground on the outside. As soon as this discovery was made Santa Anna ordered his entire division to charge and make for the gangway and hole in the roof. But most of the soldiers who showed themselves at this place got not into the Alamo, but into another world, for nearly every one of them was killed. We then found out that all the Americans were alive inside the church. During the entire siege up to this time we had not killed even a single one, except Colonel Travis and the man and boy referred to, for afterwards there were no new graves nor dead bodies in an advanced state of decomposition discovered.

By this time the front door was battered down and the conflict had become general. The entire army came pouring in from all sides, and never in all my life did I witness or hear of such a hand to hand conflict. The Americans fought with the bravery and desperation of tigers, although seeing that they were contending against the fearful odds of at least two hundred to one, not one single one of them tried to escape or ask for quarter, the last one fighting with as much bravery and animation as at first. None of them hid in rooms nor asked for quarter, for they knew none would be given. On the contrary, they all died like heroes, selling their lives as dear as possible. There was but one man killed in a room, and this was a sick man in the big room on the left of the main entrance. He was bayoneted in his bed. He died apparently without shedding a drop of blood. The last moments of the conflict became terrible in the extreme. The soldiers in the moments of victory became entirely uncontrollable, and owing to the darkness of the building and the smoke of the battle, fell to killing one another, not being able to distinguish friend from foe. General Filisola was the first one to make this discovery. He reported it to General Santa Anna, who at once mounted the walls. Although the voice of our idolized commander could scarcely be heard above the din and roar of battle, his presence together with the majestic waving of his sword sufficed to stop the bloody carnage, but not until all buglers entered the church and sounded a retreat, did the horrible butchery entirely cease.

To recount the individual deeds of valor, of the brave men who were slain in the Alamo, would fill a volume as large as the History of Texas; nevertheless there was one who perished in that memorable conflict who is entitled to a passing notice. The one to whom I refer was killed just inside of the front door. The peculiarity of his dress, and his undaunted courage attracted the attention of several of us, both officers and men. He was a tall American of rather dark complexion and had on a long cuera (buck skin coat) and a round cap without any bill, and made of fox skin, with the long tail hanging down his back. This man apparently had a charmed life. Of the many soldiers who took deliberate aim at him and fired, not one ever hit him. On the contrary he never missed a shot. He killed at least eight of our men, besides wounding several others. This fact being observed by a lieutenant who had come in over the wall he sprung at him and dealt him a deadly blow with his sword, just above the right eye, which felled him to the ground and in an instant he was pierced by not less than twenty bayonets. This lieutenant said that if all Americans had killed as many of our men as this one had, our army would have been annihilated before the Alamo could have been taken. He was about the last man that was killed.

After all the firing had ceased and the smoke cleared away, we found in the large room to the right of the main entrance three persons, two Mexican women named Juana De Melto and La Quintanilla and a negro boy, about fifteen or sixteen years old who told us that he was the servant of Colonel Travis. If there had been any other persons in the Alamo they would have been killed, for General Santa Anna had ordered us not to spare neither age nor sex, especially of those who were American or American descent.

On the floor of the main building there was a sight which beggared all description. The earthen floor was nearly shoe-mouth deep in blood and weltering there in laid 500 dead bodies, many of them still clinched together with one hand, while the other held fast a sword, a pistol or a gun, which betokened the kind of conflict which had just ended.

General Santa Anna immediately ordered every one of the Americans to be dragged out and burnt. The infantry was ordered to tie on the ropes, and the cavalry to do the dragging. When the infantry commenced to tie the ropes to the dead bodies they could not tell our soldiers from the Americans, from the fact that their uniforms and clothes were so stained with blood and smoke and their faces so besmeared with gore and blackened that one could not distinguish the one from the other. The fact was reported to Santa Anna and he appeared at the front and gave instructions to have every face wiped off and for the men to be particular not to mistake any of our men for Americans and burn them, but to give them decent sepulture. He stood for a moment gazing on the horrid and ghastly spectacle before him but soon retired and was seen no more.

When the Americans were all dragged out and counted there were 180 officers and men. Upon the other hand this four day's siege and capture of the Alamo cost the Mexican nation at least a thousand men, including killed and wounded, a large majority of this number being killed. Our officers, after the battle was over, were of the opinion that if the Americans had not made holes in the roof themselves, the Alamo could not have been taken by assault. It would either have had to have been starved out or demolished by heavy artillery.

After we had finished our task of burning the Americans a few of us went back to the Alamo to see if we could pick up any valuables, but we could not find anything scarcely, except their arms and a few cooking utensils and some clothing. I found Colonel Travis' coat, which was hanging on a peg driven to the wall just behind the cannon and from where his dead body had just been dragged away. In the pockets I found some papers that resembled paper money or bonds of some kind. His cannon was standing just as he had left it with its mouth pointing west and not towards the Alamo plaza. We did not use Colonel Travis' cannon, nor even our own, because cannons were almost useless on the day that we made the final assault.[61]

Felix Nuñez is said to have been born in Mexico in 1804. He claimed that he had been conscripted into the Mexican army at thirty-two years of age. His account comes to us third hand. Nuñez allegedly related the tale to a professor George W. Noel, who then passed it on to an unidentified staff writer for the *San Antonio Express*. It is impossible to know how much of the story comes from Nuñez himself or how much of it was editorialized by both Noel and the newspaperman. Nuñez's story has figured into the controversy over Crockett's death. Supporters of Crockett's traditional combat death believe that Nuñez's description of an unidentified Alamo defender fighting to the death is that of Crockett.

The many problems and inaccuracies in Nuñez's account were brought to light in 1990 in a critical essay by professor Stephen L. Hardin. Prof. Hardin's essay marked the first time the account had been published in its entirety in 101 years. One of the major stumbling blocks to the credibility of this account is the fact that Nuñez's description of the Alamo seems to be that of the small Alamo church, the only part of the original sprawling mission complex that still stands today or when the account was published in 1889. As with the possibility of editorializing by Noel and the newspaperman, it is unknown if Nuñez supplied this description of the Alamo or if it was the interpretation of the others trying to fit Nuñez's memory of the large Alamo complex to the only building that they were able to recognize as the Alamo in later years. Prof. Hardin criticizes the Nuñez account for its inconsistency with other descriptions of the battle from the Mexican side, most notably that allegedly written by José Enrique de la Peña. (See the comments on de la Peña's account #4.30.)[62]

3.32
Juan N. Seguin, June 7, 1890
From a letter to William Winston Fontaine

Col. Travis had no idea that Santa ana [*sic*] with his army would venture to approach the city of Bexar (now San Antonio) and for this reason, only a watch was kept on the church tower that existed where today stands the cathedral of San Antonio; this watchman was an American whose name I do not remember. About three o'clock in the afternoon he sent a messenger stating that on the road to Leon, he saw a moving body which appeared like a line of troops raising the dust of the road. Upon receipt of this notice John W. Smith, a carpenter (alias "el colorado") was sent to reconnoiter, and returned in the evening, about five o'clock saying "there comes the Mexican army composed of cavalry, infantry and artillery!" In the act of the moment Col. Travis resolved to concentrate all his forces within the Alamo, which was immediately done. As we marched "Potrero Street" (now called "Commerce") the ladies exclaimed "poor fellows, you will all be killed, what shall we do?" Santa ana [*sic*] occupied the city of Bexar at about seven o'clock in the afternoon of that same day and immediately established the siege of the Alamo, which at first was rigorously kept as the sons of a widow named Pacheco, one of whom was named Esteban, took me my meals, and by them we were enabled to communicate with those external to the Alamo.

The day following the arrival of Santa ana, the bombardment was vigorously commenced and lasted three days. Finding ourselves in such a desperate situation, Col. Travis resolved to name a messenger to proceed to the town of Gonzalez and ask for help, thinking that Sam Houston was then at that place. But, as to leave the fortification at such a critical moment was the same as to encounter death, Santana having drawn a complete circle of iron around the Alamo, no one would consent to run the risk, making it necessary to decide the question by putting it to a vote; I was the one elected. Col. Travis opposed my taking this commission, stating that as I was the only one that possessed the Spanish language and understood Mexican customs better, my presence in the Alamo might become necessary in case of having to treat with Santana. But the rest could not be persuaded and I must go. I was permitted to take my orderly Antonio Cruz and we left eight o'clock at night after having bid good bye to all my comrades, expecting certain death. I arrived safely at the town of Gonzalez, and obtained at once a reinforcement of thirty men, who were sent to the Alamo, and I proceeded to meet San Houston.

When the notice of the arrival of the thirty men was given to Santana, it is said, he gave orders to allow them entrance stating that he would only have that many more to kill.

In the city of Bexar at the time of which we speak, there were no others by the name of Seguin than my father Don Erasmo Seguin and myself. My father was the Judge of the Probate Court and I was commander of the 4th department of the West, with headquarters in Bexar.

Even though there may have been a misunderstanding between Bowie and my father, the forces of Col. Travis did not reach the Medina then.

Col. Bougham [Bonham] was about six feet in height, thin, fair complexion, brown hair, grey eyes, he was not vicious and of very honorable conduct as I knew.[63]

This account was written in the form of a letter from Seguin to William Winston Fontaine, who had been a teacher at William Carey Crane College.[64] (For other accounts by or attributed to Seguin see #3.11 and 3.30.)

3.33
Andrea Castañon de Villanueva (Madam Candelaria), 1890

According to William Corner in his book *San Antonio de Bexar—A Description and a Guide*

I asked her was she inside the fortifications of the Alamo during the fight? She answered unhesitatingly "Yes." Was she in the Alamo Church building during the last stand? She replied as before without reflection that she was, in those moments she was nursing Colonel Bowie who was in bed very ill of typhoid fever, and that as she was in the act of giving him a drink of water the Mexican soldiery rushed in, wounding her in the chin - showing an old scar - and killing Bowie in her arms. She demonstrated this scene in quite an active fashion and showed us exactly how she was holding Bowie, her left arm around his shoulders and a drinking cup in her right hand.

I next asked her what was done with the bodies of the Texans? She said all were cremated. With the bodies of the dead Mexicans? All were cremated. Were there many American families in San Antonio then? Some, but they all fled or the men took refuge within the Alamo. Did she know Mrs. Dickinson? Yes, but not well. She adopted an expression of considerable repugnance at this question, and said with some snap that Mrs. Dickinson hated Mexicans. Perhaps Mrs. Dickinson had some reason to do so! I was particular to ask her about a child of Mrs. Dickinson and she said that the husband of Mrs. Dickinson was fighting as one of the defenders of the Alamo and that when he saw the cause was lost he hastened down from the walls and took his son, a little child and tied him around his waist in front of him, got to the top of the wall at the front of the Church and jumped down among the fighting Mexicans below and both were killed. This is very dramatic but it is not I believe elsewhere recorded. Being anxious to know about the daughter of Mrs. Dickinson I asked her if she had not heard that such a child had escaped the massacre with her mother. She believed she said, that Mrs. Dickinson had taken a daughter with her in her flight, she had been told so at any rate.

She said that she recollected David Crockett before the fight. But she could not have known him well, for Crockett was only in San Antonio a few weeks before he lost his life in the Alamo. The rest of the Texans she did not know so well. Most of these men came to San Antonio just previous to the siege. She did not know anything of Ben Milam who was killed in the Veramendi House at the storming of San Antonio in December, 1835. She had not heard of him nor was she aware that he was buried on Milam Square, and that there was a stone to his memory there, though her house and jacal were almost within a stone throw of the place.

I then asked her age. The old lady said one hundred years and three months, holding out three very wrinkled fingers. Her hands were very large for a Mexican. She looked quite the age she said, or older, for that matter, great deep ridges, wrinkles and furrows of skin on her face and hands as "brown as is the ribbed sea sand." She was almost toothless, very little hair of a light yellowish color. Never suffered any sickness, quite active, alert and quick to perceive and understand. A cigarette smoker. Her eyes she feared were beginning to fail her; they were rheumish with red circles underneath.

My friend next interviewed her with his camera and took two excellent negatives in different positions. I then asked her a question upon a matter which had puzzled me and which puzzles me still, though she had a ready answer to it as she had for any other asked. She informed me that the water from the Acequia was used constantly by the defenders of the Alamo during the siege. I naturally asked why the besiegers did not cut off the water or divert it and so distress those within? She said the Indians at the Missions would not have allowed this!

She remembered perfectly that there was a roof formerly to the Alamo Church prior to the siege, but that it was destroyed during the siege by the cannonading.

She had given, when her memory was better, full depositions and statements of all her recollections to Major Teel, and that he held the same. As to Mr. Gentilz's picture that was compiled from her personal descriptions and recollection. It was very good: that it was an exact representation of the Alamo as it was at the time of its fall, and that it gave a fair idea of the fight.

She mentioned Mr. John Twohig, saying that she knew him "Como mis manos," - "Like my hands," which is a favorite idiom of the old woman. "Visitors come every day to see me to hear my story of the Alamo."

Returning to the subject of David Crockett, the old Señora said he was one of the first to fall; that he advanced from the Church building "towards the wall or rampart running from the end of the stockade, slowly and with great deliberation, without arms, when suddenly a volley was fired by the Mexicans causing him to fall forward on his face, dead."

She was quite anxious to remember everything. With reference to a man whom many regard to be an imposter and of whom no one had ever gleaned anything authentic, Señora Candelaria said she could endorse him as another child of the Alamo. She remembers his frightened condition during the bombardment. "He clutched her dress as children do," trying to hide his face.

Such are her recollections; the reader must make many allowances. So long and active a life as hers must be crowded - more - overcrowded, and jumbled with the multitude of things to remember.[65]

Andrea Castañon de Villanueva (1785-1899), the famous Madam Candelaria, has always been a controversial figure regarding the Alamo battle, since historians had never been able to reach a consensus as to whether her story was true or not. She lived to the ripe old age of 113, and in her old age she entertained a growing number of visitors with her stories of the Alamo. Her name "Madam Candelaria" derives from her marriage to her second husband, Candelario Villanueva, in 1830. This particular interview was given to William Corner in 1888, and it was included in his book *San Antonio de Bexar - a Description and Guide* two years later.[66] (For other accounts by or attributed to Madam Candelaria see #3.35 and 3.40.)

3.34
Samuel G. Bastian, October 3, 1891
Originally published in the *Philadelphia Press*

I was in the Alamo in February [1836]. There was a bitter feeling between the partisans of Travis and Bowie, the latter being the choice of the rougher party in the garrison. Fortunately Bowie was prostrated by pneumonia and could not act. When Santa Anna appeared before the place most of the garrison were drunk, and had the Mexicans made a rush the contest would have been short. Travis did his best and at once sent off couriers to Colonel Fannin, at Gonzales, to hurry up reinforcements. I was one of these couriers, and fortunately I knew the country well and spoke Spanish like a native, so I had no trouble. On the 1st of March I met a party of thirty volunteers from Gonzales on the way to the Alamo and concluded to return with them. When near the fort we were discovered and fired on by the Mexican troops. Most of the party got through; but I and three others had to take to the chaparral to save our lives. One of the party was a Spanish Creole from New Orleans. He went into the town and brought us intelligence. We were about three hundred yards from the fort concealed by brush, which extended north for twenty miles. I could see the enemy's operations perfectly.... Disguising myself, and in company with Rigault, the Creole, we stole into the town. Everything was in confusion. In front of the fort the Mexican dead covered the ground, but the scene inside the fort was awful.... We now thought it time to look after ourselves, and we made for the chaparral, where our companions were. We had nearly reached the wood when a mounted lancer overtook us. Rigault awaited and shot him dead, and so we made our escape. Our good fortune did not end here, for we had to make a detour to reach Gonzales and learned in time that the place was invested, and so were spared the fate of the garrison, for they and their commander, Colonel Fannin, were massacred by the Mexicans.[67]

Samuel G. Bastian was born in Philadelphia in 1814. His story of being a courier from the Alamo was published in the *Philadelphia Press* on October 3, 1891. It later was printed in John Henry Brown's *Indian Wars and Pioneers of Texas*. Brown declared Bastian's account as "notoriously false." Brown was a great admirer of Jim Bowie, and Bastian's account also contained a derogatory description of Bowie's earlier life. Amelia Williams included Bastian as a *probable* Alamo courier in her 1931 dissertation "A Critical Study of the Siege of the Alamo," strictly on the basis of Bastian's claim to have been one. She admitted that she could find no evidence in the Texas General Land Office or in other official documents that any man by the name of Bastian served in the Texan army during the Texas Revolution. She felt that this fact was not proof enough that his account was untrue.[68]

3.35
Andrea Castañon de Villanueva (Madam Candelaria), March 6, 1892
According to an article in the *San Antonio Express*

...[S]he was called upon a few days before the fatal attack was made to nurse Colonel Bowie, who was sick of typhoid fever.

Santa Anna made the attack on March 6. The Alamo was filled with Texans, a number of women being among them. Colonel Bowie died in my arms only a few minutes before the entrance to the Alamo by the soldiers. I was holding his head in my lap when Santa Anna's men swarmed into the room where I was sitting. One of them thrust a bayonet into the lifeless head of Colonel Bowie and lifted his body from my lap. As he did so the point of the weapon slipped and struck me in the jaw...[69]

This version of Madam Candelaria's tale appeared in the *San Antonio Express* on the fifty-sixth anniversary of the fall of the Alamo. (For other accounts by or attributed to Madam Candelaria see #3.33 and 3.40.)

3.36
Maria Jesusa Peña, 1896
According to Theodore Gentilz in his research papers for the painting *The Death of Dickinson*

[She] saw from a little window of a jacal on the west side facing the church all or part of what was happening. After the cease-fire, Santa Anna entered by the south west door. Some Texans still hiding came to kneel before him, each one with a little white flag. The foot-soldiers surrounding them hesitated to kill them; but Santa Anna in passing signalled with his head and his sword and suddenly they were pierced with blows of the bayonets.[70]

This account comes to us third hand from the papers of the artist Theodore Gentilz (1819-1906), who did a number of paintings on the subject of the Alamo. This particular statement comes from his research for the painting *The Death of Dickinson* (1896). Maria Jesusa Peña was the wife of Antonio Cruz y Arrocha, from whom Gentilz obtained this account. Cruz y Arrocha and his wife lived in a jacal close to the Alamo. On the night Juan Seguin escaped from the Alamo, Cruz y Arrocha waited for him with a horse by the acequia. He apparently accompanied Seguin on his mission. A cryptic note in the Gentilz papers states that "The account of Sr. Matias Carillo is in perfect accord with this." The Carillo account has never been located. There is no way to tell when this information was actually given to Gentilz, and it never actually became public until much later. It is given here under the year 1896 simply because that is the date of Gentilz's painting.[71]

3.37
John Sutherland, 1896
According to a version of his story that appears in the John S. Ford Papers

On the morning of the twenty-third the inhabitants were observed to be in quite an unusual stir. The citizens of every class were hurrying to and fro, through the streets, with obvious signs of excitement. Houses were being emptied, and their contents put into carts, and hauled off. Such of the poorer class, who had no better mode of conveyance, were shouldering their effects, and leaving on foot.

These movements solicited investigation. Orders were issued that, no others be allowed to leave the city, which had the effect to increase their commotion. Several were arrested, and interrogated, as to the cause of the movement, but no satisfactory answer could be obtained. The most general reply was, that they were going out to the country to prepare for the coming crop. This excuse, however, availed nothing, for it was not to be supposed that every person in the city was a farmer. Colonel Travis persisted in carrying out his order, and continued the investigation. Nine o'clock came, and no discoveries were made. Ten o'clock in like manner passed, and finally the eleventh hour was drawing near, and the matter was yet a mystery. It was hoped by Colonel Travis that his diligent investigation, and strict enforcement of the order prohibiting the inhabitants from leaving the city, would have the effect to frighten them into a belief that, their course was not the wisest for them to pursue; that, he, provoked by their obstinacy in refusing to reveal the true cause of the uneasiness, would resort to measures which might be more distasteful than any which would probably follow an open confession. But in that he was disappointed. The treacherous wretches persisted in their course, greatly to his discomfiture all the while.

Finally he was informed, secretly, by a friendly Mexican that the enemy's cavalry had reached the Leon, eight miles from the city, on the previous night, and had sent a messenger to the inhabitants, informing them of the fact, and warning them to evacuate the city at early dawn, as it would be attacked the next day. He stated further that, a messenger had arrived, a day or two before, and that, it had been the purpose of the enemy to take the Texians by surprise, but in consequence of a heavy rain having fallen on the road, their march was impeded, and they were unable to reach the place in time. Notwithstanding this statement seemed altogether plausible, and to substantiate the statement the report given by Herrera three days before, yet it wore the countenance of so many of their false rumors that it was a matter of doubt that there was any truth in it.

Colonel Travis came to me forthwith, however, and informed me of what he had learned, and wished to borrow a horse of me to send out to the Salado for his "Caballado" that he might start a scout through the country. As I had two, of course, he obtained one, when a runner was started forthwith. In company with Colonel Travis, and at his request, I proceeded to post a reliable man on the roof of the old church, as a sentinel. We all three went up, but being unable to make any discoveries, the Colonel and myself returned. The sentinel remained at his post with orders to ring the bell, if he should discover any sign, which he might deem ominous.

Colonel Travis went to his room, and I to the store of Captain Nat Lewis, who requested me to assist in taking an inventory of his goods, saying that he had some suspicion that they would soon be taken from him. We proceeded to the task, but had not been long engaged when the sentinel rang the bell, and cried out, "the enemy are in view." Immediately I went out, and ran across the plaza toward the church, when a considerable crowd soon gathered around, Colonel Travis was also there. Several persons ran up to the sentinel's post, and not being able to see anything justifying the cry, hallowed that it was a "false alarm," and that they "believed the whole tale was a lie," and "our fears useless." The sentinel exclaimed, with an oath, that "he had seen them," and "that they had hid behind a row of brushwood." The crowd disbanded, the greater part of them discrediting the report altogether.

I then proposed to Colonel Travis, that, if any one, who knew the country, would accompany me, I would go out, and ascertain to a certainty the truth or falsity of the whole. John W. Smith was soon at hand. When we started taking the Laredo road, I remarked to Travis, just as I mounted my horse, that "if he saw us returning in any other gait than a slow pace, he might be sure that we had seen the enemy." This arrangement proved of some benefit. A moderate gait soon brought us to the top of the slope, about a mile and a half west of town, where we were not surprised to find ourselves within one hundred and fifty yards of fifteen hundred men, well mounted and equipped. Their polished armor glistening in the rays of the sun, as they were formed in a line, behind the chaparral and mesquite bushes mentioned by the sentinel. The commander riding along the line, waving his sword, as though he might be giving directions to the mode of attack. We did not remain long watching their movements, but wheeled around, and started full speed back to town. In consequence of a heavy rain, through the previous night, the road was quite muddy, and my horse being rather smoothly shod, began to slip and scramble, stopped at the end [of] fifty yards where with a tumbling somersault, he pitched my gun out of my hand, throwing me some distance ahead of him, and followed himself, rolling directly across my knees. Smith dismounted, and pulled him off of me, but being slightly stunned, he had made no effort to rise, but lay perfectly still, holding me fast beneath him. After some moments he managed to get up, when by the assistance of Smith, I did likewise. When I picked pieces of my gun, which was broken off at the breech, being again mounted, we resumed our gait and were not long in getting to town.

On reaching the civil plaza we met Col. Crockett, who informed us that, Col. Travis had removed his headquarters, together with the entire force, from the city to the Alamo. Smith here left me, and went to his house.

On learning the result of our scout Col. Crockett returned with me. We crossed the river at the ford in the river below, and on our way up to the fort, we met Capt. Dimmitt and Lieut. Nobles. The former inquired where we were going. I told him. When he remarked that "there were not men enough at Bexar to defend the place, that it was bound to fall; and insisted that I go with him" Saying he "would see me safely out." Then we would go and bring reinforcements to the garrison." I replied that "I should go, and report to Col. Travis, and could not say, that I could accompany him even then." As we rode on he remarked that he would wait for me down the street at his house. It was not until attempting to dismount, in front of Travis' room, that I was sensible of the extent of the injury caused by the fall of my horse. On alighting from the saddle my knee gave way, and I fell to the ground. By the assistance of Col. Crockett I got up and went to Col. Travis' room, where we found him writing a despatch. He had watched our movements, and by this time no longer doubted that the enemy were upon him. I informed him of our discoveries, and of the accident which had happened to me and added that, "if I could be of any benefit to him I was at his service." He replied that he wished me to go forthwith to Gonzales, and rally the settlers, if possible, to his relief. Col. Crockett, yet standing by, remarked to him, "Colonel, here am I, assign me a position, and I and my twelve boys will try to defend it." Travis replied that he wanted him to defend the picket wall extending from the end of the barracks, on the south side, to the corner of the church.

At this time the Texians had well nigh consumed everything they had on hand in the way of provisions. Grant and Johnston had left them but a small supply of coffee, sugar, and salt, which had long since disappeared, and none of these necessaries were to be found, though they might have had ever so much money with which to buy them.

129

Their meats they obtained by driving the beef from the prairie, just as they needed it, and as they never had more at one time than would serve them more than twenty-four hours; so it happened they were in need just at that time. They were out of corn of which they made their bread, and had no money to purchase more. Though Travis afterwards thought that the Lord was on his side upon the promise that "he would provide for the upright," if he had claimed his favor under the circumstances it would have been upon the score that; "He chasteneth whom he loveth." While they were retiring from the city to the Alamo they met twenty or thirty beeves coming down the Alamo street, now Commerce Street, towards the river when all hands gathered around them and drove them into the Alamo. They also got their bread by chance. During the hurry, and excitement of the day, a number of Mexican "jacales," near the Alamo, had been vacated. In them they found some eighty or ninety bushels of corn. These were their supplies during the siege.

As soon as the Texans entered the Alamo they set about preparing for its defense. The beeves were secured in a pen on the north east side of the fortress, ... The corn was stored away in some of the small rooms of the barracks. They did not obtain water from the small canal which runs near, but dug a well within the walls. There being no portholes in the walls, it was necessary for them to make an arrangement by which they could shoot over it. This was done by throwing up an embankment against it on the inside. This being done they proceeded to make other arrangements necessary. Their guns were placed upon the wall, as soon as possible. Of these they had some thirty or forty pieces of various calibres, amongst them was an eighteen pounder. Most of them they had taken from the enemy, in December previous, when Cos surrendered. Though they had so many they were not all mounted, I don't think more than about twenty were put to use during the siege. They had also obtained from the same source a considerable number of muskets, swords, and bayonets, together with any amount of ammunition, which came in play, for of their own they had but a small supply. All were armed with good rifles, single barrel pistols, and good knives. Their powder they kept in a small room in the southwest corner of the church, which was covered over with an arched roof of stone, and plastered perfectly tight, so as to make it proof against sparks of fire from the enemy's shells.

So soon as Travis ascertained that the enemy were upon him he sent despatches to Col. Fannin then at Goliad, representing to him his condition, and requesting assistance, as speedily as it could be sent to him. This despatch was borne by a young man by the name of Johnson, and not by

J.B. Bonham as stated in some accounts. On the twenty-third, when Almonte arrived at Bexar, Bonham was absent from the city. He had visited Texas with a view of purchasing land, and had not attached himself to the army, though he held himself in readiness to serve the country whenever an emergency occurred. At the time the cavalry arrived he was prospecting the country in the vicinity of San Antonio, and on hearing the report of cannon in the city, started on the return. On the way to Fannin, he learned the cause of the cannon fire. He put spurs to his horse and made his way into the walls of the Alamo.

Between three and four o'clock P.M. I started as requested by Col. Travis, for Gonzales. I first rode down the river, a short distance, thinking to meet Dimmitt, but he had gone, taking the main Goliad road. On coming near the ford I fell in with J.W. Smith, also on his way to Gonzales. We halted and were paralyzed for a moment when we saw the enemy march into the Military Plaza in regular order. While we sat on our horses, for a moment, watching their movements, Capt. Nat Lewis came to us on foot. He too, was bound for Gonzales with as much of his valuables as he could carry in his saddle-bags, thrown across his shoulder, leaving the remainder in his storehouse, a contribution to the enemy.

We soon parted, Capt. Lewis taking one direction, Smith and myself another. Thinking the Mexicans might have seen us going off, and pursue us, we took the old Goliad road, which runs directly south for some distance, after going about half a mile we turned due east into mesquite and chaparral brush, following the winding paths that led through it. We crossed the Gonzales road between the city and Powder house Hill, about one mile east of town. Turning eastward over the hill, we saw three men riding in the distance across the Salado, about a mile and a half from us. We suspected, that they might be a scouting party of the enemy attempting to cut off any one leaving the city, we kept on our course rather bearing around them to the left.

On reaching the Salado, my injured leg began to stiffen and to give me such pain that I thought of turning back and should have done so if Smith had not urged me on, believing that the enemy had by that time surrounded the fort, for a few minutes had passed since we had heard a cannon shot. After resting a moment and filling our gourds for which we had just paid a Mexican, whom we met, a dollar, we went on, continuing parallel with the road and about a mile from it. After riding about sixteen miles, dark came upon us, when my pains now became so acute that I was forced to stop. We spread our blankets upon the ground, and ourselves upon them, and being somewhat relieved of my suffering, I was soon asleep.

By daylight on the morrow we were again in the saddle, and on our way to Gonzales, where after a hard days ride, and anything else than an agreeable one to myself, we arrived about four o'clock, P.M.[72]

This version of John Sutherland's account is much more extensive than his claim of 1854. It is contained in the John S. Ford papers, and it is presented at this point since 1896 is the year that Sutherland's original manuscript was presented to Ford by Sutherland's family. Sutherland's account has appeared in a number of different publications with a number of variations. For the purposes of this book the later versions will not be included. Sutherland's account and his participation in the opening stages of the Alamo siege have become an accepted part of the Alamo story. However, Tom Lindley's recent findings on the subject supply enough information to cast considerable doubt on its authenticity.[73] (For another account by or attributed to Sutherland see #3.10.)

3.38
Eulalia Yorba, April 12, 1896
From an article in the *San Antonio Express*

I remember well when Santa Anna and his two thousand soldiers on horses and with shining muskets and bayonets marched into the little pueblo of San Antonio. The news ran from mouth to mouth that Colonel Travis, Davy Crockett and Colonel Bowie and the 160 or so other Texans who had held against the Mexicans for several weeks had taken refuge in and had barricaded themselves in that old stone mission, which had been used as a crude fort or garrison long before I came to the country. It belonged to Mexico and a few stands of muskets and three or four cannons were kept there. When Santa Anna's army came they camped on the plains about the pueblo and a guard was put about the Alamo fort. That was from the last day of February to March 4. Of course, I kept at home with my little boys and never stirred out once, for we women were all terribly frightened. Every eatable in the house, all the cows, lumber and hay about the place were taken by the troops, but we were assured that if we remained in the house no personal harm would come to us.

Of course, we were hourly informed of the news. We knew that the Texans in the Alamo were surrounded by over five hundred soldiers constantly, while fifteen hundred more soldiers were in camp out on the plains. We learned that four days had been given the Texans to surrender. We heard from the soldiers that not one of the imprisoned men had so much as returned a reply to the demand for surrender and that on the morning of the 6th of March 1836, Santa Anna was going to bring matters to a crisis with the beleaguered rebels. I never can tell the anxiety that we people on the outside felt for that mere handful of men in the old fort, when we saw around hostile troops as far as we could see and not a particle of help for the Texans, for whom we few residents of the town had previously formed a liking.

The morning of Sunday - the 6th of March - ah! indeed, I could never forget that, even if I lived many years more - was clear and balmy and every scrap of food was gone from my house and the children and I ran to the home of a good old Spanish priest so that we could have food and comfort there. There was nothing to impede the view of the Alamo from the priest's home, although I wished there was. The shooting began at six in the morning. It seemed as if there were myriads of soldiers and guns about the stone building. There was volley after volley fired into the barred and bolted windows. Then the volleys came in quick succession. Occasionally we heard muffled volleys and saw puffs of smoke from within the Alamo, and when we saw, too, Mexican soldiers fall in the roadway or stagger back we knew the Texans were fighting as best they could for their lives.

It seemed as if ten thousand guns were shot off indiscriminately as firecrackers snap when whole bundles of them are set off at one time. The smoke grew thick and heavy and we could not see clearly down at the Alamo, while the din of musketry, screams of crazy, exultant Mexicans increased every moment. I have never heard human beings scream so fiercely and powerfully as the Mexican soldiers that day. I can compare such screams only to the yell of a mountain panther or lynx in desperate straits.

Next several companies of soldiers came running down the street with great heavy bridge timbers. These were quickly brought to bear as battering rams on the mission doors, but several volleys from within the Alamo, as nearly as we could see, laid low the men at the timbers and stopped the battering for a short time. Three or four brass cannons were loaded with what seemed to us very long delay and were placed directly in front of the main doors of the mission. They did serious work.

133

Meanwhile, bullets from several thousand muskets incessantly rained like hail upon the building and went through the apertures that had been made in the wood barricades at the windows and doors. The din was indescribable. It did not seem as if a mouse could live in a building so shot at and riddled as the Alamo was that morning.

Next we saw ladders brought and in a trice the low roof of the church was crowded with a screaming, maddened throng of men armed with guns and sabers. Of course we knew then that it was all up with the little band of men in the Alamo. I remember that the priest drew us away from the window and refused to let us look longer, notwithstanding the fascination of the scene. We could still hear the shouts and yells and the booming of the brass cannon shook the priest's house and rattled the window panes.

Along about nine o'clock, I should judge, the shooting and swearing and yelling had ceased, but the air was thick and heavy with blue powder smoke. A Mexican colonel came running to the priest's residence and asked that we go down to the Alamo to do what we could for the dying men.

Such a dreadful sight. The roadway was thronged with Mexican soldiers with smoke and dirt begrimed faces, haggard eyes and wild, insane expressions. There were twelve or fifteen bodies of Mexicans lying dead and bleeding here and there and others were being carried to an adobe house across the way. The stones in the church wall were spotted with blood, the doors were splintered and battered in. Pools of thick blood were so frequent on the sun-baked earth about the stone building that we had to be careful to avoid stepping in them. There was a din of excited voices along the street and the officers were marshaling their men for moving to camp.

But no one could even tell you the horror of the scene that met our gaze when we were led by the sympathetic little colonel into the old Alamo to bandage up the wounds of several young men there. I used to try when I was younger to describe that awful sight, but I never could find sufficient language. There were only a few Mexicans in there when we came and they were all officers who had ordered the common soldiers away from the scene of death and - yes - slaughter, for that was what it was. The floor was literally crimson with blood. The woodwork all about us was riddled and splintered by lead balls and what was left of the old altar at the rear of the church was cut and slashed by cannon ball and bullets. The air was dark with powder smoke and was hot and heavy. The odor was oppressive and sickening and the simply horrible scene nerved us as nothing else could.

The dead Texans lay singly and in heaps of three or four, or in irregular rows here and there all about the floor of the Alamo, just as they had fallen when a ball reached a vital part or they had dropped to their death from loss of blood. Of course we went to work as soon as we got to the mission at helping the bleeding and moaning men, who had only a few hours at most more of life; but the few minutes that we looked upon the corpses all about gave us a picture that has always been as distinct as one before my very eyes.

So thick were the bodies of the dead that we had to step over them to get a man in whom there was still life. Close to my feet was a young man who had been shot through the forehead. He had dropped dead with his eyes staring wildly open and, as he lay there, seemingly gazed up into my face.

I remember seeing poor Colonel Davy Crockett as he lay dead by the side of a dying man, whose bloody and powder stained face I was washing. Colonel Crockett was about fifty years old at that time. His coat and rough woolen shirt were soaked with blood so that the original color was hidden, for the eccentric hero must have died of some ball in the chest or a bayonet thrust.[74]

Eulalia Yorba (b. 1801) was a citizen of San Antonio de Bexar at the time of the Alamo battle. Her account was published in the *San Antonio Express* sixty years later.[75]

Juana Alsbury, 1898
According to Mary Adams Maverick in her book *The Fall of the Alamo*

Mrs. Allsbury [sic] went into the Fort with Bowie to care for his comfort, he being in feeble health, and having had to resign command to Colonel Travis. Mrs. Alsbury told me that the women and children, i.e. her son, 8 years, and her sister 13, and Mrs. Dickenson and babe fled to Colonel Bowie's room when the soldiers entered the old church - this room was upstairs. She saw the Mexican soldiers enter, bayonet Bowie, then while he still lived, carry him upon their bayonets into the Plaza below, and there toss him up and catch him upon the bayonets 'til the blood ran down upon their arms and clothes. Then a Mexican cavalry officer dashed in amongst the butchers, with drawn sword. Lashing them right and left and forced them to desist. I am sorry I have forgotten this officer's name. It should be recorded. Mrs. A. herself and children, were taken care of by Sergeant Perez of the Mexican army, who was a brother of her first husband.[76]

This account attributed to Juana Alsbury comes to us from Mary Adams Maverick (1818-1898). She was the wife of Samuel Augustus Maverick and a leading citizen of San Antonio, Texas. The Maverick home stood on what is now the northwest corner of Houston Street and North Alamo, which would have put it in close proximity with what had been the northwest corner of the Alamo compound.[77] (For another account by or attributed to Alsbury see #3.19.)

3.40
Andrea Castañon de Villanueva (Madam Candelaria), February 19, 1899
From an article in the *St. Louis Republic*, repeated in the *San Antonio Light*

When Santa Anna suddenly appeared on the prairies in sight of San Antonio, at the head of a veteran army of 10,000 men, Colonel Bowie was very sick. Hopeful as all who are afflicted with consumption, he still felt himself able to discharge the duties of a soldier. He went to the Alamo and declared that he would fight as a private. It was not long before he confined to his cot. General Houston wrote a letter to Mme. Candelaria, which she still possesses, asking her to look after his friend Bowie, and nurse him herself. All save Bowie himself realized that the hero was in the last stages of consumption.

When Santa Anna invested the city and drew a cordon of troops around the Alamo, Mme. Candelaria was inside the walls. She might easily have returned to her home, but her heart was with the patriots, and she determined to remain with them and share their fortunes. Bowie grew worse every day. He was never able to sit up more than a few minutes at any period during the time that the battle was going on. He occupied the little room on the left of the great front door, and Mme. Candelaria sat by his side. When the firing grew hot he would ask his faithful nurse to assist him to raise himself to the window. He would aim deliberately and after firing would fall back on his cot and rest. One evening Colonel Travis made a fine speech to his soldiers. Mme. Candelaria does not pretend to remember what he said, but she does remember that he drew a line on the floor with the point of his sword and asked all who were willing to die for Texas to come over on his side. They all quickly stepped across the line but two men. One of these sprang over the wall and disappeared. The other man was James Bowie. He made an effort to rise, but failed, and with tears streaming from his eyes, he said: "Boys, won't none of you help me over there?" Colonel Davy Crockett and several others instantly sprang towards the cot and carried the brave man across the line. Mme. Candelaria noticed Crockett drop on his knees and talk earnestly in low tones to Colonel Bowie for a long time. "At this time," says the heroic old lady, "we all knew that we were doomed, but not one was in favor of surrendering." A small herd of cattle had been driven inside of the walls, and we had found a small quantity of corn that had been stored by the priests. The great front door had been piled full of sand bags, and there was a bare hope that we might hold out until General Houston sent a re-enforcement.

"There were just 177 men inside of the Alamo, and up to this time no one had been killed, though cannon had thundered against us and several assaults had been made. Colonel Travis was the first man killed. He fell on the southeast side near where the Menger hotel stands. The Mexican infantry charged across the plaza many times, and rained musket balls against the wall, but they were always made to recoil. Up to the morning of the 6th of March, the cannon had done us little damage, though the batteries never ceased firing. Colonel Crockett frequently came into the room and said a few encouraging words to Bowie. This man came to San Antonio only a few days before the invasion. The Americans extended him a warm welcome. They made bonfires in the streets, and Colonel Crockett must have made a great speech, for I never heard so much cheering and hurrahing in all my life. They had supper at my hotel and there was lots of singing, story telling and some drinking. Crockett played the fiddle and he played well if I am any judge of music. He was one of the strangest-looking men I ever saw. He had the face of a woman and his manner was that of a young girl. I could not regard him as a hero until I saw him die. He looked grand and terrible standing in the door and fighting a whole column of Mexican infantry. He had fired his last shot, and had nothing to reload. The cannon balls had knocked away the sand bags, and the infantry was pouring through the breech. Crockett stood there swinging something bright over his head. The place was full of smoke and I could not tell whether he was using a gun or a sword. A heap of dead was piled at his feet and the Mexicans were lunging at him with bayonets, but he would not retreat an inch. Poor Bowie could see it all, but he could not raise up from his cot. Crockett fell and the Mexicans poured into the Alamo."

On the morning of the 6th of March, 1836, General Santa Anna prepared to hurl his whole force against the doomed fort. The duguelo [deguello] was sounded and Mme. says that they all very well understood what it meant, and every man prepared to sell his life as dearly as possible.

The soldiers with blanched cheeks and a look of fearless firmness, gathered in groups and conversed in low tones. Colonel Crockett and about a dozen strong men stood with their hands behind the sand bags at the front. The cot upon which Colonel Bowie reposed was in the little room on the north side and within a few feet of the position occupied by Crockett and his men. These two brave spirits frequently exchanged a few words while waiting for the Mexicans to begin the battle. "I sat by Bowie's side," says Mme. Candelaria, "and tried to keep him as composed as possible. He had a high fever and was seized with a fit of coughing every few moments. Colonel Crockett loaded Bowie's rifle and a pair of pistols and laid them by his side. The Mexicans ran a battery of several guns out on the plaza and instantly began to rain balls against the sand bags. It was easy to see that they would soon clear every barricade from the front door, but Crockett assured Bowie that he could stop a whole regiment from entering. I peeped through the window and saw long lines of infantry, followed by dragoons, filing into the plaza, and I notified Colonel Crockett of the fact. "All Right," said he. "Boys, aim well!" The words had hardly died on his lips before a storm of bullets rained against the walls and the very earth seemed to tremble beneath the tread of Santa Anna's yelling legions. The Texans made every shot tell, and the plaza was covered with dead bodies. The assaulting columns recoiled and I thought we had beaten them, but a host of officers could be seen waving their swords and rallying the hesitating and broken columns.

They charged again, and at one time, when within a dozen steps of the door, it looked as if they were about to be driven back, so terrible was the fire of the Texans. Those immediately in front of the great door were certainly in the act of retiring when a column that had come obliquely across the plaza reached the southwest corner of the Alamo and bending their bodies, they ran under the shelter of the wall to the door. It looked as if a hundred bayonets were thrust into the door at the same time, and a sheet of flame lit up the Alamo. Every man at the door fell but Crockett, I could see him struggling with the head of the column, and Bowie raised

Andrea Castañon de Villanueva [Madam Candelaria]
enthralled visitors with her ever-changing tales of the Alamo.

(Courtesy of the Institute of Texan Cultures)

up and fired his rifle. I saw Crockett fall backwards. The enraged Mexicans streamed into the building firing and yelling like madmen. The place was full of smoke, and the death screams of the dying, mingled with the exultant shouts of the victors, made it a veritable hell. A dozen or more of the Mexicans sprang into the rooms occupied by Colonel Bowie. He emptied his pistols in their faces and killed two of them. As they lunged towards him with their muskets I threw myself in front of them and received two of their bayonets in my body. One passed through my arm and the other through the flesh of my chin. Here, señor, are the scars; you can see them yet. I implored them not to murder a sick man, but they thrust me out of the way and butchered my friend before my eyes. All was silent now. The massacre had ended. One hundred and seventy-six of the bravest men that the world ever saw had fallen, and not one had asked for mercy. I walked out of the cell, and, when I stepped upon the floor of the Alamo the blood ran into my shoes.[78]

This account of Madam Candelaria appeared as an article in the *St. Louis Republic* and was repeated in the *San Antonio Light* shortly after her death in 1899. This version certainly does nothing to enhance the credibility of Madam Candelaria. It is yet another account which centers on the Alamo church as the scene of all the action. Everything takes place before her eyes with Bowie and Crockett never leaving her sight. In addition, many of the details given in this version are in conflict with those of her earlier accounts.[79] (For other accounts by or attributed to Madam Candelaria see #3.33 and 3.35.)

Chapter Four

20TH CENTURY

*The need of society to write a
history of major events produces
witness to fill that need.*

Katherine W. Elison and
Robert Buckhout

4.1

Benjamin F. Highsmith, 1900

According to A. J. Sowell in his book *Early Settlers and Indian Fighters of Southwest Texas*

Mr. Highsmith stayed in the Alamo with Colonel Travis until the approach of Santa Anna from Mexico with a large army, and he was then sent by his commander with a dispatch to Colonel Fannin ordering that officer to blow up the fort at Goliad and come to him with his men. Mr. Highsmith was gone five days and on his return Santa Anna's advance of 600 cavalry was on the east side of the river, riding around the Alamo and on the lookout for messengers whom they knew the Texan commander was sending from the doomed fort.

Mr. Highsmith sat on his horse on Powderhouse Hill and took in the situation. The Mexican flag was waving from the Church of Bexar across the river, and the flag of Travis from the Alamo. The country was open and nearly all prairie in the valley around San Antonio, and objects could be seen some distance from the elevated points. There was a great stir and perceptible activity in the town, and the forms of some of the doomed men at the Alamo could be plainly seen as from the walls of the fort they watched the Mexican cavalry.

The daring messenger saw there was no chance for him to communicate with his gallant commander, and slowly rode north towards the San Antonio and Gonzales road. The Mexican cavalrymen saw him, and a dense body of them rode parallel with and closely watched him. Finally they spurred their horses into a gallop and came rapidly towards him. Highsmith took one last look towards the Alamo and the trapped heroes within, and then, turning his horse east, dashed off towards Gonzales. He is the last man alive to-day who talked with Bowie and Travis at the Alamo.

The Mexicans pursued Uncle Ben six miles - two miles beyond the Salado Creek - and then gave up the chase. He went on to the Cibolo Creek, eighteen miles from San Antonio and then halted on a ridge to rest his horse. While here his quick ear caught the sound of cannon as the dull boom was wafted across the prairie. The siege and bombardment of the Alamo had commenced. Mr. Highsmith thinks that David Crockett went into the Alamo with George Kimble, A.J. Kent, Abe Darst, Tom Jackson, Tom Mitchell, Wash Cottle, and two 16-year-old boys named Albert [Galba] Fuqua and John Gaston. Crockett had a few men who came with him to Texas, and some think he did not come by Gonzales, but straight across from Bastrop to San Antonio. The men mentioned above all came from Gonzales and were led by Captain Kimble. The names are not all given here. There were thirty two of them in all. They came down the river in the night and fought their way into the Alamo by a sudden dash.

When Mr. Highsmith arrived at Gonzales he found Gen. Sam Houston there with about 300 men on his way to succor Travis, and Highsmith's report was the last reliable news before the fall. Scouts were sent back to within a few miles of San Antonio to listen for the signal gun that Travis said he would fire at sunup each morning as long as [they] held the fort. On Monday morning, March 7, 1836, the scouts listened in vain for the welcome signal. The sun arose and began to mount into the heavens, and still no token came; all was silent in the west. The scouts mounted their horses and set off again for Gonzales to inform General Houston that the Alamo had fired her last gun. On the 6th the Alamo had been stormed and all the defenders perished.[1]

Benjamin F. Highsmith (1817-1905) was born in either Mississippi or the Missouri territory. He emigrated to Texas with his parents, crossing the Sabine River on Christmas Eve 1823. Highsmith's account appears in A.J. Sowell's book *Early Settlers and Indian Fighters of Southwest Texas*, and it is narrated in the words of Sowell.[2]

Benjamin F. Highsmith's account as an Alamo courier
was the first published in the 20th century.

From *Early Settlers and Indian Fighters of Southwest Texas* by A.J. Sowell

4.2
Enrique Esparza, November 9, 1901
According to Adina de Zavala in
an article in the *Houston Chronicle*

[He] and the other Mexicans who escaped from the butchery of Santa Anna's hordes were concealed in two store rooms in the court yard of the Alamo proper in front of what is left of the old building, and that these rooms were on each side of the main entrance gate which led into the court from the outside. He also says the walls were surrounded on the outside by a ditch "as deep as two men" and that a draw bridge spanning this moat afforded the means of ingress and egress to and from the place. It is known that such a wall and moat did exist and Esparza's apparent familiarity with this is another proof of the genuineness of his story....

Esparza says she [Madam Candelaria] was not there [in the Alamo]. She had been in it frequently before it fell, he says, and was there immediately afterward, but was not present when the actual fall of the Alamo and massacre of its patriotic defenders occurred....

Early in '36 they [the Esparza family] were warned by letter from Vice President De Zavala, through Captain Roja, that the Mexican hordes were coming and advised to take their families to a place of safety. No wagons were obtainable, and so they waited. On the morning of February 22 John W. Smith, one of the scouts, galloped up to Esparza's house bearing the news that Santa Anna was near - would be upon them by night. What should they do? was the question. Flee they could not! Should they try and hide or go into the fortress of the Alamo? The Alamo was decided upon by the mother, as there her husband would be fighting for liberty. There they carried in their arms their most precious possessions - going back and forth many times - till at sunset, the mother Mrs. Anita Esparza, with her last bundles and her little daughter and four sons, passed across the bridge over the acequia into the court yard of the Alamo, just as the trumpets' blare and noise of Santa Anna's army was heard. Within the Alamo court yard were other refugees who were saved - Mrs. Alsbury and one child and sister, Gertrudis Navarro, Mrs. Concepcion Losoya, and her daughter and two sons, Vitorina de Salina, and three little girls, Mrs. Dickinson and baby (hitherto believed to have been the only ones who escaped alive), and an old woman called Petra.

No tongue can describe the terror and horror of that fearful last fight! The woman and children were paralyzed with terror and faint from hunger when the Mexican soldiers rushed in after the Fall of the Alamo. A poor paralytic unable to speak - to tell them he was not a belligerent, was murdered before their eyes, as also a young fellow who had been captured some time previous and confined in the Alamo. Brigido Guerrero, a youth, was saved, as he managed to say he was not a Texan, but a Texan prisoner.

A Mexican officer, related to some of the refugees, arrived just in time to save the women and children - but they were subjected to terrible usage and horrible abuse. Finally, someone obtained safe conduct for them at about 2 o'clock on the morning of the 7th to the house of Governor Musquiz, on Main Plaza. Here the famished prisoners were served with coffee by the Musquiz domestics. At daylight they were required to go before Santa Anna and take the oath of allegiance. Each mother was then given a blanket and two dollars by Santa Anna in person. The only two who escaped this additional humiliation were the two daughters of Navarro, who were spirited away from Musquiz' house by their father [uncle] - Jose Antonio Navarro. The body of Esparza's father, who was butchered with other Texans, was obtained by his brother, who was in the Mexican army, and was buried in the San Fernando Campo Santa, and thus he has the distinction of being the only Texan who escaped the funeral pyre.[3]

Enrique Esparza (1828-1917) was the son of Alamo defender Gregorio Esparza. His story remained unknown for sixty-five years until his part in the Alamo battle was announced by Adina de Zavala. Miss de Zavala was the granddaughter of Lorenzo de Zavala, the first vice-president of the Republic of Texas. She was also one of the driving forces behind the preservation of the modern day Alamo. Esparza's story comes to us third hand, via Miss de Zavala and through a reporter of the *Houston Chronicle*. In an article from the previous day Miss de Zavala's discovery of Esparza is described as accidental. It also explained that Esparza had kept silent for years because "...he did not know the value of his testimony or think anything about the famous battle..."[4] (For other accounts by or attributed to Enrique Esparza see #4.3, 4.8, 4.16, 4.17, and 4.28).

Adina de Zavala, one of the saviors of the modern day Alamo. Miss de Zavala made public Enrique Esparza's role in the Alamo story.

(Courtesy of the Daughters of the Republic of Texas Library at the Alamo)

Enrique Esparza, November 22, 1902
From an article in the *San Antonio Express*

My father, Gregorio Esparza, belonged to Benavides' company, in the American army ... and I think it was in February, 1836, that the company was ordered to Goliad when my father was ordered back alone to San Antonio for what I don't know. When he got here there were rumors that Santa Anna was on the way here, and many residents sent their families away. One of my father's friends told him that he could have a wagon team and all necessary provision for a trip, if he wanted to take his family away. There were six of us besides my father, my mother, whose name was Anita, my eldest sister, myself and three younger brothers, one a baby in arms. I was 8 years old.

My father decided to take the offer and move the family to San Felipe. Everything was ready, when one morning, Mr. W. Smith, who was godfather to my youngest brother, came to our house on North Flores street, just above where the Presbyterian church now is, and told my mother to tell my father when he came in that Santa Anna had come.

When my father came my mother asked him what he would do. You know the Americans had the Alamo, which had been fortified a few months before by General Cos.

"Well, I'm going to the fort" my father said.

Well, if pop goes, I am going along, with the whole family too.

It took the whole day to move and an hour before sundown we were inside the fort. [T]here was a bridge over the river about where Commerce street crosses it, and just as we got to it we could hear Santa Anna's drums beating on Milam Square, and just as we were crossing the ditch going into the fort Santa Anna fired his salute on Milam Square.

There were a few other families who had gone in. A Mrs. Cabury(?) [probably Alsbury] and her sister, a Mrs. Victoriana, and a family of several girls, two of whom I knew afterwards, Mrs. Dickson [Dickinson], Mrs. Juana Melton, a Mexican woman who had married an American, also a woman named Concepcion Losoya and her son, Juan, who was a little older than I.

The first thing I remember after getting inside the fort was seeing Mrs. Melton making circles on the ground with an umbrella. I had seen very few umbrellas. While I was walking around about dark I went near a man named Fuentes who was talking at a distance with a soldier. When the latter got near me he said to Fuentes:

"Did you know they had cut the water off?"

The fort was built around a square. The present Hugo-Schmeltzer building is part of it. I remember the main entrance was on the south side of the large enclosure. The quarters were not in the church, but on the south side of the fort, on either side of the entrance, and were part of the convent. There was a ditch of running water back of the church and another along the west side of Alamo Plaza. We couldn't go to the latter ditch as it was under fire and it was the other one that Santa Anna cut off. The next morning after we had gotten in the fort I saw the men drawing water from a well that was in the convent yard. The well was located a little south of the center of the square. I don't know whether it is there now or not.

On the first night a company of which my father was one went out and captured some prisoners. One of them was a Mexican soldier, and all through the siege, he interpreted the bugle calls on the Mexican side, and in this way the Americans knew about the movements of the enemy.

After the first day there was fighting. The Mexicans had a cannon somewhere near where Dwyer avenue now is, and every fifteen minutes they dropped a shot into the fort.

The roof of the Alamo had been taken off and the south side filled up with dirt almost to the roof on that side so that there was a slanting embankment up which the Americans could run and take positions. During the fight I saw numbers who were shot in the head as soon as they exposed themselves from the roof. There were holes made in the walls of the fort and the Americans continually shot from these also. We also had two cannon, one at the main entrance and one at the northwest corner of the fort near the post office. The cannon were seldom fired.

I remember Crockett. He was a tall, slim man, with black whiskers. He was always at the head. The Mexicans called him Don Benito. The Americans said he was Crockett. He would often come to the fire and warm his hands and say a few words to us in the Spanish language. I also remember hearing the names of Travis and Bowie mentioned, but I never saw either of them that I know of.

After the first few days I remember that a messenger came from somewhere with word that help was coming. The Americans celebrated it by beating the drums and playing on the flute. But after about seven days fighting there was an armistice of three days and during this time Don Benito had conferences every day with Santa Anna. Badio, the interpreter, was a close friend of my father, and I heard him tell my father in the quarters that Santa Anna had offered to let the Americans go with their lives if they would surrender, but the Mexicans would be treated as rebels.

During the armistice my father told my mother she had better take the children and go, while she could do ʂo safely. But my mother said:

"No!, if you're going to stay, so am I. If they kill one they can kill us all."

Only one person went out during the armistice, a woman named Trinidad Saucedo.

Don Benito, or Crockett, as the Americans called him, assembled the men on the last day and told them Santa Anna's terms, but none of them believed that any one who surrendered would get out alive, so they all said as they would have to die any how they would fight it out.

The fighting began again and continued every day, and nearly every night. One night there was music in the Mexican camp and the Mexican prisoner said it meant that reinforcements had arrived.

We then had another messenger who got through the lines saying that communication had been cut off and the promised reinforcements could not be sent. On the last night my father was not out, but he and my mother were sleeping together in headquarters. About 2 o'clock in the morning there was a great shooting and firing at the northwest corner of the fort, and I heard my mother say:

"Gregorio, the soldiers have jumped the wall. The fight's begun."

He got up and picked up his arms and went into the fight. I never saw him again. My uncle told me afterwards that Santa Anna gave him permission to get my father's body, and that he found it where the thick of the fight had been.

We could hear the Mexican officers shouting to the men to jump over, and the men were fighting so close that we could hear them strike each other. It was so dark that we couldn't see anything, and the families that were in the quarters just huddled up in the corners. My mother's children were near her. Finally they began shooting through the dark into the room where we were. A boy who was wrapped in a blanket in one corner was hit and killed. The Mexicans fired into the room for at least fifteen minutes. It was a miracle, but none of us children were touched.

By daybreak the firing had almost stopped, and through the window we could see shadows of men moving around inside the fort. The Mexicans went from room to room looking for an American to kill. While it was still dark a man stepped into the room and pointed his bayonet at my mother's breast, demanding"

"Where's the money the Americans had?"

"If they had any," said my mother, "you may look for it."

Then an officer stepped in and said:

"What are you doing? The woman and children are not to be hurt."

The officer then told my mother to pick out her own family and get her belongings and the other women were given the same instructions. When it was broad day the Mexicans began to remove the dead. There were so many killed that it took several days to carry them away.

The families, with their baggage, were then sent under guard to the house of Don Ramon Musquiz, which was located where Frank Brothers store now is, on Main Plaza. Here we were given coffee and some food, and were told that we would go before the president at 2 o'clock. On our way to the Musquiz house we passed up Commerce street, and it was crowded as far as Presa street with soldiers who did not fire a shot during the battle. Santa Anna had many times more troops than he could use.

At 3 o'clock we went before Santa Anna. His quarters were in a house which stood where L. Wolfson's store now is. He had a great stack of silver money on a table before him, and a pile of blankets. One by one the women were sent into a side room to make their declaration, and on coming out were given $2 and a blanket. While my mother was waiting her turn Mrs. Melton, who had never recognized my mother as an acquaintance, and who was considered an aristocrat, sent her brother, Juan Losoya, across the room to my mother to ask the favor that nothing be said to the president about her marriage with an American.

My mother told Juan to tell her not to be afraid.

Mrs. Dickson [Dickinson] was there, also several other women. After the president had given my mother her $2 and a blanket, he told her she was free to go where she liked. We gathered what belongings we could together and went to our cousin's place on North Flores street, where we remained several months.[5]

This version of Esparza's story appeared in the *San Antonio Express* in 1902. The paper repeated the story a few years later and finally published an expanded version in 1907. This article explains that Esparza was not available up to 1897 since he had been living on his farm in Atascosa County. It also reassures the reader of Esparza's veracity with a left-handed compliment, "Although he is a Mexican, his gentleness and unassuming frankness are like the typical old Texan." The article describes Esparza as being eight years old at the time of the battle.[6] (For other accounts by or attributed to Enrique Esparza see #4.2, 4.8, 4.16, 4.17, and 4.28).

4.4
Martin Perfecto de Cos, August 1904
According to William P. Zuber in a letter to Charles Jeffries

When we thought all the defenders were slain, I was searching the barracks, and found, alive and unhurt, a fine-looking and well-dressed man, locked up, alone, in one of the rooms, and asked him who he was. He replied: "I am David Crocket [*sic*], a citizen of the State of Tennessee and representative of a district of that State in the United Sates Congress. I have come to Texas on a visit of exploration; purporting, if permitted, to become a loyal citizen of the Republic of Mexico. I extended my visit to San Antonio, and called in the Alamo to become acquainted with the officers, and learn of them what I could of the condition of affairs. Soon after my arrival, the fort was invested by government troops, whereby I have been prevented from leaving it. And here I am yet, a noncombatant and foreigner, having taken no part in the fighting."

I proposed to introduce him to the President, state his situation to him, and request him to depart in peace, to which he thankfully assented. I then conducted him to the President, to whom I introduced him in about these words: "Mr. President, I beg permission to present to your Excellency the Honorable David Crockett, a citizen of the State of Tennessee and Representative of a district of that State in the United States Congress. He has come to Texas on a visit of exploration; purposing, if permitted, to become a loyal citizen of the Republic of Mexico. He extended his visit to San Antonio, and called in the Alamo to become acquainted with its officers and to learn of them what he could of the condition of affairs. Soon after his arrival, the fort was invested by Government troops, whereby he has been prevented from leaving it. And here he is yet, noncombatant and foreigner, having taken no part in the fighting. And now, Mr. President, I beseech your Excellency to permit him to depart in peace."

Santa Anna heard me through, but impatiently. Then he replied sharply, "You know your orders;" turned his back upon us and walked away. But as he turned, Crockett drew from his bosom a dagger, with which he smote at him with a thrust, which, if not arrested, would surely have killed him; but was met by a bayonet-thrust by the hand of a soldier through the heart; he fell and soon expired.[7]

William P. Zuber had already given us tales of two Alamo leaders: Travis and the famous "line;" and Bowie's mutilation and death. It is only fitting that he complete the Alamo trium- virate by relating a tale concerning Crockett. The origin of this story is as convoluted as Zuber's others. General Cos allegedly told Dr. George M. Patrick, who allegedly told Zuber, who related the story to Charlie Jeffries in a letter in 1904.[8] General Cos had led one of the attack columns during the Alamo bat- tle. There is no independent information by Cos or by Dr. Patrick to confirm that this event ever took place, and they both had died before Zuber broke this story. This story may have been another concoction of Zuber, but even he did not intend that it be taken seriously. At the end of his letter to Jeffries he states, "This story by Cos, though a gross falsehood, shows what Santa Anna would have done if it were true."[9]

4.5
Charles Bledsoe, August 23, 1904
From an article in the *San Antonio Express*

Eighty-two years ago he was born near Lexington, Ky., his people moving while he was a child to Missouri. Here while he was a boy of 10 or 12 years, well grown for his age, he ran away with his two uncles Jim and John Bledsoe who had joined a party of adventurers bound for Texas under the leadership of a man named Blair. These thirty men came from Missouri and Arkansas. They had heard of the adventures of Crockett and Bowie and other pioneers in Texas history, and determined to cast in their lot with them.

Their journey was not without adventure. They met while in Texas small bands of Mexican soldiers, and several skirmishes took place, until one morning at a place called Little Creek near San Antonio, they encountered another band of soldiers, and while engaged with them heard the firing of the pioneers who were hotly pursued by an over- whelming force of Mexicans.

The two bands came together during a running fight of several hours, and were pursued by the Mexican forces to the Alamo. With the Mexi- cans on their heels, the panting men rushed into the Alamo and barricaded the doors. Several were shot down while they were crashing in.

At once the building was surrounded by troops. Mexicans climbed on the old earthen roof and began to tear holes in it and the Texans fired through the roof into them until blood dripped in and the red stain ran down the walls in streams.

Texans shot through the head as they tried to fire through the windows, fell back upon their comrades, and the building reeked with powder smoke. There was no water, and the men fought with powder-blackened faces and parching tongues from early in the afternoon until dusk.

Outside, through the windows in lulls of the firing, could be seen rows and rows of dead Mexican soldiers, the wounded crawling off to shelter. Little by little the firing of the Americans ceased, for their powder was giving out, until only an occasional shot was fired through the blood spattered windows. The floor was slippery with blood, and the dead and wounded were so thick on the floor that movement was impossible.

"Open the door for God's sake," someone shouted, and the Texans throwing down their useless flintlocks, drew their long knives and made for the heavy door on which the Mexicans had already begun an assault with timbers. Other soldiers climbed in the windows and shot down the men inside.

The door was forced open a little and the long knives and Spanish bayonets slashed in the opening, red with blood. The firing had already ceased, and the heavy breathing of the men could be heard.

As the door opened Bledsoe dodged under the clashing weapons, ran around the building and made for the river. Several soldiers saw him and followed shouting, but he gained the river in safety, and notwithstanding a jagged wound across the soldier [shoulder] made by a bullet earlier in the day, managed to swim or crawl for several miles below where he crawled out on the shore, almost dead from fear and exhaustion. Before him loomed the gray walls of a Spanish mission. He thought it a Spanish castle or house, and climbed a mesquite tree to see if there were Mexicans about. Then he followed the river, coming out several miles lower down....

He did not hear of his companions in the Alamo until long afterward when their fate was told him in New Orleans....

He says he can still see the blood dripping down, and can hear the awful hell of noise inside the walls, but he remembers little of the outside view, for he was "in too big a hurry" when he got out. He saw the bodies of several Mexicans, though, as he ran.[10]

The tale of Charles Bledsoe appeared in the *San Antonio Express* in August of 1904. According to the article Bledsoe was eighty-two years old and had arrived in San Antonio from Arizona after an absence of fifty years. His reason for returning was that "he wanted to see if all his old friends were dead." There is no record of Bledsoe having taken part in the Alamo battle, and there is no record of his uncles having been killed there. Bledsoe's is another account that conveys the idea that the Alamo was simply one building, the roofed over Alamo church, rather than the sprawling mission complex it actually was. This view of the Alamo would have been accurate at the time Bledsoe was telling his story but not at the time of the siege and battle.[11]

4.6
Pablo Diaz, July 1, 1906
According to Charles Merritt Barnes in the *San Antonio Daily Express*

After Cos surrendered, that portion of the army of the Constitutionalists that remained for a while was quartered in the barracks vacated by the Mexicans on Military Plaza, but soon after the arrival of Davy Crockett the small band moved over to the Alamo, because the defenses were better and more substantial than the ones on the West Side of the city. The weakness of the military fortress or Presidio, as it was called, on Military Plaza, had been demonstrated by the facility with which Milam's forces had dislodged the soldiers under General Cos. As soon as the coming of Santa Anna, which had been heralded, was known the Constitutionalists retired to the Alamo and commenced to fortify it. Up to this time it had not been used as a military fortification, but was a church and convent.

The arrival of Santa Anna was announced by the firing of a gun from in front of the Alcalde's house on Main Plaza. His red flag was hoisted over the Cathedral. I heard the gun fired from the plaza and saw the flag floating from San Fernando. From the Mission I could see also the flag of the Constitutionalists floating from the Alamo. The latter flag was not the flag that was afterward adopted by the Texas Republic, with its blue field and single star and a stripe of white and one of red, but was the flag of Mexico under the Constituion and prior to the usurpation and assumption of the Dictatorship by Santa Anna. When Santa Anna hoisted his red flag it was his announcement that no quarter would be shown those opposing him. This was well understood by those in the Alamo. They knew that unless Houston, on whom they vainly relied, sent them succor they were lost.

For six days I heard the rattle of musketry and the roar of cannon. I did not dare to leave my refuge near the mission lest I become involved in the terrible slaughter which I knew was going on there. Messengers frequently came out to the mission and told us of the terrible devastation and butchery in progress and of the brave and dauntless defense of the heroic Constitutionalists. The cannon shots became louder and more frequent as Santa Anna's soldiers got closer and closer to the Alamo. Finally, on the sixth day, after a fierce fusillade, there was silence, and I saw the red flag of Santa Anna floating from the Alamo where the Constitutional flag before had been. Then I knew that the battle was over, that the invading tyrant and his horde had won and that the price paid for their stubborn defenses by the Constitutionalists had been their lives. I had several personal friends among the brave men in the Alamo. One of them was named Cervantes. His descendants lived on the Alameda for many years, and some of them are now residing on Losoya Street.

Next I saw an immense pillar of flame shoot up a short distance to the south and east of the Alamo and the dense smoke from it rose high into the clouds. I saw it burn for two days and nights and then flame and smoke subsided and smouldered. I left my retreat and came forth cautiously, coming along Garden Street to town. I noticed that the air was tainted with the terrible odor from many corpses and I saw thousands of vultures flying above me. As I reached the ford of the river my gaze encountered a terrible sight. The stream was congested with the corpses that had been thrown into it. The Alcalde, Ruiz, had vainly endeavored to bury the bodies of the soldiers of Santa Anna who had been slain by the defenders of the Alamo. He had exhausted all of his resources and still was unable to cope with the task. There were too many of them. Nearly 6000 of Santa Anna's 10,000 had fallen before they had annihilated their adversaries and captured their fortress. I halted, horrified, and watched the vultures in the revel and shuddered at the sickening sight. Then involuntarily I put my hands before my eyes and turned away from the river, which I hesitated to cross. Hurriedly I turned aside and up La Villita and went to South Alamo. I could not help seeing the corpses which congested the river all around the bend from Garden to way above Commerce Street and as far as Crockett Street is now.

They stayed there for many days and until finally the Alcalde got a force sufficient to dislodge them and float them down the river. But while this was a most gruesome sight. The one I saw later filled me with more horror. I went on to the Alameda. It was then a broad and spacious, irregularly shaped place, flanked on both sides with huge cottonwood trees, from which it gets its name. I turned into the Alameda at the present intersection of Commerce and Alamo Streets.

Looking eastward I saw a large crowd gathered. Intuitively I went to the place.

It was just beyond where the Ludlow now stands. The crowd was gathered around the smouldering embers and ashes of the fire that I had seen from the mission. It was here that the Alcalde had ordered the bodies of Bowie, of Crockett, Travis and all of their dauntless comrades who had been slain in the Alamo's unequal combat to be brought and burned. I did not need to make inquiry. The story was told by the silent witnesses before me. Fragments of flesh, bones and charred wood and ashes revealed it in all of its terrible truth. Grease that had exuded from the bodies saturated the earth for several feet beyond the ashes and smouldering mesquite faggots. The odor was more sickening than that from the corpses in the river. I turned my head aside and left the place in shame....

The pyre was a very long one, as it had to consume nearly 200 corpses, and it may be that some of the bodies may not have been burned in the main one, but have been burned on the opposite of the Alameda, but if they were I did not see the ashes. I am not prepared to say there were no bodies burned anywhere but at the spot I shall indicate, and it is not unlikely that they were burned here. It is probable that all of the bodies that were not carried away from the Alamo at the same time of the Constitutionalists all separated from the Federals at the same times, so the story that some of the bodies were burned on the south side of the Alameda and where stands the Post House, belonging to Dr. Herff Sr. and now called the Springfield House, may be true. But the main funeral pyre was about 200 yards east of where St. Joseph's Church now stands and just beyond this big red brick house (meaning the Ludlow) and thence for fifty to sixty yards north.

[Reporter Charles Merritt Barnes narrates:]

The spot was then pointed out to me by Señor Diaz and I have it now definitely located in my mind. The location is confirmed by [Antonio] Perez, who states that when he was a little boy and used to play on the Alameda he was frequently shown the same spot as the place where the bodies of the Alamo heroes were burned. Perez goes further than Diaz and says that for many years there was a small mound there under which he was told the charred bones that the fire did not consume were buried by some humane persons who had to do so secretly, and that he was familiar with the spot as the burial place of Bowie and Crockett. Perez states that about thirty years ago these bones were exhumed and placed in the Old City Cemetery, the first one located on the Powder House Hill, but he does not know the part of that cemetery they were placed in.[12]

Pablo Diaz was born in Monclova, Mexico ca. 1818. He and his older brother Francisco moved to San Antonio, arriving in February of 1835. Diaz remained neutral during the Texas Revolution, explaining, "I held that, having been born in Mexico, it was not right for me to take up arms against my native land, but I held that as I was living in this country [Texas] it was not right for me to fight against it." Diaz's story was one of several related by reporter Charles Merritt Barnes (1855-1927) in the *San Antonio Express*.[13] (For other accounts by or attributed to Pablo Diaz see #4.12 and 4.15).

4.7
Felix Rodriguez, May 4, 1907
From an article in the *San Antonio Express*

[W]hen the war of the Texas Rebellion broke out he joined the Mexican Army. His courage was soon noticed by the leaders and he was given charge of the paymasters' wagons, which hauled the money for the army.

When the battle of the Alamo occurred he had just arrived from Mexico with a caravan and reached San Antonio soon enough to participate in the fight.

Before his death the old Aztec is said to have often spoken of the cruel massacre of the Texans, and to have described it as one of the most horrible events that he ever witnessed.[14]

Felix Rodriguez's alleged role in the Alamo battle comes in the form of a death notice that appeared in the *San Antonio Express*. In the article he is described as an "Aztec Indian, and one of the last of his race." His age at the time of his death is given as 110 years.[15]

4.8

Enrique Esparza, May 12 and May 19, 1907
According to Charles Merritt Barnes
in the *San Antonio Express*

All of the others are dead. I alone live of they who were within the Alamo when it fell. There is none other left now to tell its story and when I go to sleep my last slumber in the campo de los santos there will then be no one left to tell.

You ask me do I remember it. I tell you yes. It is burned into my brain and indelibly seared there. Neither age nor infirmity could make me forget, for the scene was one of such horror that it could never be forgotten by any one who witnessed the incidents.

I was born in one of the old adobe houses that formerly stood on the east side of what we then called El Calle de Acequia or the street of the acequia or ditch, but now known as Main Avenue. The house in which I was born was but a short distance north of Salinas Street. I am the son of Gregorio Esparza.

You will see my father's name on the list of those who died in the Alamo. This list is at Austin. It is on the monument in front of the Capitol. That monument was built there in honor of those who fell with the Alamo. I have made several pilgrimages to it just to read the inscription and list of names because my father's name is on the list. There is no monument here to those who fell in the Alamo and died there that Texas might be free. There are none here with the means to do so who have ever cared enough for those who died there to mark the spot where their bodies were buried. Though this be so, those who died there were all brave, both men and women.

My mother was also in the Alamo when it fell, as were some of my brothers and a sister. She told me I was born in the month of September and in the year 1824.

I was then a boy of 12 years of age; was then quite small and delicate and could have passed for a child of 8. My father was a friend and comrade of William Smith. Smith had expected to send my father and our family away with his own family in a wagon to Nacogdoches. We were waiting for the wagon to be brought to town. My father and Smith had heard of the approach of Santa Anna, but did not expect him and his forces to arrive as early as they did. Santa Anna and his men got there before the wagon we waited for could come.

My father was told by Smith that all who were friend to the Americans had better join the Americans who had taken refuge in the Alamo. Smith and his family were there and my father and his family went with them.

Santa Anna and his army arrived at about sundown and almost immediately after we sought refuge in the Alamo. Immediately after their arrival Santa Anna's personal staff dismounted on Main Plaza in front of the San Fernando church. Santa Anna went into the building at the northwest corner of Main Plaza which has been superseded by that now occupied by S. Wolfson. That building had been occupied by the Texans and before them by the soldiers of Mexico and still earlier by the soldiers of Spain. It had been a part of the presidio or old fort, and the part where the officers had their headquarters. The Texans had left this structure and gone over to the Alamo because the latter offered more advantages for defense.

I have often heard it said that Santa Anna immediately upon his arrival in San Antonio dismounted in the West side of Military Plaza and hitched his horse to an iron ring set into the wall of the old building where the Spanish Governors dwelt and where the combined coats of arms of Spain and Austria form the keystone of the arch above its portal. This is not so, I saw Santa Anna when he arrived. I saw him dismount. He did not hitch the horse. He gave its bridle reins to a lackey. He and his staff proceeded immediately to the house on the Northwest corner of Main Plaza. I was playing with some other children on the Plaza and when Santa Anna and his soldiers came up we ran off and told our parents, who almost immediately afterward took me and the other children of the family to the Alamo. I am sure of this for I saw Santa Anna several times afterward and after I came out of the Alamo.

It was twilight when we got into the Alamo and it grew pitch dark soon afterward. All of the doors were closed and barred. The sentinels that had been on duty without were first called inside and then the openings closed. Some sentinels were posted up on the roof, but those were protected by the walls of the Alamo church and the old Convent building. We went into the church portion. It was shut up when we arrived. We were admitted through a small window.

I distinctly remember that I climbed through the window and over a cannon that was placed inside of the church immediately behind the window. There were several other cannon there. Some were back of the doors. Some had been mounted on the roof and some had been placed in the Convent. The window was opened to permit us to enter and it was closed immediately after we got inside.

We had not been in there long when a messenger came from Santa Anna calling on us to surrender. I remember the reply to this summons was a shot from one of the cannon on the roof of the Alamo. Soon after it was fired I heard Santa Anna's cannon reply. I heard his cannon shot strike the walls of the church and also the Convent. Then I heard the cannon within the Alamo buildings, both church and Convent, fire repeatedly during the night. I heard the cheers of the Alamo gunners and the deriding jeers of Santa Anna's troops.

My heart quaked when the shot tore through the timbers. My fear and terror was overwhelming but my brave mother and my dauntless father sought to soothe and quiet my brothers and myself. My sister was but an infant and knew naught of the tragic scenes enacted about us. But even child as I was I could not help but feel inspired by the bravery of the heroes about me.

If I had been given a weapon I would have fought likewise. But weapons and ammunition were scarce and only wielded and used by those who knew how. But I saw some there no older than I who had them and fought as bravely and died as stolidly as the adults. This was towards the end and when many of the grown persons within had been slain by the foes without. It was then that some of the children joined in the defense.

All who had weapons used them as often as they had the chance to do so. Shots were fired fast. Bullets flew thick. Both men and women fell within the walls. Even children died there. The fighting was intermittent. We must have been within the Alamo 10 or 12 days. I did not count the days. But they were long and full of terror. The nights were longer and fraught with still more horror. It was between the period of fierce fighting and all too short armistice that we got any rest.

Crockett seemed to be the leading spirit. He was everywhere. He went to every exposed point and personally directed the fighting. Travis was chief in command, but he depended more upon the judgment of Crockett and that brave man's intrepidity than upon his own. Bowie, too, was brave and dauntless, but he was ill. Prone upon his cot he was unable to see much that was going on about him and the others were too engrossed to stop and tell him. Although too weak to stand upon his feet, when Travis drew the line with his sword Bowie had those around him bring his cot across the line.

I heard the few Mexicans there call Crockett "Don Benito." Afterward I learned his name was David, but I only knew him as "Don Benito."

One day when I went to where Bowie was lying on his cot I heard him call those about him and say:

"All of you who desire to leave here may go in safety. Santa Anna has just sent a message to Travis saying there will be an armistice for 3 days to give us time to deliberate on surrendering. During these 3 days all who desire to do so may go out of here. Travis has sent me the message and told me to tell those near me."

When Bowie said this quite a number left. Travis and Bowie took advantage of this occasion to send out for succor they vainly hoped would come to the Alamo and those within before it fell. William Smith and Alsberry [*sic*] were among those who were sent for succor then, Seguin claimed also to have been so sent. Among the surnames of those I remember to have left during the time of this armistice were Menchaca, Flores, Rodrigues, Ramirez, Arocha, Silvero. They are now all dead. Among the women who went out were some of their relatives.

Rose left after this armistice had expired and after the others had been sent for succor. Rose went out after Travis drew the line with his sword. He was the only man who did not cross the line. Up to then he had fought as bravely as any man there. He stood by the cannon.

Rose went out during the night. They opened a window for him and let him go. The others who left before went out of the doors and in the daytime. Alsberry left his wife and sister-in-law there. His sister-in-law afterward married a man named Cantu. She and Mrs. Alsberry stayed in the Alamo until it fell. They feared to leave believing the Mexicans under Santa Anna would kill them.

Bowie asked my father if he wished to go when the armistice of 3 days was on. My father replied:

"No, I will stay and die fighting." My mother then said:

"I will stay by your side and with our children die too. They will soon kill us. We will not linger in pain."

So we stayed. And so my father died, as he said, fighting. He struck down one of his foes as he fell in the heap of slain.

The end came suddenly and almost unexpectedly and with a rush. It came at night and when all was dark save when there was a gleam of light from the flash and flame of a fired gun. Our men fought hard all day long. Their ammunition was very low. That of many was entirely spent. Santa Anna must have known this, for his men had been able during the day to make several breeches in the walls. Our men had fought long and hard and well. But their strength was spent. Many slept. Few there were who were awake. Even those on guard besides the breeches in the walls dozed. The fire from the Mexicans had slacked and finally ceased. Those who were awake saw the Mexican foeman lying quietly by their camp fires and thought they likewise slept. But our foes were simulating sleep or if they slept, were awakened by their savage chief and his brutal officers.

After all had been dark and quiet for many hours and I had fallen into a profound slumber suddenly there was a terrible din. Cannon boomed. Their shot crashed though the doors and windows and the breeches in the walls. Then men rushed in on us. They swarmed among us and over us. They fired on us in volleys. They struck us down with their escopetas. In the dark our men groped and grasped the throats of our foeman and buried their knives into their hearts.

By my side was an American boy. He was about my own age but larger. As they reached us he rose to his feet. He had been sleeping, but like myself, he had been rudely awakened. As they rushed upon him he stood calmly and across his shoulders drew the blanket on which he had slept. He was unarmed. They slew him where he stood and his corpse fell over me. My father's body was lying near the cannon which he had tended. My mother with my sister was kneeling beside it. My brothers and I were close to her. I clutched her garments. Behind her crouched the only man who escaped and was permitted to surrender. His name was Brigido Guerrera.

As they rushed upon us the Mexican soldiers faltered as they saw a woman. My mother clasped her babe to her breast and closed her eyes. She expected they would kill her and her babe and me and my brothers. I thought so too. My blood ran cold and I grew faint and sick.

Brigido Guerrera pleaded for mercy. He told them he was a prisoner in the Alamo and had been brought there against his will. He said he had tried to escape and join Santa Anna's men. They spared him. They let him out, an officer going with him.

They took my mother, her babe, my brothers and I to another part of the building where there were other women and children huddled. Another of the women had a babe at her breast. This was Mrs. Dickinson. There was an old woman in there. They called her Donna Petra. This was the only name I ever knew her by. With her was a young girl, Trinidad Saucedo, who was very beautiful. Mrs. Alsberry and her sister were there also and several other women, young girls and little boys. I do not remember having seen Madam Candalaria there. She may have been there and I shall not dispute her word. I did not notice the women as closely as I did the men.

After the soldiers of Santa Anna had got in a corner all of the women and children who had not been killed in the onslaught, they kept firing on the men who had defended the Alamo. For fully a quarter of an hour they kept firing upon them after all of the defenders had been slain and their corpses were lying still. It was pitch dark in the Eastern end of the structure and the soldiers of Santa Anna seemed to fear to go there even after firing from the Constitutionalists from there had ceased. Santa Anna's men stood still and fired into the darkness and until someone brought lanterns.

The last I saw of my father's corpse was when one of them held his lantern above it and over the dead who lay about the cannon he had tended.

It has been said that one of the women who claims to have been in the Alamo during its siege and capture, has also claimed that she brought water into the Alamo from the ditch outside. This is not true. When we got into the Alamo, which was before access to the ditch had been entirely cut off by the soldiers of Santa Anna, such occurrence had been foreseen and forestalled by inmates of the Alamo chapel. They had already sunk a well in the church and the water there from was then being drunk by the occupants instead of the water from the ditch. A number of cattle had also been driven into the court of the Convent. These later furnished food for the besieged up to the day of the fall of the Alamo. I do not recollect the inmates having suffered for either food or water during the entire period of the siege. The only article that was scarce was ammunition. This got scarcer and scarcer each day, with no chance or hope of replenishing.

The old Convent had been used for barracks by Bowie, Travis, and Crockett's men and was so used until the besiegers had driven them to seek final refuge in the chapel after a number of breeches had been made in the Convent wall. Communication was constantly kept up between the Convent & the church buildings. This was done through a door connecting them. I was in the Convent several times, but stayed most, and practically all of the time in the church, as it was considered safest. Crockett who, as I said before they called Don Benito, went into the Convent and stayed there for some time. But he was everywhere during the siege and personally slew many of the enemy with his rifle, his pistol and his knife. He fought to his last breath. He fell immediately in front of the large double doors which he defended with the force that was by his side. Crockett was one of the few who were wide awake when the final crisis and crash came. When he died there was a heap of slain in front and on each side of him. These he had all killed before he finally fell on top of the heap.

Travis spent most of his time directing the firing from the roof of the church. He too, seemed not only dauntless but sleepless. He encouraged the gunners. Whenever a good shot was made with the cannon he commended them. He told them where to aim and where to fire efficaciously, the cannon fire from the roof of the church being most of the time under his direct personal supervision. Crockett and he both, however, looked after the cannonading from the Convent as well, both making repeated visits to that locality and at frequent intervals.

Bowie, although ill and suffering from a fever, fought until he was so severely wounded that he had to be carried to his cot, which was placed in one of the smaller rooms on the north side of the church. Even after he was confined to his cot he fought, firing his pistol and, occasionally, his rifle at the enemy after the soldiers of Santa Anna had entered the church and some of them got into his room. He loaded and fired his weapons until his foes closed in on him. When they made their final rush upon him, he rose up in his bed and received them. He buried his sharp knife into the breast of one of them as another fired the shot that killed him. He was literally riddled with bullets. I saw his corpse before we were taken out of the building.

Mrs. Alsbury and my mother were among those who nursed and ministered to his wants. Mrs. Alsbury was near him when he was killed, while my mother and I were in the large main room of the church and by the cannon near the window where my father fell.

The shot and shells tore great holes in the walls. They also sawed out great jagged segments of the walls of both the Convent and the church. The roof of the Convent was knocked in, the greater part of it falling, as also did a considerable portion of the roof of the church. Nearly one-half of the walls of the Convent were knocked off....

Although I do not remember to have seen any one killed in the Convent, because I was not in there when they were, I am told and believe that many of the defenders of the Alamo perished there....

After all of the men had been slain, the women and children were kept huddled up in the church's southwest corner in the small room to the right of the large double door of the church as one enters it. A guard was put over them. They were held there until after daylight when orders were given to remove them. We were all marched off to the house of Señor Musquiz. Here all of the women were again placed under guard. Musquiz owned a suerte on South Alamo Street not very far from where the Beethoven Hall now is. My mother and father were well acquainted with the Musquiz family. At about 8:00 we became very hungry, up to then not having been given any food. My mother, being familiar with the premises, began to look about for food for herself and children as well as her other comrades. While she was doing so Musquiz told her that it was dangerous for her to be moving about and leaving the place, and room in which she was under guard. She told him she did not care if she was under guard or not, she was going to have something to eat for herself, her children and her companions whom she intended to feed if Santa Anna did not feed his prisoners. Musquiz admonished her to silence and told her to be patient and he would get them some food from his own store.

After urging my mother not to leave the room, Musquiz disappeared and went to his pantry, where he got quite a quantity of provisions and brought them to the room in which the prisoners, some 10 or a dozen in number, were and distributed the food among them. There was some coffee as well as bread and meat. I recollect that I ate heartily, but my mother very sparingly.

We were kept at Musquiz's house until 3:00 in the afternoon when the prisoners were taken to Military Plaza.

We were halted on the plaza and in front of the place where Wolfson's store now is. Mrs. Alsbury and her sister, Mrs. Gertrudes Cantu [Navarro], were the first ones to be taken before Santa Anna. He questioned them and after talking with them for a few minutes, discharged them from custody and they left. Mrs. Cantu afterwards removed to the Calaveras where she married and resided up to the time of her death.

Mrs. Dickinson, the wife of Lieutenant Dickinson, the woman whom I told you, like my mother, had a babe at her breast, was the next to be summoned before Santa Anna. He spent some time in questioning her after which he dismissed her.

My mother was next called before the dictator. When she appeared before him baby sister pressed closely to her bosom, I with my brother followed her into his presence. My brother was clinging to her skirt, but I stood to one side and behind her. I watched every move and listened to every word spoken. Santa Anna asked her name. She gave it. He then asked, "Where is you husband?" She answered sobbing: "He's dead at the Alamo." Santa Anna next asked where the other members of the family were. She replied a brother of my father's, she was informed, was in his (Santa Anna's) army. This was true. My father had a brother whose name was Francisco Esparza, who joined the forces of Santa Anna. It was this brother who appeared before Santa Anna later and asked permission to search among the slain for my father's corpse. The permission was given. My uncle found my father's body and had it buried in the Campo Santa where Milam Square is now. I did not get a chance to see it before it was buried there, as the burial, as all others incident to that battle, was a very hurried one. It was probable that my father was the only one who fought on the side of the Constitutionalists, and against the forces of the dictator, whose body was buried without having first been burned.

Santa Anna released my mother. He gave her a blanket and two silver dollars as he dismissed her. I was informed that he gave a blanket and the same sum of money to each of the other women who were brought from the Alamo before him.

I noticed him closely and saw he was the same officer I had seen dismount on the Main Plaza about sundown of the night when I went into the Alamo. After our release we went back to our home and my mother wept for many days and nights. I frequently went to the Main Plaza and watched the soldiers of Santa Anna and saw him quite a number of times before they marched away towards Houston where he [Santa Anna] was defeated. He had a very broad face and high cheek bones. He had a hard cruel look and his countenance was a very sinister one. It has haunted me ever since I last saw it and I will never forget the face or figure of Santa Anna.[16]

This account of Enrique Esparza comes to us from Charles Merritt Barnes in the *San Antonio Express*. Barnes began working for the paper in or about 1880. It is likely that the many articles published about the Alamo survivors and witnesses between this time and the early 1900s could be attributed to Barnes even if he did not receive a by-line for some of them. In 1910 Barnes published *Combat and Conquests of Immortal Heroes*, a collection of stories regarding nineteenth-century personalities and events of San Antonio including the Alamo. It is unknown if Barnes may have coached Esparza in some of his reminiscences of the Alamo, but Esparza's account is somewhat different in 1907 than his earlier ones. For instance, in his account of 1901, Esparza's comments indicate that he and his family were housed in the Alamo in what is known as the "low barracks," a structure which comprised the south side of the Alamo compound and which contained the Alamo's main gate. In the 1907 version Esparza indicated that he and his family spent most of their time, including the battle, within the Alamo church. It is unknown whether this was confusion on the part of the elderly Esparza or if Barnes felt compelled to relate Esparza's comments to the most recognizable building of the Alamo mission that was still standing while Barnes was writing his stories.

In another example Esparza is described in the 1907 article as having been twelve years old at the time of the battle. In earlier articles he is described as having been eight years old. Once again it is unknown if this was confusion on Esparza's part or if Barnes determined that the memory of a person who had been twelve years old at the time of the event carried more weight than that of a boy who was eight. Contemporary records indicate that Esparza was eight years old in 1836.[17] (For other accounts by or attributed to Enrique Esparza see #4.2, 4.3, 4.16, 4.17, and 4.28).

4.9
Antonio Menchaca, June 22 to July 27, 1907
From his memoirs

On the 13 January, 1836, David Crockett presented himself at the old Mexican graveyard, on the west side of the San Pedro Creek, had in company with him fourteen young men who had accompanied him from Tennessee, here. As soon as he got there he sent word to Bowie to go and receive him, and conduct him into the City. Bowie and A. [Menchaca] went and he was brought and lodged at Erasmo Seguin's house. Crockett, Bowie, Travis, Neill and all the officers joined together, to establish guards for the safety of the City, they fearing that the Mexicans would return. On the 10 February, 1836, A. [Menchaca] was invited by officers to a ball given in honor of Crockett, and was asked to invite all the principal ladies in the City to it. On the same day invitations were extended and the ball given that night. While at the ball, at about 1 o'clock, A.M. of the 11th, a courier, sent by Placido Benavides, arrived, from Camargo, with the intelligence that Santa Ana, was starting from the Presidio Rio Grande, with 13,000 troops, 10,000 Infantry and 3,000 Cavalry, with the view of taking San Antonio. The courier arrived at the ball room door inquired for Col. Seguin, and was told that Col. Seguin was not there. Asked if Menchaca was there, and was told that he was. He spoke to him and told him that he had a letter of great importance, which he had brought from P.B. [Benavides] from Camargo, asked partner and came to see letter. Opened letter and read the following: "At this moment I have received a very certain notice, that the commander in chief, Antonio Lopez de Santa Anna, marches for the city of San Antonio to take possession thereof, with 13,000 men." As he was reading letter, Bowie came opposite him, came to see it, and while reading it, Travis came up, and Bowie called him to read that letter; but Travis said that at that moment he could not stay to read letters, for he was dancing with the most beautiful lady in San Antonio. Bowie told him that the letter was one of grave importance, and for him to leave his partner. Travis came and brought Crockett with him. Travis and Bowie understood Spanish, Crockett did not. Travis then said, it will take 13,000 men from the Presidio de Rio Grande to this place thirteen or fourteen days to get here; this is the 4th day. Let us dance to-night and to-morrow we will make provisions for our defense. The ball continued until 7 o'clock, A.M.

There Travis invited officers to hold a meeting with a view of consulting as to the best means they should adopt for the security of the place. The council gathered many resolutions were offered and adopted, after which Bowie and Seguin made a motion to have A.M. [Menchaca] and his family sent away from here, knowing that should Santa Anna come, A. [Menchaca] and his family would receive no good at his hands. A. [Menchaca] left here and went to Seguin's ranch, where he stayed six days, preparing for a trip. Started from there and went as far as Marcelino to sleep; then three miles the east side of Cibolo, at an old pond at sun up next morning. Nat Lewis, passed with a wallet on his back, a-foot from San Antonio, and A. [Menchaca] asked him why he went a-foot and he was answered that he could not find a horse; that Santa Anna had arrived at San Antonio, the day previous with 13,000 men. A. [Menchaca] asked what the Americans had done. He said they were in the Alamo inside the fortifications. A. [Menchaca] asked why N. [Nat Lewis] did not remain there and he answered that he was not a fighting man, that he was a business man. A. [Menchaca] then told him to go then about his business.[18]

José Antonio Menchaca (1800-1879) was a citizen of San Antonio de Bexar at the time of the Texan Revolution. He took part in the battle of San Jacinto on April 21, 1836. Later Menchaca served for several terms as alderman and in 1838 as

Charles Merritt Barnes, reporter for the *San Antonio Express*, recorded many eyewitness stories of the Alamo for his paper.

(Courtesy of the Daughters of the Republic of Texas Library at the Alamo)

mayor pro tem of San Antonio. Menchaca dictated his memoirs to Charles Merritt Barnes of the *San Antonio Express*. They were first published in the *Passing Show* in San Antonio in weekly installments from June 22 to July 27, 1907. They later appeared in 1937 as a publication of the Yanaguana Society.[19]

4.10
Maria de Jesus Buquor, July 19, 1907
From an article in the *San Antonio Express*

Her words translated one to the past and one seems to see Travis and Crockett at the home of her, who was then Maria de Jesus Delgado, on the day that Santa Anna marched to San Antonio. Maria de Jesus steps out into the yard and beholding many men approaching calls to her mother to question her concerning them. It is the Mexican army and Travis and Crockett hastily bid their friend farewell and hastened to the fortress and glorious death.

Then Mrs. Buquor, for the little Maria de Jesus was she, gave Travis his first warning of the actual approach of the enemy although, of course, rumors of this enemy's coming had been heard for many days. Mrs. Buquor says that this was not the last that she saw of the Texas patriots by any means as for days before the final onslaught by the Mexican troops Travis, Crockett and others of the garrison would wave greetings to their friends in this city and bid them goodbye, knowing full well that their doom had been sealed and that death was very near.

During the siege Mrs. Buquor says she and her family as well as the other citizens suffered severe hardships and were harshly treated by the Mexican soldiers from whom they had no protection. The Delgado family, consisting of her mother, father, three sisters and four brothers and herself, she says was forced to give up their home, which is still standing on the river bank in the vicinity of the electric power house, to the Mexican soldiers. The members of the family sought refuge at the old Arciniega home which stood on the street which now bears his name. Here they were forced to dig and seek refuge in a cellar where they were safe from the bullets which swept the streets of the city at the moments of attack.

Childhood's idea of humor has not wholly departed from the now aged woman for she laughed slightly as she remembered the efforts of an aged blind woman to get into the cellar and the woman's fall into the same just in time to avoid a bullet which whistled by.

During the siege, Mrs. Buquor says she saw General Santa Anna many times and she bears testimony to his well known penchant for amours in that she related how he seized a young girl living near her home and held the maiden captive during his stay in the city.

She says that she did not see any of the Texas dead after the last final attack by she plainly remembers seeing the smoke arising from the burning bodies of the Texans when their remains were destroyed in this way a sacrificial fire on the altar of Texas Liberty. She however, fails to remember much concerning the departure of the Mexican troops from the city....

She related yesterday the death of seven Texans who tried to make [their] escape from the Alamo and were killed on the river bank near her house as vividly as if it were an event of the past few days.[20]

Maria de Jesus Buquor was born in 1826 and moved to San Antonio with her family in 1830. Her story is another that comes to us as an article in the *San Antonio Express*. Mrs. Buquor is described as "...well preserved," and that "...her memory is wonderful considering her age. Save that she is a little confused as to dates, her memory is very clear."[21]

4.11
Juan Díaz, September 1, 1907
From an article in the *San Antonio Light*

It was while he was playing with his sisters and some of the neighbor children that the sound of martial music broke on the air. Díaz says he was old enough to know something of what war meant and that the first thing he did was to send his sisters home. Then he scampered to the tower to watch the army, and later clambered down and stood in awe-struck wonder near the plaza as the big guns of the Mexicans began to roar and boom and send deadly cannon balls hurtling against the solid walls of the sacred Alamo.

"I will never forget how that army looked as it swept into town," said the old man as he told the story of what he knew and saw of the fall of the Alamo to a Light reporter yesterday. "At the head of the soldiers came the regimental band, playing the liveliest airs, and with the band came a squad of men bearing the flags and banners of Mexico and an immense image that looked like an alligator's head. The band stopped on Main Plaza and remained there until after the fall of the fort. The artillery was planted where the French Building now stands and the cannoneers had a clean sweep to the Alamo, for at the time there were no buildings between it and the San Fernando Cathedral."

Díaz tells how he watched the progress of the battle from a distant point of vantage, how, after the cannon had ceased to boom, he saw the six columns of Mexican soldiers form in line and go straight for the walls of the Alamo. He was not too far away to see the soldiers go scrambling up and up, only to be hurled back onto their comrades who, all undaunted, stepped into the breaches and fought their way to the top of the battle-scarred walls.

"I did not go to the plaza when the dead were burned," said Díaz. "I had no desire to see that great funeral pyre, but the odor of it permeated every part of the city. It was sickening and for weeks and months people shunned the Alamo. Some of the men who went there during the crema-tion told us that the Texas and Mexican soldiers were all piled in a heap and burned together."

Many of Santa Anna's staff officers had quarters at the San Fernando Cathedral and were fed by Díaz's mother. He says the general gave orders that their home was to be safe from the soldiers and that a guard was constantly on watch to see that no damage was done.

The aged Mexican says that for days after the battle there was the most intense excitement, but he asserts that Santa Anna kept his victori-ous soldiers well under control and that but a few cases of damage resulted from their depredations.[22]

Juan Díaz was the young son of Antonio Díaz, the custo-dian of the San Fernando Cathedral in San Antonio. His story appeared as an article in the *San Antonio Light* in 1907. A varia-tion of his story also appeared in James T. DeShields' *Tall Men With Long Rifles* in 1835. DeShields reassured us that Juan Díaz is considered "...an honorable and reliable Mexican, being a native of San Antonio...."[23]

4.12
Pablo Díaz, October 31, 1909
From an article in the *San Antonio Light*

When asked why he was not in San Antonio during the siege; why he continued to work in the "labor," [at Mission Concepción], he said "No quiere la guerra" (I do not like war).

Going on with his story he tells how on the fateful morning of March 8 [*sic*] at two o'clock began the last act in the terrible tragedy, when the Mexicans made a night attack upon the chapel and with crowbars and ladders scaled the walls and began the hand-to-hand encounter which ended in the massacre of all the brave little band who fought for their lives.

Then fell a great silence in the gray dawn, the fight was over and drawn by curiosity to learn what was the outcome of the "guerra," Pablo Díaz fared his way to San Antonio de Béxar and learned the details of the fall of the Alamo.

Forgetting then his English, he tells in Spanish, with words stumbling over each other in their liquid flow, how the Mexicans dragged branches of trees and limbs of trees through the streets and made a funeral pyre in the plaza off to the side of the Alamo. First a layer of wood and then a layer of corpses until the pyre was completed, Pablo Díaz declared was the work of Santa Anna, the Napolean of the west.

When asked if he saw the flames which leaped to heaven consume their human sacrifice on the altar of liberty his voice trembled and tears gathered in his dim old eyes and he replied, Sí, sí. No era bueno, no era bueno." (Yes, yes. It was not good; it was not good).[24]

This version of Pablo Díaz's account appeared in the *San Antonio Light*. Much of the descriptive language in the account probably is that of the reporter. (For other accounts by or attributed to Pablo Díaz see #4.6, and 4.15).

4.13
Joe, 1909
From the published diary of William Fairfax Gray

The garrison was much exhausted by incessant watching and hard labor. They had all worked until a late hour on Saturday night, and when the attack was made sentinels and all were asleep, except one man, Capt. _____, who gave the alarm. There were three picket guards without the fort, but they, too, it is supposed, were asleep, and were run upon and bayonetted, for they gave no alarm. Joe was sleeping in the room with his master when the alarm was given. Travis sprang up, seized his rifle and sword, and called to Joe to follow him. Joe took his gun and followed. Travis ran across the Alamo and mounted the wall and called out to his men, "Come on, boys, the Mexicans are upon us, and we'll give them *Hell*." He discharged his gun; so did Joe. In an instant Travis was shot down. He fell within the wall, on the sloping ground, and sat up. The enemy twice applied their scaling ladders to the walls, and were twice beaten back. But this Joe did not well understand, for when his master fell he ran and ensconced himself in a house, from which he fired on them several times, after they got in. On the third attempt they succeeded in mounting the walls, and then poured over like sheep. The battle then became a *melee*. Every man fought for his own hand, as he best might, with *butts of guns*, pistols, knives, etc. As Travis sat wounded on the ground General Mora, who was passing him, made a blow at him with his sword, which Travis struck up, and ran his assailant through the body, and both died on the some spot. This was poor Travis' last effort. The handful of Americans retreated to such cover as they had, and continued the battle until one man was left, a little, weakly man named Warner, who asked for quarter. He was spared by the soldiery, but on being conducted to Santa Anna, he ordered him to be shot, and it was done. Bowie is said to have fired through the door of his room, from his sick bed. He was found dead and mutilated where he lay. Crockett and a few of his friends were found together, with twenty-four of the enemy dead around them. The negroes, for there were several negroes and women in the fort, were spared. Only one woman was killed, and Joe supposes she was shot accidently, while attempting to cross the Alamo. She was found lying between two guns. The officers came around, after the massacre, and called out to know if there were any negroes there. Joe stepped out and said, "Yes, here is one." Immediately two soldiers attempted to kill him, one by discharging his piece at him, the other with a thrust of the bayonet. Only one buckshot took effect in his side, not dangerously, and the point of the bayonet scratched him on the other. He was saved by Capt. Baragan. Besides the negroes, there were in the fort several Mexican woman, among them the wife of a Dr._____ and her sister, Miss Navarro, who were spared and restored to their father, D. Angel Navarro, of Bejar. Mrs. Dickenson, wife of Lieut. Dickenson, and child, were also spared, and have been sent back into Texas. After the fight was over, the Mexicans were formed in a hollow square, and Santa Anna addressed them in a very animated manner. They filled the air with loud shouts. Joe describes him as a slender man, rather tall, dressed very plainly - somewhat *"like a Methodist preacher,"* to use the negro's own words. Joe was taken into Bejar, and detained several days; was shown a grand review of the army after the battle, which he was told, or supposes, was 8,000 strong. Those acquainted with the ground on which he says they formed think that not more than half that number could form there. Santa Anna questioned Joe about Texas and the state of its army, and if more were expected, and said he had men enough to march to the city of Washington. The American dead were collected in a pile and burnt.[25]

This final account of Joe appeared in the diary of William Fairfax Gray published in 1909 and is listed under the diary entry for March 20, 1836. It is slightly different from the account related by Gray in May of 1836 (see Joe's account #2.6). For example, in this version a woman is mentioned as having been killed, but she is not identified as a Negro woman as in account #2.6. In another instance Crockett's body is described as having been surrounded by twenty-four bodies of Mexican soldiers. In the account of May 25, 1836, the number is twenty-one. This is a minor difference, but it is an unusual one since the version appearing in 1909 was supposedly written earlier than the version appearing in 1836 (March versus May). Traditionally the passage of time tends to increase numbers (combatants, casualties, etc.) involved in the Alamo story rather than decrease them.[26] (For other accounts by or attributed to Joe see #2.3, 2.4, and 2.6).

4.14
Juan Vargas, April 3, 1910
According to Louis de Nette in an article in the *San Antonio Light*

I remember how the troop of Santa Anna marched into San Antonio de Béxar. I remember how they overawed all, taking what they wanted with no thought of pay. They had come to suppress a rebellion and one way to do it was to take the worldly goods of the rebels. They camped to uncounted numbers within the city, close to the Alamo and yet far enough away to escape the leaden hail which the Texans poured into them. As for me, I was with them. They had taken me in passing, I waited on them performed kitchen and equipage tasks about camp. They said I did not know how to shoot and they would not trust me with a gun. Little did they know that I had fought with Padre Hidalgo and with Iturbide.

Things are dim to me now. As the light of day has gone from my eyes, so the light of memory has left my mind. But never can I forget the battle of the Alamo. I did not fire a shot, neither did I storm the old fort when the Mexicans rushed in to cut to pieces the last remnant of the gallant band. They did their own work, I refusing to go to the Alamo. For this they threatened execution when the day was won, but could not at that time waste a shell on me. One shell might mean victory or defeat. They used their shells on the Texans.

Back in the camp I heard the roar of the artillery. Shriek of shell mingled with groan of dying; soldiers mutilated and torn stumbled into camp to be bound up; dozens and scores were dragged in with gaping wounds through which their lifeblood had trickled; ever and anon the cry of "Muerte a los Tejanos" echoed; carnage and a hell of battle reigned; Mexican were mowed down as though a scythe passed; the uncounted dead were piled in camp, while sort of service was rendered the living by doctors, aided by myself and others who, like me, had been impressed for this service.[27]

Juan Vargas (b. 1796) is described as an Indian who claimed descent from the Aztecs. He was a citizen of San Antonio de Bexar during the Alamo siege and battle. He related his story to the *San Antonio Light* at the age of 114.[28]

4.15
Pablo Díaz, March 26, 1911
According to Charles Merritt Barnes in an article in the *San Antonio Express*

My parents fled with me. I was a child then. I had a brother older than I who espoused the cause of Santa Anna and fought in his army. After the Alamo had fallen we returned from the Calaveras, where we had gone. On our approach we saw a huge pillar of flames and smoke shooting up to a considerable height to the south and east of the Alamo. The dense smoke from this fire went up into the clouds and I watched it while the fire burned for two day and two nights. Then it subsided and smoldered. During this time we had been hiding in the southern part of the city and left our retreat, coming back to town by way of Garden Street.

I noticed that the air was tainted with a terrible odor from many corpses and that thousands of vultures were circling in the sky above us. They were hovering over the city and especially along and above the river's course. As I reached the ford of the San Antonio River at the old Lewis Mill site I encountered a terrible sight. The stream was congested with corpses that had been thrown into it.

Ruiz, the Alcalde at that time, had vainly striven to bury the dead soldiers of Santa Anna's command who had been slain in the struggle during the siege. After exhausting every effort and all of his resources, he was unable to give burial to but a very limited number these principally being officers. Being unable to bury them in the earth he was compelled to dispose of them otherwise. He had them cast into the swiftly flowing stream. But they were so numerous that they choked up the stream, finding lodgement along the banks of the short curves and bends of that stream.

They obstructed the stream for some time until Ruiz was able to get a sufficient force to push the bodies away from the banks as they lodged against them and floated them down the stream for a considerable distance below, where they remained until devoured by the vultures and wolves.

I stopped and looked at the sickening sight, which made me shudder, and I became ill. I was told afterward that the sight and stench had even nauseated Santa Anna himself so that he had complained and reprimanded Ruiz for not getting rid of the dead. Involuntarily I put my hands before my eyes and turned away from the river which I hesitated to cross and went to the right along the settlement of La Villita, but even then could not help seeing the corpses, for they lined the river's course and banks all the way from Crockett Street to more than a mile below.

But while the bodies of the Mexican soldiers in the river was a revolting spectacle the one that met my vision later was even more gruesome. It filled me with the greatest horror. I had passed along La Villita to South Alamo Street and thence north to the Alameda. This was a broad and spacious place used as a promenade and also as a highway of ingress to and egress from the city on the east side of the river. It has since become a part of East Commerce Street. On each side of the Alameda was a row of large cottonwood trees. From them the place took its name Alameda. It commenced at about where St. Joseph's Church now stands, this having been the western extremity about half a block from South Alamo Street.

It was Santa Anna himself who had given the orders to Ruiz to have the bodies of all who perished while defending the Alamo incinerated. By intuition I went straight to the place. I did not need a guide. The whole story was told by the spectacle I saw. The witnesses were silent but eloquent ones. They were the charred skulls, fragments of arms, hands, feet and other members of the bodies of the dead defenders. In carts the slain, among whom were Travis, Crockett, Bowie, Bonham and Jameson, as well as all of the others, had been removed from the Alamo mission, where they fell, to the Alameda, where they were burned on two different pyres. These were about 250 yards apart and one was on each side of the Alameda. The one on the north side was the smallest, while that on the south side was the largest. The latter was probably about twenty feet longer than the former. Both were about the same width - about eight or ten feet. Both pyres were about ten feet high when the flames were first kindled and the consuming of the corpses commenced.

In alternate layers the corpses and wood were placed. Grease of different kinds, principally tallow, was melted and poured over the two pyres. They were then ignited and burned until they burned out, leaving but a few fragments of different members. Most of the corpses were entirely consumed.

When I reached the spot I saw ashes, as well as the blackened chars of the different anatomical fragments. They emitted an odor even more sickening than did the corpses of those who had been thrown into the river and to me were much more nauseating.[29]

This version of Pablo Díaz's account appeared in an article in the *San Antonio Express* by Charles Merritt Barnes that also featured accounts by Enrique Esparza and Juan Antonio Chávez. (For other accounts by or attributed to Pablo Díaz see #4.6, and 4.12).

4.16
Enrique Esparza, March 26, 1911
According to Charles Merritt Barnes in an article in the *San Antonio Express*

Enrique Esparza... states he was a child eight years old when the siege and fall of the Alamo took place and that he was in the Alamo with his parents and one of his brothers. He said that his father and the brother mentioned were killed in the Alamo and his mother and he were taken before Santa Anna after it had fallen. Esparza says that Mrs. Dickinson, the wife of Lieutenant Dickinson, who became a mother during the siege and was taken with her infant to Santa Anna at the same time as also Mrs. Alsbury and several other women and children.

Santa Anna gave each of the women two silver pesos, of Mexican "dobe" dollars when he ordered their release. Esparza says:

After this we went to look for the body of my father and my brother, but when we got to the Alamo again all of the bodies had been removed and taken to the Alameda. They were put in two piles, one on each side of the Alameda, and burned, both Mexicans and Americans, and my father and brother were among them, but we could not find them in either pile, for the soldiers would not let us get close enough to examine or claim them.

They set fire to them and burned them. My mother placed her mantilla before her face and ran screaming from the scene, dragging me by the hand with her. After the bodies were burned we went back several times to the two places until all of the fragments had been removed and the ashes had been scattered in every direction.[30]

This account by Enrique Esparza appeared in the same article as the previous one. It is markedly different from his other accounts in that it mentions only one brother being in the Alamo with him and his parents, and that brother being killed. In this account Esparza claims that the bodies of his brother and father were burned. Other accounts, including a deposition by Esparza's uncle Francisco, describe Gregorio Esparza's body being removed from the Alamo and buried in El Campo Santa. This account also describes Susanna Dickinson as giving birth during the Alamo siege, a detail that is verified by no other source.[31] (For other accounts by or attributed to Enrique Esparza see #4.2, 4.3, 4.8, 4.17, and 4.28).

4.17
Enrique Esparza, August 27, 1911
According to Charles Merritt Barnes in an article in the *San Antonio Express*

He states that he and his mother, who were in there [the Alamo] during the combat, escaped slaughter, she on account of her sex and he on account of his tender youth, he being at the time under ten years of age. He details the episodes incident to the memorable combat and those that transpired subsequent to it. He vividly describes the circumstances of his mother and himself being taken before Santa Anna, together with several other women and children, among the former being Mrs. Dickinson, wife of Lieutenant Dickinson, and Mrs. Alsbury. He also saw the incineration of the bodies of those slain during the defense of the Alamo and say they were burned on the Alameda.[32]

This account of Esparza is another one reported in the pages of the *San Antonio Express* by Charles Merritt Barnes. In the same article he made mention of Juan Díaz and Juan Antonio Chávez without going into their accounts in any great detail. He described Esparza as "...nearing the ninety-year mark," and "...perhaps the most interesting of all the Mexican aged citizens." He also mentions that "There is no doubt that his [Enrique Esparza's] father and *one of his brothers* [my italics] perished there, as their names appear on the roll of the slain."[33] (For other accounts by or attributed to Enrique Esparza see #4.2, 4.3, 4.8, 4.16, and 4.28).

4.18
Trinidad Coy, November 26, 1911
According to Andrés Coy in an article in the *San Antonio Light*

According to the story told to Captain Coy by his father, the command under Colonel Travis believed that they were unable to withstand a concerted attack by the Mexican army, if it were true that Santa Anna really was headed towards San Antonio.

Plans were being discussed as to the advisability of resisting the attack or of moving out of San Antonio for the purpose of augmenting the forces available for actual fighting. There was considerable discussion until finally Davy Crockett, who wanted to be right before he went ahead, proposed a plan.

"If it is true that Santa Anna is coming to San Antonio," he said, "then our plans must be made one way. If he is not coming to San Antonio, they must be made another way. The proper thing to do is to find out whether he is coming to San Antonio. Isn't that so? Well, let's send out men to find out where he is and what he intends to do."

The suggestion met with instant approval from Travis and from Bowie, who was listening to the conversation from his cot in the next room, where he lay ill. So it was decided to send out a reconnaissance party to locate the army of Mexicans under Santa Anna and to discover their probable destination.

Among the men sent on this errand was Trinidad Coy, father of the present police captain. He mounted his horse and faced to the south, in an attempt to follow the trail of rumor that led from San Antonio back to the Mexican forces.

As he proceeded on his way the scent grew warmer. Day by day he became convinced that there was truth in the rumor, that Santa Anna was on his way to the city of San Antonio. Several times he was sent off on a cold trail — he traveled roads that led him farther and farther from his quest. Then he would retrace his way and pick up the trail where he had left it.

He was without news from home. Days had passed now and he was without the least intimation that would lead him to believe that he should continue on his quest. By day he would ride and ride, stopping now and then to inquire the latest news of a farmer, or to verify a report that had come to him further up the road. Sometimes he passed hours without seeing a human being. Then, when he had stopped for the night and was rolling a cigarette at the home of some lone farmer, or when the coals of his campfire glowed brightly in the clear nights, he would begin to wonder whether, after all, he had better not give up the search and return to San Antonio.

Coy was a brave man. He knew that Travis' forces were inadequate to withstand any attack from a great force. He knew the tremendous importance of the coming battles and realized the need Travis had of every possible rifleman.

[At this point Coy's narrative breaks with events at the Alamo and in San Antonio and describes Coy's actions on his scouting mission for Travis. A good portion of this part of the story describes Coy's horse getting stoned on loco weed and Coy being captured by Mexican troops and brought back to San Antonio. His story continues:]

They carried him back to the main army. With them, as a prisoner, he was taken to San Antonio. One day they appeared before the city. Coy afterwards learned that their appearance was entirely unexpected. The defenders were taken by surprise.

He was kept in the Mexican camp while preparations were made to attack the band of faithful heroes in the little church. With great avidity he saw the work go forward that was to destroy his comrades, to whom he should have brought word. He cursed the luck that had tied his hands in this important of all important hours.

The preparations of warfare went on. The attack commenced. With unholy joy, he saw the Mexican troops beaten back, only to surge forward again, overpowering the brave defenders by sheer weight of numbers. He longed to join his friends.

Looking hastily about him he saw that the camp was deserted. All the hangers-on had followed the line of soldiery. He worked his bonds against a stone until they parted. He made his way out of the camp, followed a well-known path that led around the city, and in another hour he had arrived at a point in back of the chapel of the Alamo, from where he could join his comrades.

Only a bank of cottonwood trees hid them from his view. He forced his way through the underbrush. The Alamo lay before him. There were no signs of fighting. All was quiet. Only, before his eyes, there rose the heavy black cloud from a smoking pile.

It was the funeral pyre of his friends.[34]

Trinidad Coy's story of the Alamo was related by his son, Andrés Coy, a San Antonio police officer, to the *San Antonio Light*.[35]

4.19
A Mexican Soldier, 1911
According to Adina de Zavala in her book
The Story of the Siege and Fall of the Alamo

The Texans fought like tigers. The proportion was one to one-hundred, yet no quarter was asked and each sold his life as dearly as possible. The last moments of the conflict were terrible. The darkness of the rooms, the smoke of the battle and the shrieks of the wounded and dying all added to the terror of the scene. Unable to distinguish friend from foe, the Mexicans actually brained each other in their mad fury. After the battle was over and all were dead, the scene beggared description. The floor of the main building was nearly shoe deep in blood, and weltering there were hundreds of dead men, many still clenched together with one hand while the other hand held the sword, pistol or knife which told how they had died in that last terrible struggle.[36]

The account of this unidentified Mexican soldier appeared in *The Story of the Siege and Fall of the Alamo* by Adina de Zavala (1861-1955). Miss de Zavala did not identify this Mexican soldier, but the account obviously comes from that of Felix Nuñez in 1889.[37] (See account #3.31).

4.20
José María Rodriguez, 1913
From his memoirs

…Colonel Travis was put in command and he stayed at the Alamo. Colonel Travis was a fine looking man of more than ordinary height. I recollect him distinctly from the very fact that he used to come up to our house from the Alamo and talk to my father and mother a great deal. Our house was the first one after you crossed the river coming from the Alamo and Col. Travis generally stopped at our home going and coming. He was a very popular man and was well liked by everyone. My father was always in sympathy with the Texas cause, but had so far not taken up arms on either side.

Soon after this, a report came to my father from a reliable source that Santa Ana was starting for San Antonio with 7,000 men, composed of cavalry, infantry and artillery, in fact a well organized army. My father sent for Colonel Travis and he came to our house and my father told him about this coming of Santa Ana and advised him to retire into the interior of Texas and abandon the Alamo. He told him he could not resist Santa Anna's army with such a small force. Colonel Travis told my father that he could not believe it, because General Cos had only been defeated less than three months, and it did not seem possible to him that General Santa Ana could organize in so short a time as large an army as that. Colonel Travis, therefore, remained at the Alamo, and at the last, Travis told my father, "Well we have made up our minds to die at the Alamo fighting for Texas." My father asked him again to retire as General Sam Houston was then in the interior of Texas organizing an army. The Mexicans in San Antonio who were in sympathy with the war of Independence organized a company under Colonel Juan Seguin. There were twenty-four in the company including my father and they joined the command of General Sam Houston. My mother and all of us remained in the city.

One morning early a man named Rivas called at our house and told us that he had seen Santa Ana in disguise the night before looking in on a fandango on Soledad Street. My father being away with General Houston's army, my mother undertook to act for us, and decided it was best for us to go into the country to avoid being here when General Santa Ana's army should come in. We went to the ranch of Dona Santos Ximenes. We left in ox carts, the wheels of which were made of solid wood. We buried our money in the house, about $8000.00; it took us nearly two days to get to the ranch.

A few days after that, one morning about day break, I heard some firing, and Pablo Olivarri, who was with us, woke me up. He said, "You had better get up on the house, they are fighting at the Alamo." We got up on the house and could see the flash of the guns and hear the booming of the cannon. The firing lasted about two hours. The next day we heard that all the Texans had been killed and the Alamo taken. A few days after that an army consisting of about 1200 men under General Urrea came by from San Antonio on their way to Goliad to attack Fannin. I saw these troops as they passed the ranch.

There has been a great deal of discussion with reference to what had been done with the bodies of the Texans who were slain in the Alamo. It is claimed that Colonel Seguin wrote a letter in which he stated that he got together the ashes in the following February and put them in an iron urn and buried them in San Fernando Cathedral. This does not seem possible to me, because nothing of that kind could have happened without us knowing that and we never heard of any occurrence of that kind. Seguin did not return from Houston's army until my father did, both of them being in the same command, my father a first Lieutenant and he a Colonel. It is true that the bones were brought together somewhere in the neighborhood or a little east of where the Menger Hotel is now and were buried by Colonel Seguin, but that any of them were ever buried in the Cathedral, I have never heard nor do I believe that to be true.[38]

José María Rodriguez (1829-1913) was born in San Antonio, Texas. He was educated in Texas and New Orleans and served Texas in later life in positions such as the tax assessor and collector of Bexar County, the alderman of San Antonio, and county judge of Webb County. His memoirs were published after his death by a family friend, Leonard Garza, at the request of Rodriguez's family.[39]

4.21
Juan Antonio Chávez, April 19, 1914
From an article in the *San Antonio Express*

We did not remain tranquilly at home very long. Profiting by our former experience [of abandoning San Antonio during the siege and battle of Bexar in late 1835] and as advised by numerous friends, my father on the approach of Santa Anna's forces again left the house two and a half months later and went back to the ranch, where we remained until the siege of the Alamo was over. When we returned the bodies of those that had perished in the Alamo were still burning on two immense pyres on the old Alameda. I went to look at them and the sight indelibly impressed itself upon my memory. One pyre occupied a position on the site of where the new Halff building is. The other was diagonally across the street on what is now known as the lawn of the Ludlow House and the recently built house adjoining it on the east. The bodies burned for several days and the wood and tallow fuel used for consuming them was frequently replenished. I made several trips to the scene, which so fascinated me I could not stay away until all of the bodies had been consumed. They were all reduced to ashes except a few charred heads, arms, and legs that were scattered about. These were gathered up and placed in a shallow grave where the Ludlow House lawn now is.

All of the officers and some of the privates of Santa Anna's army, according to Dan Antonio Chávez, were buried in the cemetery where Milam Park now is, but the slain Mexicans were so numerous it was thought the quickest and best way of getting rid of the bodies was by throwing them in the San Antonio river, then a swift and deep stream. There were so many bodies they choked its flow. Many of them lodged in the curves of the river.[40]

Juan A. Chávez was a young citizen of San Antonio de Bexar at the time of the Alamo battle. He did not actually witness the battle since he fled the town with his family on the approach of the Mexican army and spent the time at their ranch on Calaveras Creek. His story appeared in the *San Antonio Express* in 1914.[41]

4.22
Susanna Dickinson, 1921
**According to Rena Maverick Green, editor
of *Memoirs of Mary A. Maverick***

The first attack of the Mexicans was over, and all seemed peaceful, when one day Lieutenant Dickinson came hurriedly up to their home on Main Plaza, saying:

"Give me the baby; jump on behind me and ask me no questions."

They galloped down to the crossing, at the point where the "Mill Bridge" now is, but not in time to escape being fired at by the incoming Mexicans; However, they succeeded in crossing and hastened over to the Alamo.

Mrs. Dickinson said she saw no fighting - only the noise of the battle reaching her and the few Mexican women inside the Alamo.

On the day of the fall, Sunday, her husband kissed her goodbye in the morning, and she never saw him again.

Probably she and the Mexican women, who were her companions, saw the bayoneting of the last American; when the shooting was over, a soldier crawled into the room where they were, not to seek refuge, but to carry out an order previously given, and generally understood, which was that if the garrison fell someone was to try to fire the powder supply; and this man named Evans, wounded and spent with weariness, was killed while making his painful way to the powder room.

One of the Mexican officers, always thought by Mrs. Dickinson to be General Almonte, chief of Staff to Santa Anna, who spoke broken English, stepped to the door of the room in which the women were, and asked:

"Is Mrs. Dickinson here?"

As she feared to answer and kept quiet, he repeated: "Is Mrs. Dickinson here? Speak out, for it is a matter of life and death."

Then she answered, telling who she was, and he took her in charge over to Main Plaza. Here she and her child were held and cared for some days, when she was given a horse and a bag of provisions and told to go. She and her baby and a colored manservant journeyed safely eastward to the town of Washington, then the Capital, where she lived some years, later returning to visit San Antonio.[42]

This version of Susanna Dickinson's story appears in *Memoirs of Mary A. Maverick*, edited and published by her granddaughter. This version is most likely a third-hand account since it is explained in the memoirs that "Mrs. Dickinson told Dean Richardson of the St. Mark Episcopal Church the following story of the 'Fall of the Alamo' several times; once when the transfer of the Alamo property from the Church to the State was about to be made (1883). At this time she walked with him and a party of others to an inner room in the Alamo, and pointed it out as the one in which she and the Mexican women were asked to stay, and where they were when the Alamo fell."[43] (For other accounts by or attributed to Susanna Dickinson see #2.1, 2.5, 3.18, 3.20, 3.22, 3.23, 3.28, and 3.29).

William Sanders Oury, 1930
According to Col. William G. Smith in his "Life of William Sanders Oury"

I know messages were carried from Travis on the Colorado; and from his camp at San Antonio; and from the Alamo; and I was sent out with one a few days before the massacre.[44]

This cryptic remark is attributed to William S. Oury (1817-1887), a leading and controversial figure in the history of Arizona. This statement is repeated in several works on Oury by his descendants, and it is his only link with the Alamo battle. From this sentence alone, Oury has been recognized as a participant in the Alamo siege. He may have served as a courier for Travis. He may even have made his way into the Alamo and then carried a message out; however, there is no other documentation that places him at the Alamo during the siege or battle.[45]

Rafael Soldana, 1935
According to James T. DeShields in his book *Tall Men With Long Rifles*

During the siege which began on the twenty-third of February, every available means was employed to harass and weaken the defenders of the fortress. One of the measures employed was that of constant alarms during the hours of the night. At intervals, when silence reigned over the Alamo and all was still in camp, the artillery would open, a great shout would be raised by the besieging forces and this uproar, supplemented by volleys of musketry, was intended to make the impression that a night assault had been planned, and also to make it appear to the beleaguered that their expected reinforcements, while trying to make their way into the Alamo had become engaged with the enemy and were being destroyed. These continued - almost hourly - alarms throughout the night were supposed to keep every American in position ready to repel the attack, thus through loss of sleep and increasing anxiety unfitting him for the final assault.

These men were defiant to the last. From the windows and parapets of the low buildings, when taunted by the Mexican troops, they shouted back their defiance in the liveliest terms. A tall man, with flowing hair, was seen firing from the same place on the parapet during the entire siege. He wore a buckskin suit and a cap all of a pattern entirely different from those worn by his comrades. This man would kneel or lie down behind the low parapet, rest his long gun and fire, and we all learned to keep at a good distance when he was seen to make ready to shoot. He rarely missed his mark and when he fired he always rose to his feet and calmly reloaded his gun seemingly indifferent to the shots fired at him by our men. He had a strong, resonant voice and often railed at us, but as we did not understand English we could not comprehend the import of his words further than that they were defiant. This man I later learned was known as "Kwockey."

When the final assault was made upon the walls these men fought like devils. [When asked by Creed Taylor if any begged for quarter he replied by saying that:] ...he had never heard that any of them offered to surrender or that a single man had begged for his life. "Kwockey" was killed in a room of the mission. He stood on the inside to the left of the door and plunged his long knife into the bosom of every soldier that tried to enter. They were powerless to fire upon him because of the fact that he was backed up against the wall and, the doorway being narrow, they could not bring their guns to bear upon him. And, moreover, the pressure from the rear was so great that many near the doorway were forced into the room only to receive a deadly thrust from that long knife. Finally a well-directed shot broke this man's right arm and his hand fell useless at his side. He then seized his long gun with his left hand and leaped toward the center of the room where he could wield the weapon without obstruction, felling every man that came through the doorway. A corporal ordered the passage cleared of those who were being pressed forward, a volley was fired almost point blank and the last defender of the Alamo fell forward - dead.

[Creed Taylor narrates] Señor Soldana told me there were three or four Mexicans who went down with Travis at the Alamo. He did not know of any Mexican women being in the fortress when when it fell. He had heard that nine men deserted Travis before the Alamo was invested but did not see them and did not know what became of them.[46]

This account and the three that follow come to us in a convoluted manner that is typical for many of the accounts of the

Alamo. The alleged witness tells his or her story to a second party who relates it to a third party who publishes it many years later. In this and the following three accounts, the second person is Creed Taylor who, according to tradition, was an active participant in the Texas Revolution, the Mexican War, as well as assorted Indian battles with the Texas Rangers. He passed his stories on to James T. DeShields (1861-1948) who allegedly induced the "grizzled old veteran ... to dictate his recollections of the Texas War of Independence."[47] According to Taylor he related only such facts "...which were told to me by soldiers who took part in the tragedy and citizens who lived in Bexar and were cognizant of all that transpired during those eventful days." Taylor also assures us that "True, these were Mexicans but I accepted no narrative as related without corroborative evidence, and the facts herein recorded were substantiated by statements of a number sufficient to guarantee the veracity of these statements."[48] DeShields published Taylor's reminiscences as *Tall Men With Long Rifles* in 1935.

The first account from the Taylor/DeShields connection is attributed to Rafael Soldana, who according to Taylor was a captain in the Tampico battalion and led his company during the final assault on the Alamo. Taylor states that he obtained this information from Soldana at Corpus Christi, Texas, at the end of the Mexican War. Soldana's account as the others related here by Taylor are not verified by any independent sources.[49]

4.25
Juan Ortega, 1935
According to James T. DeShields in his book *Tall Men With Long Rifles*

During the night of the twenty-fourth, two batteries commanding the Alamo were planted, and at dawn on the morning of the twenty-fifth these opened fire on the garrison which in turn responded with vigor. A brisk fire was maintained by both sides during the day until late in the evening firing ceased and a deep silence fell upon the town and fortress. During the night two entrenchments were constructed along the alameda of the Alamo and, while details of men were working on these entrenchments, nine men came over from the fortress and asked to be conducted into the presence of Santa Anna. As the General was asleep at that hour and no one cared to disturb his slumbers these men were held under guard until morning. Señor Ortega told me [Creed Taylor] that one of these men spoke Spanish sufficiently fluent to make their wants known, but he did not learn whether they were Texans or volunteers.[50]

Creed Taylor told James DeShields that Juan Ortega was a sergeant of the Dolores Regiment of the Mexican army and that he died in Brownsville, Texas, in June of 1862. He also stated that "...his story was corroborated by several others whom I [Taylor] knew personally."[51]

4.26
Unidentified Captain, 1935
According to James T. DeShields in his book *Tall Men With Long Rifles*

He [the unidentified captain] said Crockett was the last man slain and that he fought like an infuriated lion. He stated that his last stand was in a small room and with gun in hand he brained every Mexican that tried to enter the door. He used his gun as a club until a shot from without the door broke his right arm, and his gun barrel (the stock had been broken off) fell to the floor. Seeing this the Mexican soldiers made a rush into the room with fixed bayonets, but drawing a large knife with his left hand he rushed upon his assailants and, parrying their thrusts, killed several before he was finally slain. He said he did not hear of a sick man being bayoneted while helpless on his bed but there was a sick man who got out of bed when the Mexicans entered the fortress and died fighting with the rest. He also stated that Santa Anna could not have done otherwise than to put the defenders of the Alamo to the sword, since they were in open rebellion, held a government fortress, and had refused all overtures looking to a surrender.[52]

This account allegedly came to Creed Taylor from a Mexican gentleman traveling from Matamoras to Austin just prior to the U.S. Civil War. At Domingo Creek he and a few companions were set upon by bandits. The man received a wound to his arm. On the following day he arrived at Taylor's ranch where he recuperated for a week and related his tale. Taylor describes him as having been a captain in the Mexican army.

He also reassures us that while he had been guarding prisoners at Saltillo following the battle of Buena Vista, he had spoken with two Mexican soldiers who had been at the storming of the Alamo, and their version of this story was "...along the same lines as that given by the wounded captain." Like many of the other accounts that mention a description of Crockett's last moments, there is no explanation as to how this individual would have known Crockett or would have recognized him.[53]

4.27
Rodriguez, 1935
According to James T. DeShields in his book *Tall Men With Long Rifles*

During the siege of the Alamo the Mexican women in San Antonio remained indoors, praying, and when the final assault began on Sunday morning, every woman was on her knees pleading for the repose of the fallen, foes as well as friends.... [O]ne young woman who was enamored of one of the garrison and who went into the Alamo when the carnage had ceased, found the object of her affection among the slain, folded his hands across his breast, wiped the grime from his pallid face, placed a small cross on his breast, and when ordered away, she dipped her handkerchief in his blood and carried it away in her bosom.[54]

Rodriguez is simply described by Taylor as an "old Mexican ...who lived in Bexar all of his life."[55]

4.28
Enrique Esparza, 1936
According to Howard R. Driggs and Sarah S. King in their book *Rise of the Lone Star*

As I told you the Alamo was left and it fell into ruins. When the Texas soldiers came and drove Cos away, they camped round the old Mission. I heard some of them say it was too big; they did not have enough men to hold it. I thought that the Texans could do anything. There seemed to be many, many men in the fortress when they gathered there; but they were only a few when we think of Santa Anna's army. Anyway I was sure that these brave men could whip Santa Anna and all of his men.

There was great cheering when Señor Crockett came with his friends. He wore a buckskin suit and a coonskin cap. He made everybody laugh and forget their worries. He had a gun he called "Betsey." They told me that he had killed many bears. I knew he would kill many of Santa Anna's soldiers. One thing that frightened me was the cannon the Texans brought. They placed these big guns on the top of the thick walls and pointed them every way. The noise they made was terrible to me.

Santa Anna had many men and much "thunder." I mean powder. The Indians called it "thunder." A man told my mother he was like a king with much power and many servants. It was said he ate from plates made of silver and gold. I could not believe that, but I have read from books it is true. He was very proud. He said that the Texans could not get away from him. A Mexican woman told this to the men at the Alamo. One day Santa Anna demanded that the Texans surrender. Colonel Travis answered with a shot from one of the big cannons. Then Santa Anna ran a blood-red flag to the top of the tower of the cathedral of San Fernando. Someone said that this meant he would kill every one on the side of the Texans. The Texans did not seem to be excited. At night they would sing and dance. No fighting came for several days.

Travis was a brave leader. He had been asked by Señor Bowie, who was ill, to take command. Father would rather follow Bowie, because they were friends. I saw Señor Bowie while he was ill. The soldiers let me go about among them.

This good friend did not forget us. When the mothers and children fled to the Alamo, Señor Bowie had driven in some beeves and found some corn. He gave part of this food to us. We were too scared to think much of eating, but mother made some atole, a sort of mush, for all the children. She ground the corn and boiled it and almost poured it down our throats. Mother was a sensible woman and kept her head. Some of the other women were almost helpless.

When the trumpets of Santa Anna were heard, we had rushed to the Alamo. When father told her she had better go to a safer place, she said, "No; if you are to die, I want to be near you!" We gathered up the few things we had - metate, two chairs, four skins and some cooking utensils. In one bundle was my baby sister. My small brothers and I carried what we could. I was the oldest - nine years.

We all went into a small store room near the monastery. Here we slept on hay and under hay. With us were other Mexican mothers and children. The women helped by grinding corn and cooking for the men. Mrs. Dickerson and her baby were with us. She seemed not to know what to do in this condition. I heard my mother say, "povrecita," and take the lady some food.

At first we got our water from the ditch in front of the Alamo. Later the enemy cut off this supply and we had to use an old well. One night father captured a Mexican who was prowling round, and kept him a prisoner. He was one of Santa Anna's soldiers. During the siege he would tell the Texans what the bugle calls of the enemy meant. I heard that this poor fellow was afterwards killed because Santa Anna thought he was a deserter. Then came the days of the terrible fighting. It was so frightful - but what could one do except just watch and wait? The roof of the old Alamo was off. Along the south side was a dirt wall or embankment up which the Texans would run and fire. Some of them were killed when they did this - Lieutenant Dickerson was among these. His sorrowful wife and babe were left with us.

Señor Crockett seemed everywhere. He would shoot from the wall or through the portholes. Then he would run back and say something funny. He tried to speak Spanish sometimes. Now and then he would run to the fire we had in the courtyard where we were to make us laugh.

When Señor Smith came from Gonzales with the band of men he had gathered, there was great shouting. The Texans beat the drums and played on a flute. Colonel Travis sent Señor Smith off again to get more men.

Captain Seguin was also sent for help. I saw him go. The way I remember was he rode Señor Bowie's horse. We were afraid he could not get by Santa Anna's soldiers. They were getting closer and closer to the Alamo. Afterwards I heard that the Captain was stopped by them, but he said he was a Mexican rancher. This was true; and they let him go. He tried to gather men to get back to help the Texans; but the ways were long in those days, and not many men to get. Before he and Señor Smith could return, the battle was all over.

One brave man that did get back was Señor Benham [Bonham]. He had been sent to Goliad to get Fannin to send help. He rode right past the sentinels of Santa Anna. They fired but he escaped. My mother knelt and said her beads and thanked the good God. Señor Benham, had a white handkerchief tied to his hat. If he was shot while trying to get back to his friends in the Alamo, this handkerchief was a sign he had seen Fannin, Benham came through the danger unharmed. He was one of the great heroes that fell there fighting for liberty.

At times Señor Travis looked very sad and stern. One day he said to Bowie, "Help will come." But help did not come. When he felt that they must fight it out alone, he gave his men a chance to say whether they would stay by him to the end. I saw him draw the line with his sword, and heard him say, "All who are willing to die cross this line." I think all jumped across. Señor Bowie said, "Boys, lift my cot across that line."

My heart was in my mouth. My eyes were like coals of fire; but I would stay and listen. Some blame the great Bowie and Travis and Crockett because they did not hasten away. Can men do more than give their lives, Señorita? I heard a great man tell that these heroes of the Alamo saved Texas. If Santa Anna had not been stopped there, he would have marched over all Texas before an army could be gathered to defeat him. This sounds right to me. I did not know that these men were heroes.

At last there came fire and guns and bayonets with many men. The soldiers of Santa Anna scaled the walls to be met by the fighting Texans. It was early morning. I ran out to the courtyard from a deep sleep. I was fastened to the ground. The Texans killed many of Santa Anna's men but more and more kept coming up the ladders. My father was killed. The brave Travis while shooting a cannon was shot down. I wish I could tell you all the great bravery of these few Texans fighting against that host. It would take great words like in your Bible and in your songs. I do not know these words.

Santa Anna's men broke down the outside walls and came into the courtyard. The Texans went to the second wall and fought them back. They clubbed with their rifles, and stabbed with their bowie knives. At last the few Texans that were left drew back into the monastery and shot the enemy as they came into the courtyard.

The women and children had hidden themselves where they could. I crawled under the hay. I would open my eyes and shut them again. I could not keep myself from looking and hearing. The awful sights still come to my eyes and the sounds ring in my ears. The soldiers of Santa Anna came on thick as bees. Inch by inch they gained ground but for every Texan they killed five of them fell. Poor fellows - many of them cared not to fight. It was the will of their tyrant leader. Mexico builds not one statue to Santa Anna. It is a lesson to all. He was a self-seeking, cruel ruler.

I did not stay in the courtyard. I was afraid. Long before this I had heard Señor Bowie tell Señor Smith, "We must hold the Alamo. We must keep Santa Anna back from Gonzales. If we don't even the women and children will be murdered." I had kept close to Señor Bowie. He knew my language and I could feel his strength. Though he was ill I felt he would yet find a way to overcome Santa Anna. When he and the other brave fighters were slain fear seized me.

I hid with other frightened children and their mothers. Some of Santa Anna's men shot into the room. One boy was killed, but the rest of us escaped alive. We could see little in the dark corner where we had huddled. As soon as it was light enough, some of the soldiers came searching through the rooms.

One of them put his bayonet against my mother and said, "Where is the Texans' money?"

"If they had any find it," she said.

The soldier struck her and I screamed. An officer appeared and ordered the soldier to go and leave the women and children alone.

When it was broad daylight, the families were sent to the home of Don Musquiz at the southwest corner of Main Plaza. A servant there gave us coffee and tamales. We were very hungry. That afternoon we were taken before Santa Anna. He had his headquarters on the Plaza. I saw a pile of silver on the table where he sat.

Mrs. Dickerson was more excited than any of the other women. My mother was very quiet and very sad, but not afraid of Santa Anna. I was scared. The Texans had told me that he would cut off my ears if he ever caught me. I did not cry out, but clung to my mother. Santa Anna, I remember, was dressed up very fine and he had a pleasant voice; but he looked angry. He thought us traitors. He was kind to Mrs. Dickerson, at least his voice sounded different when he spoke to her.

He asked the Mexican women, "Why do you fight your countrymen?"

"They are not our countrymen," my mother answered; "we are Texans."

"I suppose if I let you go you will raise your children to fight Mexico."

"Yes," my mother said. Her sorrow over the death of my father had made her not afraid to die, I think.

"You ought to have your ears cut off," he replied.

This made me and the other children scream.

"Get the mob out!" Santa Anna said. "Give each woman two dollars and a blanket."

The officer led us away. As we were going out he said in a low voice, "Vamonos." We did.

Mrs. Dickerson sat there before Santa Anna when we left. She was crying. Señor Travis had a negro slave named Joe, who was also standing there. We heard afterwards that Santa Anna sent Mrs. Dickerson on a horse to Gonzales with Joe to help her along. Deaf Smith and some of Houston's scouts met her on the way. After hearing the sad story from her, some of them hurried on to Gonzales with the news.

We stayed in San Antonio with my uncle. He had taken no part in the war. He was too old. Uncle found my father's body among the slain and buried it. It took three days for the soldiers of Santa Anna to gather up their dead and bury them. In after years I was told that six hundred of them had been killed by the one hundred and eighty-two Texans who died fighting at the Alamo.

"Did you see them burn the bodies of these Texans, Señor Esparza?" some one questioned.

No, but I heard that they did burn the bodies. Later, when Santa Anna had been defeated I learned that Captain Seguin had come to San Antonio and gathered up the ashes of these brave men and given them honorable burial near the spot where they had died fighting for freedom. Alcalde Ruiz helped to burn and bury many of the bodies.

After the battle of the Alamo we moved away to San Pedro Creek. I was frightened until Santa Anna had left San Antonio. He did not stay long. We were all happy when he was beaten in battle by General Houston.

The old Alamo was left in ruins. It stood like a haunted place - full of many memories for me.

"Do you know how many Mexicans were in the Alamo fighting as Texans against Santa Anna?" came a question.

I heard Guerrero, an old man, tell that the names were Fuentes, Losoya, Jimenes, and my father; also Captain Badilla of Nacogdoches. Guerrero was there, too, I was told but escaped because he said he was a prisoner of the Texans. It is a sin for a man to carry a lie to his grave.

There was a monument made and the names on it were many, but I heard that no Mexican name was cut in the marble. My father and other Mexicans died for Texas. These of English tongue could do no more, so why not every name? Yet I blame no one. It was thought by too many that all people with dark faces and foreign tongues were wicked like the cruel Santa Anna.

That is not so. Many of my people loved liberty just as did the Americans who came to help settle Texas. I am glad to tell this story of the Mexicans who gave their lives for freedom. It is good to come and tell it to you American boys and girls.

Gray hairs cling to old memories. I live by the soil and with the soil. I talk to few about the Alamo and the old days. Some believe me not; some know it all. I talk now and then to friends of understanding and sympathy.[56]

This final account attributed to Enrique Esparza appeared in the book *Rise of the Lone Star* by Howard R. Briggs and Sarah S. King. Miss King was the long-time principal of the Bowie School in San Antonio and a respected leader and inspiration in education and civics. The account apparently was supplied

Enrique Esparza survived the battle as a child. He related a number of accounts between 1901 and 1907.

(Courtesy of Ray Esparza and the Daughters of the Republic of Texas Library at the Alamo)

by her since the chapter in which it is contained begins, "The principal of the Bowie School one day introduced to her pupils an old Mexican gentleman … 'I am so glad you could come Señor Esparza.…'"[57] The account is related in the form of a class visit and lecture by Esparza. For some unexplained reason he is called "Gregorio" in this book. Did this actually take place? Is the story accurate? The story is related as if someone were actually addressing a group of school children. If it did occur, it would have taken place years before *Rise of the Lone Star* was published in 1936. Esparza is said to have described himself as being eighty years old, so it could have taken place at any time from 1908 until his death in 1917. Miss King would have had to transcribe what Esparza was saying at the time or record everything from memory years afterward. It is possible that this visit by Esparza did take place since he was acquainted with the King family. Miss King's mother, Emily Brackett King, stated in a 1917 newspaper story that she "…heard the story [of the Alamo] from Mrs. Allsbury [*sic*] and also from Esparza."[58] (For other accounts by or attributed to Enrique Esparza see #4.2, 4.3, 4.8, 4.16, and 4.17.)

4.29
José Juan Sanchez-Navarro, 1938
According to his alleged handwritten journal and published by Carlos Sanchez-Navarro y Peón

[March] 2
At eleven I arrived at Bejar I was not able to speak to His Excellency. The cold is horrible, they walked during the day … 19 [leagues].
Leagues from Leona Vicario to Béjar … 197.

[March] 3
At ten in the morning I left his excellency the President to reconnoiter the camps and batteries. Señor Cos followed, who I accompanied.

Two batteries of ours were situated one at the highest point of the city overlooking the direction of the river to the West of the Alamo served with a cannon of 8 [pounder], one of 6 [pounder] and a howitzer of 7p. spread out 200 toesas; and another between North and East of said fortification with four pieces as the previous. The distance was 150 toesas; It is not noticed that the batteries cause serious damage. The enemy does not appear from behind his parapets.

A contrast is formed to the eagerness that his excellency presents himself to needless danger (God holds him in his hand) and the care that general Sesma takes to withdraw from places even where there is no danger.

Our troops generally make camp in the open field.

[March] 4

Reconnoitering as the previous day. In the outer trench his excellency learned, by a courier, that general Urrea had beaten the enemy in San Patricio. He continued to expose the man to death unnecessarily.

The battalions of Zapadores [Sappers], Aldama and Toluca have arrived. They are hungry and cold; but no resentment because we are expected to do what we are ordered to do.

The enemy shows no change. It is only known that there are men in the Alamo by the cannons and rifles that they fire; and because no more is heard than the blows of hammers and extensive vulgarities.

News had slipped out that they had mined the exterior and interior of the fort in order to blow us up together if we attack, it appears that tomorrow a breach will be opened.

[March] 5

In fact, last night our troops worked with much endurance, while our generals were in conference, it is said that his excellency favored the assault and all were for the negative. A trench was placed to the North and East half a rifle shot, but at five this morning it was not toyed with but for a quarter of an hour.

The assault has been decided upon. Why does señor Santa Anna always want his triumphs and defeats marked with blood and tears?

General Cos commands the first column, he has ordered me to the lead. God protect us all!

[March] 6

Long live the country, the Alamo is ours!

Today at five in the morning the assault was made by four columns commanded by general Cos and colonels Duque, Romero and Morales. His excellency the President commanded the reserve. The fire lasted for half an hour. Our chiefs, officers and troops as if by magic topped the walls at one and the same time and they threw themselves inside continuing the conflict by the sword. By six thirty in the morning none of the enemy existed. I saw actions that I envied, of heroic valor. Some cruelties horrified me, among others the death of an old man they called "Cocran" and of a boy approximately fourteen years. The women and children were spared. Travis, the Commander of the Alamo, died as a brave man. Buy [Bowie], the braggart son-in-law of Beramendi, as a coward. The troop was granted plunder.

They had taken away from the enemy a fortified point, twenty pieces of various calibres, many arms and ammunition; they killed two hundred fifty seven men whose bodies I have seen and counted; but it was not able to cheer me because we have lost eleven officers dead and nineteen wounded, among these the valiant Duque and Gonzales; of troops two hundred forty seven wounded and one hundred ten dead.

It is well said: "With another such victory we will be carried away to the devil."[59]

José Juan Sanchez-Navarro (d. 1849) was born in Saltillo, Mexico, and was a career military man. At the time of the Texan campaign he held the rank of captain and had served as the adjutant inspector of Nuevo León y Tamaulipas. He was present in San Antonio de Bexar when Texan forces defeated Gen. Cos in December of 1835. He returned with Cos's force in the spring of 1836.

The appearance of Sanchez-Navarro's account marked the beginning of a new stage of firsthand Alamo accounts in which the story was related via a handwritten document. By the 1930s all of the participants in the Alamo battle were long gone. Enrique Esparza had died in 1917, and Alejo Perez Jr., the son of Juana Alsbury and youngest survivor of the battle, had passed away in 1918. Perez had been too young to have remembered any of the events of the battle. If his mother had related any details to him, he took them to his grave without passing them on.[60] Also, by this time there were few, if any, people around who could claim to have spoken to or interviewed eyewitnesses. The only way for firsthand accounts of the Alamo battle to become known were through "newly discovered" handwritten documents.

Sanchez-Navarro's account appeared in the form of a handwritten narrative of the Texan campaign tucked away on the blank pages of two large ledger books that contained indexes of official records from his days as adjutant inspector of Nuevo León y Tamaulipas. Texas writer Lon Tinkle wrote that this account was discovered in 1936, which coincidentally was the centennial of the Texas Revolution. The account was first published in 1938 by Carlos Sanchez-Navarro y Peón as *La Guerra de Tejas - Memorias de un Soldado*. There is no record of the account before that time, and Sanchez-Navarro y Peón gives no record of where it came from.[61]

The ledger books in which the account is contained are somewhat suspicious. They contain official records dated from 1831 to 1839, which means that if Sanchez-Navarro used them for his personal journal then he, or someone else, continued to use the books for official records after the Texan campaign. The very use of these ledger books by Sanchez-Navarro is suspect. The books are large and would have been very cumbersome to take along on a campaign. Also, Sanchez-Navarro was a scion of the richest land holding family in Mexico and was also an army officer and official of the Mexican government. It is unlikely that these ledger books would have been the only things at his disposal to record his personal journal.[62]

The ledger books are now part of the Nettie Lee Benson Latin American Collection at the University of Texas at Austin. Information on the university's acquisition of the document is described as "sketchy," and the little information there is "...fails to indicate from whom the university bought the material or what price was paid."[63]

Some of the description of the Alamo battle resembles that found in the letter of the unidentified Mexican soldier of March 7, 1836. This resemblance caused writer Walter Lord to conclude that the unidentified soldier was actually Sanchez-Navarro. However, the possibility cannot be eliminated that some later individual found the ledgers of Sanchez-Navarro, half filled with mundane official records, and filled in the unused pages with an account of the Texan campaign, incorporating information from other sources such as that from the letter of the unidentified Mexican soldier.[64]

4.30
José Enrique de la Peña, 1955
According to the final draft of his alleged handwritten diary, and published by Jesús Sanchez Garza

In a council of war held on the fourth of March in the house of the general in chief, he stated the need of making the assault. Generals Ramírez y Sesma, Cos, Castrillón and colonels Almonte, Duque, Amat, Romero, Salas and the casual major of San Luis, attended to him, giving him deference. The controversy revolved about the manner of doing this. Castrillón, Almonte and Romero were agreed that a breech should be opened, that eight or ten hours would be enough to do this practically. There were field pieces on the way and colonel Bringas aid to the general president, marched with the purpose of hurrying them along. It was decided to summon the commander of artillery and to come to an agreement with him and notwithstanding that the artillery was to arrive in a day or another, and that the resolution would have remained unresolved, on the fifth the order was given for the assault. Some who approved this resolution in the presence of the general in chief, disapproved when they were not in front of him, this contradiction manifests their weakness; others adopted the party of silence, persuaded that he not accept contradictions because he was only pleased to hear that which flattered his decisions, discarding all observations which were apart from his. None of those chiefs bore in mind that we had no aid stations, nor surgeons to save our wounded and that for some it would be less bad to die than to come out wounded, as will be seen after the assault.

When in this or in another of these discussions it was of what would have to be done with prisoners, in the case that before the assault the enemy surrendered, the example of Arredondo was cited, that in the time of the Spanish government he had hanged eight hundred odd colonists, after he had won an action and this was taken as a model. General Castrillón and colonel Almonte poured out with the principle motives of the rights of people, philosophical and humane principles which did them honor. They repeated these afterward, when preparations were made to shoot the prisoners who had been taken by general Urrea but their reasons were fruitless.

We had no officers or engineers who could have given knowledge of the Alamo force and its defenses; because the section of this corps, named by the army, yet remained in Mexico; but the Sappers were not lacking those who could have made this examination and the information given by general Cos, by the wounded officers left in Béjar and some residents of that city who were believed sufficiently. These later feared the force of the garrison who were in the Alamo and of the little provisions and munitions that they counted on. They had enclosed themselves hurriedly and they did not have much time to supply themselves.

The firmness of Travis was to be defeated: for several days his own people had goaded him to surrender arguing the lack of provisions and scarcity of munitions, but he calmed their restlessness with the hope of quick recourse, something which was not difficult to make them believe after they had seen reinforcements enter. They had, nevertheless, worried him some that on the fifth he promised them that if in the night of that day some aid did not arrive, they would surrender the following day, or try to escape with the help of darkness, these details were told to us by a lady of Béjar, a negro, the only man who escaped and various women who were saved by colonels Morales and Miñon. The enemy was in communication with some of the citizens of Béjar, who were devoted to them, and it is said for certain in those days, that the general President had knowledge of the resolution made by Travis, and because of this he hurried the assault, because he wanted to create a sensation and had felt that to take possession of the Alamo without noise and without spilling blood, without which some believe there is no glory.

Once the order was given preparations were made to fulfill it, yet there were those who were not for it: none doubted we would conquer, but predicted that the strife would be bloody and it was in fact. All the afternoon of the fifth was passed in preparations, night came and with it the most serious reflections. Our soldiers, it is said, lacked the cold courage that was necessary for the assault, but they are dauntless and those that survive will not have to be ashamed. Each one privately lifted and prepared his soul for the terrible moment, made his preparations, arranged silently and with cold blood the preparedness which precedes a duel. There was a general sorrow in that it was important to us for it to turn out with honor. No proclamation preceded this combat, but the example given stated in the most eloquent language and the most urgent order. Our spirited officers left nothing to be desired in the hour of trial, and if anyone failed in his duty, if anyone spotted his honor it was so insignificant that his fault remained confused in the obscurity and in the scorn. Actions of valor were seen in which many fought hand to hand and also some infamies.

The Alamo was an irregular fortifications, without flanking fire, which a prudent general would have taken with little loss; we lost more than three hundred brave men.

Four columns were employed for the assault. The first was under the command of general Cos, composed of the battalion of Aldama and three companies of the active [battalion] of San Luis, which had to ascend the front of the West [wall] that over looked the city. The second, under the orders of colonel Duque, composed of the battalion under his command had of the other three companies of San Luis, had to do it [attack] the front that faced north which had the farthest curtain of batteries standing out. These two columns had a force of seven hundred men. The third, under the command of colonel Romero, composed of the companies of fusiliers of the battalions of Matamoras and Jimínez, had cut strength, and amounted to less than three hundred or so men, had to assault the front on the East which was the strongest because of its raised work, because of the number of openings of fire which were defending it, three of these situated in a battery constructed above the ruins of the church, which had come to be a space for high gentlemen. The fourth column was commanded by colonel Morales, composed of one hundred or so cazadores, who had to take the entrance of the fort and the entrenchments which defended it.

The battalion of Sappers and five companies of grenadiers formed the reserve column with a force of four hundred men. The general in chief had to command this column according to the text of the secret order that he had given for the assault, and its formation was put in the hands of colonel Amat, who led it into danger.

This was the general plan and although minor arrangements were to be made, almost all were omitted.

Our chief made much merit of the bravery of Travis, since it saved him from the insult of an insinuation that it would have been enough in the critical circumstances surrounding him, to save the army a great sacrifice.

From one in the morning of the sixth the columns were set in motion, and at three they commenced to advance silently toward the river, which they crossed marching by some weak and narrow wooden bridges which hardly fit one or two men across. They examined some small obstructions to arrive without being noticed by the enemy to a point which personally had been designated by the general in chief, and they placed themselves in it resting with arms in hand. He reordered silence and prohibited smoking. The moon had risen, but the density of the clouds which cover it, did not permit more than dull light to reach us, and in this manner they appeared to contribute to our plan. This half light, the silence which guarded us hardly interrupted by a noiseless murmur, the fresh air, the calmness of the weather, which lengthened the hours and the dangers that well we would soon run to, all made grave our position: we were all breathing and we were all able to understand; inside of a few minutes, many of us would not be able to answer the questions asked of us having already returned to the nothing from which we had come; others, badly wounded would remain torn for hours without anyone remembering them, fearing still that an enemy's shot would whistle over his head and die at his feet giving an end to his pain. Nevertheless, hope gave us life and within a few moments it made disappear this anguished uncertainty: an outrage to our arms had to be avenged and the blood of our friends spilled three months before, within these same walls that we were about to assault. The horizon began to lighten, the beautiful dawn was about to be seen to leave its golden curtain: a sound of a trumpet call to attention was the signal agreed upon and well soon was heard the terrible bugle call of death which stirred our hearts, which changed our countenances and drew us all out, suddenly, from our pensive reflections. Worn out by fatigue and drowsiness, I had hardly closed my eyes to doze when this fatal sound reached to strike my ears. A bugler of the sappers (José Maria González) was the one who impelled us to despise life and to face death. A few moments the horror of this hastened to flee from us, honor and glory taking its place.

The columns advanced with as much swiftness as was possible, and a short time after undertaking the march they were ordered to start to fire, being still distant, not aiming and so far as to not be able to distinguish [a target], but there was a chief who acting prudently ignored this signal. The enemy advised of our attack, by the signal answered by all of the columns, quickly answered our fire, which was not able to harm them, and whose execution [of fire] partly delayed our advance. Travis, in order to make up for the scanty number of the defenders, had placed three or four loaded rifles at the side of each one of them; and the first fire was very active and deadly. Our columns left in their path a wide trace of blood, of wounded and dead. The bands of all the corps, gathered around our chief, playing the call of attack, and this sound which electrified our hearts, which elevated our souls and made others shudder, was seen to fill us with more lively ardor and enthusiasm. The second column, carried away by this, broke forth in cheers for the Republic and the general President. The officers were not able to repress this imprudence, which was

paid for dearly. Called to the attention of the enemy, by this circumstance, at the same moment in which the light was to permit the
perception of objects redoubled his fire on the columns, and he was able
to discharge more of his blows. It was seen that a single shot of shrapnel
knocked down all of a half of the company of cazadores of Toluca, which
was advancing some paces from the column, captain don José María
Herrera, who commanded it died a few moments later, and Vences, lieutenant of it, was equally wounded. Another shrapnel shot left many gaps
in the first ranks in the lead, one of them being colonel Duque who was
pierced in a thigh; having remained on foot, not without astonishment,
one of the two sole assistants of the chief, who marched immediately to
his side, since the other was not able to witness this act. It is he who
speaks who fate preserved this time although don José Maria Macotela,
captain of Toluca, gravely wounded, died a few days later.

It has been seen what the plan of attack was, but various arrangements taken to execute it, were almost all omitted. It had been ordered
that the columns carry crow bars, axes and ladders, but until the precise
hour I noticed that all were insufficient and that the ladders were badly
constructed.

The columns threw themselves forward with firm step, in a horrible
shower of bullets and shrapnel and persevering with ardor in their resolution, had reached the foot of the walls, less the third which a battery of
three cannons on a barbette made deep furrow in its left side, and at the
time it was being attacked at the front from the height of the quarters it
was necessary to seek a less bloody entrance, rapidly went toward the
right corner of the front to the north. The few and poor ladders which
we were carrying had not arrived, because their carriers had perished in
the transit or they had hidden. Only one was seen of all which had been
planned. General Cos, seeking a favorable position to ascend, had ended
up with his column at the front where the second and third were. All met
at a point, mixed and forming a confused mass. Fortunately the covering
of this front was of wood; its ditch was hardly begun, and the height of the
parapet was of some eight or nine feet; it had leaned and although with
difficulty, it was able to be climbed. But disorder had been introduced:
officers of every rank were shouting being hardly heard. The most valiant
of our veterans tried to climb first, and after attaining this had to make
horrible shouts in order to make room, and climbing up and over these
same companions. Others very crowded together made useless efforts,
mutually impeding one another, hindering the most agile and knocking
over those who had already topped [the wall] with dauntless effort. A

lively rifle fire, directed from the flat roof of a barrack and from other points made a painful havoc, and increased the confusion of our disordered crowd. The first who climbed were knocked down by the bayonets already waiting for them behind the parapet or by pistol fire; but the valor of our soldiers was not intimidated seeing their companions fall dead or wounded and hurried to occupy their place to avenge them, climbing over their bleeding bodies. The explosion of the rifles, the whistle of the bullets, the moans of the wounded, the vague cries of the crushed, the cries for help and sighs of the dying, the arrogant exhortations of the officers, the clamor of the military instruments, and the upsetting shouts of the attackers which were raised spiritedly, deafened all and made critical and terrible this moment. The shouting of those being attacked was no less noisy and from the beginning they had wounded our ears with their furious shouts, terrible shouts of alarm in a language which we did not understand.

General Santa Anna from the battery where he had placed himself contemplated with anxiety this horrible scene and, deceived by the difficulty presented to him about the climbing and by the movement that had been made by the third column, he believed that we were being repelled; he ordered colonel Amat with the rest of the reserve, since the Sapper battalion had already been ordered to the columns in assault, arriving and climbing at the same time as them. Then he also ordered all of his Army Staff and all who were by his side. This brave reserve was to increase the clamor and the victims, so much more regrettable since there was no need for them to engage in the combat. Advancing in the middle of a shower of bullets and shrapnel and before the Sapper battalion arrived at the foot of the walls half of their officers were wounded. Another of these said officers, young Torres, died inside the fort in the same moment of taking the flag of the enemy. He died of a single blow, without complaining, covered in glory and his companions filled with feeling. A rare thing happened to this corps, it had four officers as casualties and twenty one soldiers, but among these were none of the rank of sergeant, as is known, are more numerous than that of the former.

Approximately a quarter of an hour had passed that our soldiers remained in this terrible situation, tiring themselves out trying to find a less obscure death than they would receive crammed together in one mass, and when after much effort, they gained in sufficient number to top the parapet, without distinction of corps, the terrified defenders trampled over one another to lock themselves up in the rooms placed to the right and left of the small plaza which formed their second line of defense.

They had loopholed and entrenched the doors, but in order to form these trenches they had to make some inner ditches, which were harmful to them. Not all of them locked themselves up since some remained in the open, looking at us before firing and as if astonished by our audacity. Travis was seen to hesitate, but not in the death which he chose. He took some steps and stopped turning his face to us with an air to discharge his shots, well he fought like a soldier. Finally he died, but he died after having sold his life very dearly. None of them died with more heroism and they all died. Travis behaved as a hero, it is necessary to do him justice, since with a handful of men without discipline he resolved to face men accustomed to war and in numbers very superior to his, without provisions, with little ammunition, and against the wishes of his subordinates. He was a good looking blond with a physique as robust as his spirit was strong.

Meanwhile colonel Morales with the cazadores having fulfilled the instructions which he had received, was exactly in front of us, a few paces distance and basically fearing that they would be hurt by our fire he had lodged in the entrenchments which they had conquered, attempting to harm without harming us. It had been very good that the other columns reunited in the front because being in the small enclosure, the tearing apart by each other could be avoided in part. Nevertheless, some had the pain of falling by the shots of their companions, a regrettable wound indeed and an even sadder death. They had overloaded the soldiers with ammunition, since the reserve and all of the preferred companies carried six on parade. It seems that they wanted to say with this that the soldier not rely on his bayonet, which is the weapon that is made use of in the assault, while some riflemen support the attackers with their fire; but always on these occasion great mistakes are committed which are impossible to correct. This time there were many.

Our soldiers some by recklessness and other carried away by fury threw themselves into the quarters of the entrenched enemy, from which loopholes made on us an infernal fire. After these entered others, either drawing near the doors and blinded with courage and with a cloud of smoke discharged their shots against friends and enemies and in this manner many more of us were sadly lost. On the other hand they belittled them by using the same enemy cannons to demolish the doors of the quarters of these latter, and made in these a horrible carnage concluding with some of them beaten to death. The tumult was immense, the disorder frightful, it seemed as if the furies had been set loose upon us: different groups of soldiers were firing in all directions on their companions, on their officers and in the same manner one expected to receive death at the hands of a friend as at that of the enemy. In the midst of this clamor was found bewilderment and no command was able to be understood, even when the orders were shouted as much as possible. Some believe that this story is exaggerated, but those who were witnesses confess that it is exact and to tell the truth all exaggeration is cut out.

Finally it was time to conclude the disorder which was increasing our victims, and on my arguments, and my urgent request, general Cos ordered the fire to be silenced, but the bugler Tamayo of the sappers exhausted in vain his instrument, since it did not cease until no one was left to kill and when they had wasted some fifty thousand cartridges. He who doubts this can make the approximate calculation that I had made with the data I have given.

Among the defender there were some thirty or more colonists and the rest were pirates, accustomed to challenging dangers, to scorn death and to fight with much spirit, circumstances which in my opinion made them worthy to be granted mercy which finally some of them asked for themselves and others not able to give it to them because of ignorance of the language. In fact, when these men noted the lack of their leader and they saw that they were being attacked by very superior forces, lost their courage. Some in a pronunciation hardly intelligible desperately cried "Mercy, valiant Mexicans;" others by a loophole or by the door stuck out the point of a bayonet with cloth, sign of peace and some even stuck out their stockings. Our soldiers who saw these demonstrations confidently entered the quarters, but those of the enemy who had not asked for mercy, who were not thinking of surrendering, nor counting on any other recourse than to sell their lives dearly, received them with pistol shots or the point of a bayonet; ours who believed themselves betrayed were enraged anew and every moment renewed partisan fights were joined with new rancor. The order had been given to spare no more than the women and this was compiled with; but this slaughter was useless and had we avoided it we could have saved much blood on our part. The enemy who tried to escape were to fall under the sabers of the cavalry which had been stationed with this purpose and even as they fled they defended themselves. An unfortunate father was seen with a little son in his arms throw himself from a considerable height and both perished at the same blow.

For nearly an hour which you may picture for yourself, this scene of destruction went on when the curtain of death covered and ended it; shortly after six in the morning all was concluded; the corps were beginning to form, they had begun to recognize one another, showing in their sad countenances the loss that they noticed in their very diminished files of their officers and their companions, when the general in chief appeared. He was able to see the same for himself the orphaned state of the battalions and that small enclosure sown with corpses, of scattered limbs, scattered with bullets, of weapons and destroyed uniforms. Some of these were already burning together with the corpses and gave off a filthy odor, which nauseated the stomach. These corpses with their faces blackened and bloody, disfigured by a desperate death, their clothes and hair burning at the same time presented a horrible and truly hellish appearance. What trophies those of the field of battle! Very soon some were left naked by the fire and others by a degrading rapacity and especially ours. Those of the enemy were distinguished by their whiteness, by their robust and bulky forms. What a sad spectacle that of the dead and dying…! With what horrors passed in review to encounter the remains of friends…! With what anxiety did they ask for others and with what rapture they embraced! The questions which followed one after the other when bullets still whispered and in the middle of the moans of the wounded and of the exhausted sighs of the dying.

The general addressed our mutilated battalion to praise their valor and to thank them in the name of the Country, but it was not noticed in his words that charm which Napoleon spills in his, from which as the count of Segur assures that it was impossible to defend oneself. They seconded his vivas with coldness and the silence would have hardly been interrupted if I, in one of those fits which brought about the enthusiasm, or which one forms to avoid reflection and paves over the sensibility, had not addressed the valiant cazadores of Aldama, to cheer the Republic and them, an act made in the presence of the leader, to whom without merit such importance has been given, proves on my part it is certain, that I never flatter power.

As the speech of Santa Anna very nearly proceeded an unpleasant event which, happened when the heat of the strife had already passed, was seen as contemptible murder and greatly contributed to the coldness noted. Some seven men had survived the general massacre and guided by general Castrillón, who sponsored them, were presented to Santa Anna. Among them was one of great stature, well formed and of regular features, in whose countenance there was imprinted the sentiment of adversity, but in which was noted certain resignation and nobility that commended him. He was naturalist David Crocket, very well known in North America for his strange adventures, who had come to travel over the country and had been in Bejar in the moments of surprise had locked himself up in the Alamo, fearful that his quality as a foreigner would not be respected. Santa Anna answered the intervention of Castrillón with a gesture of indignation and immediately directing the sappers, who were the troops nearest to him, ordered them to shoot them [the prisoners]. The chiefs and officers were irritated by this behavior and did not second the voice, hoping that the first moment of fury had passed, these men would be saved; but various officers who were around the President who perhaps had not been there in the moment of danger, were made notable by an infamous act; exceeding the soldiers in cruelty, they placed themselves before them, in order to flatter their chief, and sword in hand they threw themselves upon these unfortunate defenseless ones, in the same way that a tiger throws itself upon its prey. They tormented them before they were made to die, and those unfortunate ones died moaning, but without humiliating themselves to their executioners. It is said that general Ramírez y Sesma had been one of them: I do not testify to this, because although I was present, I turned aside from this sight horrified in order not to see such a barbarous scene. Remember, companions that fierce moment, that horrified us all equally, and which shook our souls, which a short while ago had thirsted for vengeance. Do not our hearts beat quickly, filled with indignation against those who so vilely bloodied their swords. As for me, I must confess I shake only at the memory and the sound is always in my ears the pitiful and penetrating tone of the victims.

To whom was this sacrifice useful, and what was the fruit that was obtained of increasing the number of victims? Rather dearly it was, though it could have been obtained otherwise, making these men travel over the carpet of corpses, over which we put our feet; and enabling them generously, to command them to tell their companions the fate which awaited them if they did not desist in their unjust cause. They could have made notice of the power and resources that their enemy had. According to the papers of theirs found and the later notices, one hundred eighty two men were the force which had been inside the Alamo; and according to that counted on our part, it is two hundred fifty three. It is unquestionable that the total did not exceed either of those two numbers, and even the sum of those is lower than the number which was mentioned by the general in chief in his message, where it is assured that in the excavations and entrenchments alone there had remained buried more than six hundred corpses. What objective was gained by this deceit? Some have believed that it was to give more importance to this act and others to excuse our own loss and to make it less regrettable.*

Death united friends and enemies in the same place. A funeral pyre converted into ashes, in a few hours, those men who a short time before had such spirit, who in a blind fury wasted their lives and had met their ends in the fight. The greater part of ours were buried by their companions, and the enemy, who seems to have some respect for the dead, attributed the great pyre that took them up to the result of our hatred. I desiring to count them for myself, arrived at the moment the flames began to redden and to consume them.

---

*   See Annex No. 9 [Santa Anna's letter of March 6 and a numerical list of dead and wounded by battalion compiled by general Amador]... The second of which manifests exactly the loss we had. Of those wounded they died in great part because of bad assistance, lack of beds, shelter, surgical instruments, etc. etc. The enemy all perished, only having remained alive an old woman and negro slave, whom the soldiers pardoned with compassion, and because it was supposed that only force had kept them in this danger. The dead, in as much, of the enemy, were 150 volunteers, 32 residents of the town of Gonzáles, who with the aid of darkness of the night got in to the fort two days before the assault, and some twenty residents or merchants, of the same city of Béjar.[65]

José Enrique de la Peña (1807-ca. 1842) was born in Jalisco, Mexico. In 1825 he embarked on a military career that lasted a troubled fifteen years. During the Texan campaign he marched north with the rank of lieutenant and as an aide to Colonel Francisco Duque, commander of the Toluca battalion. The account attributed to de la Peña comes to us from a lengthy handwritten document that was long thought to be de la Peña's personal "diary" of the Texan campaign. It was published in book form in Mexico by Jesús Sanchez Garza in 1955. Sometime in the late 1960s or early 1970s the handwritten manuscript was purchased by John Peace, who brought it to Texas and granted custodianship of it to the Special Collections of the University of Texas at San Antonio. In 1975 the manuscript was translated and edited by Carmen Perry and published in book form in Texas.[66]

de estatura, bien formado y de facciones regulares en cuyo
semblante estaba impreso el sentim.^to de la adversidad pero
en el cual se notaba cierta resignacion
y nobleza q.^e le recomendaban. Era el
naturalista David Croket, muy cono-
cido en el Norte-america por un orij-
nely aventurero, q.^e habia venido a re-
correr el pais y q.^e hallandose en Bejar
en los mom.^tos de sorpresa se habia encerrado en el Alamo temeroso de
no ser respetado por su calidad de ex-
trangero. S. A.^ma ma contestó a la in-
terbencion del Castrillon con un
gesto de indignacion y dirigiendose
en seguida á los Zap.^s que eran la
tropa q.^e tenia mas serca mandó
q.^e los fusilaran. Sargentos y oficia-
les &c.^a

One of the most controversial of alleged eyewitness passages, the de la Peña
"Diary's" description of Crockett's capture and presentation before Santa Anna.

(Courtesy of the special collections of the University of Texas at San Antonio)

The de la Peña document bears many of the same problems as the Sanchez-Navarro journal. There is no record of it before its first publication in 1955, and its original owner, Sanchez Garza, never gave any hint as to where he had obtained it. The de la Peña account bears many indications of being a modern day fake. Not the least of these is the fact that the dramatic scenes describing the battle of the Alamo appear to have been compiled from other accounts of the Alamo published long after de la Peña's death. When the account was published in English in 1975, revisionist historians focused on the scene describing the execution of Crockett. The account was quickly elevated to the "best" and "most reliable" of its kind without anyone ever trying to establish whether or not this is an authentic document actually written by de la Peña.[67]

In 1998 the de la Peña papers were auctioned off by their owners with much fanfare and publicity. They were purchased by Tom Hicks and Charles Tate, who then donated the papers to the Center for American History at the University of Texas at Austin. In May of 2000 a symposium was held at the Center to install the papers as authentic, which was done to the satisfaction of the press, those who bought the papers, and those who always believed in their authenticity anyway. To those who question the authenticity of the papers, the symposium was little more than a slick public relations ploy. Actually very little time at the symposium was devoted to presenting evidence as to the authenticity of the papers. One panelist presented uncontested argument in favor of the papers' authenticity. A good deal of time was devoted to ridiculing the motives and methods of those who question the document. No one who questions the authenticity of the papers was invited to be on the panel.

Regarding the question of whether or not Crockett was one of those executed after the Alamo battle, the de la Peña papers are no longer the source of unquestionable accuracy. Don Carlton, who organized the symposium, stated his belief in the authenticity of the papers but conceded that his belief did not extend to the accuracy of the information contained therein.

Professor James Crisp, a leading proponent of the authenticity of the papers, admitted that "It [the de la Peña manuscript] is not the best evidence we have about what happened to Davy Crockett." Thomas Ricks Lindley, perhaps the leading researcher on the battle of the Alamo, once believed in the authenticity and accuracy of the de la Peña account but now believes that the manuscript is a forgery, based on his examination of the evidence. Lindley also points out that "Writer Steve Harrigan [*Gates of the Alamo*] sees the chronicle as a research-driven narrative history and believes it is unreliable. Historian William C. Davis [*Three Roads to the Alamo*], while he does not think the account is a forgery, feels its Alamo execution data is unreliable."[68] (For another account by or attributed to de la Peña see #4.35.)

Jesús Sanchez Garza, original owner and publisher of the de la Peña "Diary."

(Courtesy of Clyde Hubbard)

Antonio Lopez de Santa Anna, August 1956

According to Jackson Burke in his article "Secret of the Alamo" published in *Man's Illustrated* magazine

When we entered the fortress we found few defenders still alive. We disposed of them instantly, after a brief interrogation which brought out some startling information. Of course we knew the stand-or-die order had been given long before our attack. And then I discovered the strange reason why this fort, manned by very able fighters such as the famous Crockett and Bowie was so easily taken. No less than 30 of these men had mutinied. This was divulged by Crockett before he died. He died, however, before we could extract from him the manner in which the mutiny had been brought under control. But the mute answer to this question lay before us in the center of the fortress itself. A pile of bodies lay in the middle of the compound. All of these had been shot in the chest as if they had been executed. Those bodies that we found on the ramparts, however, showed the usual combat wounds in the usual variety, bullet holes in the head and face, saber cuts about the head and shoulders from our troops who scaled the walls and so forth. I could only conclude that there had indeed been a mutiny, as Crockett had testified when he said, "If they had not mutinied we would have held you off from now until Armageddon." Clearly the mutiny had been put down by summary execution. It is quite possible that had it not been for this incident the battle would have gone against us. On the other hand, if the commander of these poor men had not issued his insane stand-or-die order, I would never have given the no-quarter signal, and these brave men would not have died in vain. If this officer was not a madman, he was a fool![69]

This account attributed to Santa Anna appeared in a little known article by Jackson Burke in *Man's Illustrated* magazine. It is the next in the series of suddenly discovered firsthand documents describing the Alamo battle. According to Burke it is a translation from the memoirs of Santa Anna resting in the archives of the Mexican government in the military history section of the national library. The article featured a blurry photograph of the alleged memoir, a two-page handwritten document complete with a very official looking seal and ribbon attached. Befitting a 1950s men's magazine, the article is as lurid as the account is ridiculous. The article begins with

Sam Houston himself, with his ".45 drawn," capturing Santa Anna and announcing "Hey, you men! Git on over here and see what I've done caught me!" Besides the colorful prose of the article, we are left with the account itself: The freedom loving rebels within the Alamo executing thirty of their comrades and neighbors for mutiny.[70] (For other accounts by or attributed to Santa Anna see #1.9, 1.11, 1.15, 3.1, and 4.33).

4.32
Isaac Millsaps, 1964
From an alleged letter by him to his family

We are in the fortress of the Alamo a ruined church that has most fell down. The Mexicans are here in large numbers they have kept up a constant fire since we got here. All our boys are well & Capt. Martin is in good spirits. Early this morning I watched the Mexicans drilling just out of range they were marching up and down with such order. They have bright red and blue uniforms and many canons. Some here at this place believe that the main army has not come up yet. I think they are all here even Santanna [sic]. Col. Bowie is down sick and had to be to bed I saw him yesterday & he is still ready to fight. He didn't know me from last spring but did remember Wash. He tells me that help will be here soon & it makes us feel good. We have beef and corn to eat but no coffee, bag I had fell off on the way here so it was all spilt. I have not seen Travis but 2 times since here he told us all this morning that Fanning was going to be here early with many men and there would be a good fight. He stays on the wall some but mostly to his room I hope help comes soon cause we can't fight them all. Some says he is going to talk some tonight & group us better for Defence [sic]. If we fail here get to the river with the children all Texas will be before the enemy we get so little news here we know nothing. There is no discontent in our boys some are tired from loss of sleep and rest. The Mexicans are shooting every few minutes but most of the shots fall inside & do no harm. I don't know what else to say they is calling for all letters, kiss the dear children for me be well & God protects us all....

If any men come through there tell them to hurry with powder for it is short I hope you get this & know - I love you all.[71]

Isaac Millsaps (1795-1836) was a defender of the Alamo from the town of Gonzales, Texas. The "Millsaps letter" was supposedly written during the siege of the Alamo, but it is entered at this date since it generally became available to the public in 1964 when it was donated to the University of Houston and added to the collection of its library. The letter only appeared to the general public a year or two before its acquisition by the University. It had been well known in the subculture of buyers and sellers of Texas documents before that time. The letter came to the University in the collection of E.B. Taylor of Dickinson, Texas, who had obtained his whole collection of Texana from C. Dorman David. David is now recognized as a forger of documents related to the Texas Revolution. David has admitted to faking other documents, but he steadfastly denies any responsibility in the Millsaps letter. In fact he considers it an honor that anyone thinks him responsible for such a well-done piece. David acquired the letter from Robert E. Davis, who had acquired it from William Morrison, who had acquired it from someone in Houston. David thinks it may have been Louis Lenz. The letter was only one item of a collection that included "Travis letters and a bunch of stuff." David traded an Egyptian sarcophagus for the collection. In 1989 Gregory Curtis, editor of *Texas Monthly* magazine, exposed the many questionable aspects of this document in an article on forgeries. Since then historians have generally come to recognize this letter as a fake.[72]

4.33
Antonio Lopez de Santa Anna, 1967
According to his alleged memoirs and published by Ann Fears Crawford in her book *The Eagle — The Autobiography of Santa Anna*

Our army's crossing into Texas was the cause of great surprise on the part of the filibusters, for they believed that Mexican soldiers would not cross again into Texas. Frightened by our invasion, they ran to a fortress called the Alamo, a solid fortress erected by the Spaniards. A garrison of six hundred men under the command of Travis, a leader of some renown among the filibusters, mounted eighteen cannons of various calibers. Confident that aid would come, Travis replied to my proposition of surrender, "I would rather die than surrender to the Mexicans!"

The self-styled "General," Samuel Houston, said to the celebrated Travis, in a letter we intercepted: "Take courage and hold out at all risks, as I am coming to your assistance with two thousand men and eight well-manned cannons." We did not hesitate to take advantage of this information that fell into our hands.

I felt that delay would only hinder us, and ordered an immediate attack. The filibusters, as was their plan, defended themselves relentlessly. Not one soldier showed signs of desiring to surrender, and with fierceness and valor, they died fighting. Their determined defense lasted for four hours, and I found it necessary to call in my reserve forces to defeat them. We suffered more than a thousand dead or wounded, but when the battle was over, not a single man in the Alamo was left alive. At the battle's end, the fort was a terrible sight to behold; it would have moved less sensitive men than myself.[73]

This account of Santa Anna comes from his memoirs alleged to have been written in 1874. These memoirs were the property of Santa Anna's grandson, a Jesuit priest, Father Antonio Lopez de Santa Anna III. Father Santa Anna died before realizing his goal of writing a biography of his grandfather based on his memoirs. The original document is part of the collection of the University of Texas Library. It was published in Spanish in 1906 and finally translated and published in English by Ann Fears Crawford in 1967.[74] (For other accounts by or attributed to Santa Anna see #1.9, 1.11, 1.15, 3.1, and 4.31)

4.34
Unidentified Mexican Officer, ca. 1994
In the form of a handwritten journal of the Mexican army's Active Battalion of San Luis, part of the de la Peña papers

Feb. 23 - In Bejar. General Ramirez [y Sesma] having advanced with 160 cavalry in sight of it [Bejar] at 7 in the morning at which hour the enemy did not know of our arrival. The remainder of the division were in sight between 12 and 1 but by that time the enemy had rung the general call to arms and retired to its fortification of the Alamo. There they had approximately fifteen pieces of artillery but not all mounted nor in a state of service for want of cannon balls. One of 16 [pounder] and another of 8 [pounder] they have brought to bear on this population. After the

Division had rested a half hour behind a hill half league distance the President General mounted his horse and directed it towards the city with his E.M. [probably "mounted escort"], 3 companies of Cazadores commanded by colonel Morales, 3 of grenadiers commanded by colonel Romero, two howitzers and the cavalry of general Sésma, putting the remainder of the division to march under the orders of gen. D. Ventura Mora to the camp of Concepcion. The President at the town of Bejar ordered Colonel Miñon with half the cazadores to take the church not knowing it was abandoned. As the column of the President entered the plaza they fired from the Alamo a [round of] grapeshot with the 16 pounder piece. Immediately the principal commander of artillery Ampudia was commanded to position the howitzers and they fired four grenades, they [the Texans] raised a white flag, ceased the fire and one came with an official communication which said Bowia [Bowie] to the commander of the troops invading Texas that he wanted [illegible]. The President ordered an answer by word of mouth that he would not treat with bandits, who had no more means of escape than surrender at discretion. Then he prepared the troops for action, eating and resting, making return to Bejar all he had march to Concepcion.

[February] 24 - Location in Bejar. His Excellency left at 9 in the morning, he ordered to be distributed in his sight shoes to the preferred companies he directed immediately an assault on the Alamo and made to break the suspension of fire from the afternoon before. He positioned a battery of two pieces of an 8 [pounder] and a howitzer and it commenced to beat the enemy fortification which answered the fire. Had no misfortunes. The enemy robbed six mules of cargo from the bn [battalion] the night before. We began to open and inventory the stores of the Americans. At 11 in the morning his Excellency marched with the cavalry to reconnoiter the besieged.

[February] 25 - In the same [place] at 9 1/2 [9:30] His Excellency presented himself in the battery he ordered to march to the other side of the river the column of cazadores and the battalion of Matamoras, crossing himself. Our soldiers fought in pistol range against the parapets. The soldier of the 3rd Epitacio Hernandez was wounded. The division had two dead and six wounded. In the night they made works to cover the lines that was put in la Villita by the order of colonel Morales.

[February] 26, 27, 28 - Not a notable thing has happened. The fire of the artillery and rifle they have made on these days, similar. It has been opposed without any misfortunes to the division.

[February 29] - Location in Bejar. The siege of the Alamo continues. About 7 and a half [7:30] this night was killed by the enemy the soldier of the 1st Secundino Alvarez as he approached the Alamo by order of the President.

March 1 - As usual.

[March] 2 - Location in the same [place]. The cazadore Trinidad Delgado drowned bathing in the river. The siege of the Alamo continues.

[March] 3,4 and 5 - Location in the same [place]. The siege follows without a notable thing in these three days. The day 3 the battalions Zapadores, Aldama and Toluca arrived.

[March] 6 - Location in the same [place]. At five thirty five in the morning the bugle resounded by order of the President General playing the agreed signal for the 4 attack columns to strike the assault on the Alamo. The fire of attack and defense endured twenty minutes and at 8 and a half in the morning finally none of the enemy existed. At 10 they began to march to Bejar and immediately afterwards they began to collect the dead and wounded, resulting two hundred thirty enemy of the first [dead] and among those the rebel leader Bowie commander of the Alamo, Trevis [Travis] his second and Crocker [Crockett] who had willingly interfered three nights before; wounded or prisoners none. Of the Mexican troops there resulted dead and wounded, twenty-one officers, and two hundred ninety-five troopers. The battalion has dead Lieutenant ag [breveted] D. Yrcineo Guerrero, 1st sergeant ag [breveted] second lieutenant Don Antonio Carricarte, 2nd Sergeant Anastacio Valarquer of the 1st, grenadiers[:] Victoriano Perez, Casadores: German Sanchez and Victoriano Tenorio, fusiliers: Leonardo Ramos of the 2nd Cornelio Rosalis of the 3rd and Francisco Ordas of the 4th. Wounded: Grenadiers, Felipe Santiago, and sapper Antonio Obudo: 1st [company] sergeant 2nd grade Manuel Vargas, corporal Macedonio Rocha, soldiers Juan Ysidoro Cruz, José Maria Avila, Paulin Morales, Valentin Peña, Nepomuceno Hernandez, Francisco Laredo, Lorenzo Martinez, Justo Castillo, Turto[?] Martinez, Ygnacio Nuñez, Francisco Rivera: 2nd [company] Serafin Puga, José Torres, Estevan Reyes, Francisco Martinez, Homobono[?] Zapata, Candelario Ramirez, Onofrio Carrabés, Vitale Arias; Fiburcio Quebedo; 3rd [company] Corporal Antonio Artega, soldiers José Maria Martinez 2nd, Santanna Moctezuma, Vicente Galvan, Anactacio Vega, Francisco Martinez, José Antonio Martinez, Alvino Vasquez[?], Luciano Cruz: 4th [company] Soldiers Manuel Chavez; Carlistas Castros, Morico Lara: Cazadores Mariano Hernandez.

The corps that gathered at the assault were the following: Permanent Battalions, Zapadores, Aldama, Matamoras, Jimenes, Active [battalions] Toluca, and San Luis. The regiments of Dolores, Presidials, and piquets of the regiments of Tampico and Veracruz under the orders of general Ramirez [y Sesma] were extended through open country to pursue those who ran away, of those were killed 68. The columns of attack were 4. The 1st under the orders of General D. Martin Perfecto de Cos was composed of seven companies of Aldama and two of San Luis: These were divided in three sections, the 1st commanded by the General, the 2nd I, and the 3rd Romero first aide of Aldama. The 2nd column under the orders of D. Francisco Duque was composed of the cazadores and fusiliers of Toluca, and 80 fusiliers of San Luis. The 3rd Column under the orders of colonel D. José Maria Romero was composed of the companies of grenadiers of all of the corps of infantry and of the battalion of Zapadores, under the orders of the General in chief. The 1st column attacked the side that looks toward Bejar, the 2nd opposed the gate at the end, the 3rd that looks toward the cavalry camp, and the 4th the gate at the end that looked toward la Villita. The enemy dead were burned.[75]

This account comes from the alleged journal of an unidentified officer of the San Luis battalion and is part of the handwritten de la Peña papers. It was recognized as such by Professor James Crisp in his scrutiny of the papers during the early 1990s. This account was used by the author of the de la Peña "diary" to provide information on details of the Alamo siege prior to de la Peña's arrival in San Antonio on March 3. If this journal is authentic, it may have provided de la Peña with such details.[76]

4.35
José Enrique de la Peña, ca. 1994
In the "rewritten diary," section of his alleged
diary and part of the de la Peña papers

[March] 3 - The 3rd day of March, between 8 and 9 in the morning, after the troops were lined up, we marched for Béjar, which we entered between 4 and 5 in the afternoon. At some six or seven miles I received the order to advance so as to receive those of His Excellency the general in chief and I arrived when the happy encounter with General Urrea was being precipitated in San Patricio. We traveled 21 or 22 miles.

[March] 4, 5, 6 - The 4th and 5th we were allowed to rest and on the 6th the attack on the fortress of the Alamo was made the details of which are described separately. Before going onward we shall express what occurred between the entrance of the 1st Division and our arrival, transferring here the part of a diary that has been sent to me.[77]

[At this point the author of this account copied the Journal of the San Luis Battalion. See account #4.34.]

When the de la Peña papers began to come under intense scrutiny in the early 1990s, it was determined that the papers contained two distinct tellings of the Texan campaign. Proponents and opponents of the authenticity of the papers agree that there is no original "dairy," supposedly written by de la Peña while on campaign. The two distinct accounts in the papers are now called the "rewritten diary" a part of which is reprinted here, and a "final draft" that is generally believed to have been written by de la Peña months or years after the campaign. The segment printed here is part of the "rewritten diary," and it only includes the dates on which de la Peña would have been in San Antonio to witness events at the Alamo. (For another account by or attributed to de la Peña see #4.30.)

4.36
William Cannon, 1995
From an 1893 letter to J.S. Hogg

David Crockett and James Bowie came to San Antonio several months before this trouble; and William Barrett Travis, Mr. Bonham and Mr. Wilson, with their companies, came just shortly before the fight. My father's family consisted of himself, his wife, myself and older brother John Henry, and three sisters, to-wit: Susan (wife of Lieutenant Dickinson), Martha and Mary. My father moved into the Mileno Blanco where some of the troops were stationed. He then built inside of the walls, to which himself, mother and all of the children moved. My oldest sister, who was Mrs. Dickinson, lived in the Alamo in the right hand room going in. We were living in the walls three of four weeks perhaps before Travis, Bonham and Wilson came with their companies.

James Bowie was in the left hand room going in, lying sick with typhoid fever. He was moved also out of the Mileno Blanco to that place a month or so before the fight. Mrs. Candelaria took care of him there. She was taking care of the sick generally.

Two week before the trouble commenced Gen'l Las Vegas came to the Alamo from towards San Pedro Springs, bearing a white flag. Mr. David Crockett, with three or four men, went out to meet him. He told Crockett that he wanted ammunition. The answer of Crockett was, that all the ammunition he had to give would be given through the guns.

We had nine Mexican Women and Mrs. Candelaria living inside the walls, and had been living there for some time.

On the first day of March the companies of Bonham, Wilson, Crockett and Travis, and part of Bowie's (not over twenty or twenty-five men) were drawn up in line inside the Alamo walls. I was enrolled into the army that day with my brother John Henry, my father saying that a bullet from our guns was as strong as that from a man's, and that we needed all the help we could get. I was enrolled under Mr. Bonham. There was a cotton-wood block that had been used to hold back the Alamo door and keep it from shutting in the wind. After we formed in line I rolled this block of wood down to the end of the line and sat on it while someone made a sketch of the company. I have seen this sketch, and this block of wood looks like a drum in the picture. I remember that the picture was a hastily made one, for it was finished on the next day. My recollection is that the picture hung on the walls of the Alamo throughout the whole fight and was not touched. Three years ago I learned from my niece Susan Griffiths, granddaughter of Mrs. Dickinson, that she had seen it in some show-window in San Antonio. I do not know where it is now, but some one in Houston told me recently that he saw the picture in Galveston.

On Thursday the 3rd of March the Mexicans commenced heaving in sight on the West side of the river, and camped near the old Mission of San Jose. On that day six of our men went out to drive in some beeves. Four of them returned with the cattle, but I never heard of the other two afterwards. Others also drove in two carts of corn, amounting to forty finegas (Mexican measure), or about one hundred bushels. This corn was brought in carts by oxen yoked by their heads. It was carried into the right hand room, first floor, and scattered in the room, and the sacks were filled with sand and placed at different places on the walls. The men continued the work of fortifying during Friday, Saturday they were busy entrenching two pieces of artillery. The Mexicans in the mean time were moving closer to the walls, and were re-enforced Friday night and Saturday morning. That evening all the Mexican women left the Alamo, one of whom returned about sun-down. The others did not return at all.

The next morning (Sunday) the Mexicans held what they called early mass. The walls of the Alamo plaza ran down to the river on each side. There was no wall connecting these two ends, as the river banks were perpendicular and about fifteen feet high. There was no chance for Santa Anna to cross there except by bridging, which would have to be done in the face of the defenders. After mass was over, and when the sun was about an hour risen, Santa Anna sent a flag of truce in front of the walls across the river at the place above named, telling the men that the women and children would be permitted to retire before the battle began, if they wished. My sister, Mrs. Dickinson, then stated to some of the commanders that if she were furnished with means of transportation she could carry the news to Gen'l Sam Houston of the besieged condition of the garrison. She thought the Mexicans would not fire upon her, as she was a weakly woman with a child in her arms. There were two horses in the walls: one a bay belonging to Bonham; and the other, a gray, belonging to William Barrett Travis. They put her on the gray horse, handed her the baby, and a negro man belonging to Travis got up behind her, and they opened the gates and she went out to risk their lives and reach Sam Houston for reinforcements if possible. Mrs. Alsbury and girl child about six years old went out about the same time. Miss Hess went also. The firing took place immediately, and my sister, whether by accident or intention, was wounded in the right limb. Of Mrs. Alsbury and her child I never heard anything afterwards, and was never able to find out what became of her. Miss Hess was taken prisoner by Yellow Wolf, of the Comanche tribe, who made her his wife. She died some few years ago in the Comanche tribe in the nation, leaving grand children and great grand-children, some of them who could be found here at the present time, having blue eyes and red hair. The negro who went out on the horses behind Mrs. Dickinson left her shortly after they got out of the Alamo. He was taken prisoner also by the Comanche tribe, and remained with them some time. He afterwards went to the Mescalero Apaches; then to the Yutes; from there to the Crows; thence to Colorado state in 1857 to where Denver now stands on Cherry Creek. While there he married a negro woman. After her death some years later, he went to the Crows and died chief of the Crow Nation. He called himself James Beckwith.

To return to the Alamo: After all the women and children had gone out the fight commenced. It was brisk and hot, not lasting over an hour. The ammunition of the artillery gave out before that time, and the gunners had to cease firing. The Mexicans advanced from the direction of San Pedro Springs, crossing the river above the fort. They ran their artillery so close to the walls as to shake them with their discharges. I was using a rifle, and think I shot twenty-seven times. The Mexicans were at close range - not over forty yards; and I am sure I never missed a single shot. We were afraid to waste ammunition, as it was very scarce. After the walls were battered down the Mexicans rushed over and continued firing as our men retired slowly into the Alamo building. Several fell in the door of the Alamo. William Barrett Travis was in the act of moving some fallen men from the door-way so he could shut it, when he was shot and fell over them. The Mexicans then rushed inside the Alamo. I had gotten inside, and Mrs. Candelaria and I were upstairs in the room where James Bowie had been carried during the fight. The Mexicans came up while we where there, and killed Bowie by stabbing him with bayonets as he lay on his bed. Mrs. Candelaria and I then rushed for the stairs, I holding to her dress. When we reached the bottom, Crockett lay about fourteen or fifteen feet distant. He attempted to throw us a piece of brown paper, but his strength was not sufficient and it fell almost at his hand. I picked it up and placed it in my bosom. Afterwards, on my escape, I concealed it in the Mission where it remained until I took it way about two months afterward while Gen'l Houston was there looking after the Alamo, which was just before the making of the treaties with the Indians. I gave the piece of paper to Gen'l Houston then he made a copy of it. The original remained in my possession until it became worn out by time and usage, but I retained a copy of it, which is as follows: "Let the goddess of the free dedicate an altar. Make it of the materials of the Alamo. Let these stones speak, that their immolation be not forgotten. The blood of heroes has stained them."

We then ran out the door - Mrs. Candelaria and I - and a Mexican struck her on the left cheek with the butt of his gun, making a terrible gash and knocking her down. I was not touched, and continued to run through the horses until I got to the end of the house. Then I recollected myself and ran back to her and found her on her feet. We then ran to the wall without being further noticed. Some of our men were still fighting with their knives. My mother was killed about this time outside the Alamo near the walls. My sisters were killed on the inside. My father was with the artillery, and he fell down by the guns at the back of the river inside the walls. My brother was killed between there and the door, and Mr. Wilson about a hundred and fifty yards from the door down towards the artillery, and a great many of his company were killed there also.

Mrs. Candelaria and I got out of the walls and went to Dr. Levario's house where the Menger Hotel now stands. He lived in a story and a half doby house. I was put up stairs. There was a window in my room covered with domestic, or some kind of cloth, from which I could see over the wall not knocked down, and see what was going on inside. I saw some of the Mexican soldiers caring for their wounded, while others were bringing in wood on their backs from the hill where the cemetery now is Southeast of the Alamo. I saw them start the fire, and could see them pile the dead, and I supposed some of the wounded, on this fire and they were burned. I remained at Dr. Levario's until dark. He was afraid to keep me any longer, and Mrs. Candelaria went with me from there to the San Jose Mission, where I was concealed. She would bring me provisions when she had a chance, sometimes once a day, sometimes twice and sometimes once in two days, telling me to keep still, that the Mexicans were still hunting me. I was in the mission over a month. I then made up my mind to venture out and get to my sister if she had made her escape, or to go to Gonzales, which I did. I was five days on the way, living on prickly pears during the time. When I reached Gonzales my sister was there with her child, and she told me how she came through the lines. A French officer had come to her and conducted her through. She also told me that she had sent word to Gen'l Houston of the danger to the Alamo, not knowing until I arrived that all had been killed and the Alamo taken. I stayed at Gonzales a couple of days and then started out on the trail of Gen'l Houston, reaching him after the battle of San Jacinto and the capture of Santa Anna. I reported to Gen'l Houston the fate of the Alamo; and that all the men had been killed, and it was no use to hurry there until everything where he was had been fixed up. Afterwards troops were sent there but I did not return with them.

Those are the particulars as far as I remember them at this time, not having any records to refresh my memory.

Four or five years ago the Mexicans that were buried between the Alamo and the place where the Menger hotel now stands were taken up. It seems that Mrs. Candelaria did not tell of the burning of the dead nor the place where the Mexicans were buried until I came back to Texas six years ago with Chief Jeronimo, when I told him of it in San Antonio, and she confirmed my account.[78]

The account of William James Cannon comes to us in the form of a letter he had written to Texas governor J.S. Hogg apparently in an attempt to obtain some type of payment for his service and losses to his family at the Alamo. Although the letter was written in 1893, it is included at this point since it was first made public by Thomas Ricks Lindley in a 1994 article in the *Alamo Journal*. If the account had been made public one hundred years earlier, without being challenged, it is safe to say that some of its details would have been woven into the Alamo story and now would be part of its history. Lindley subsequently discovered a document by Susan Griffith Sterling, the granddaughter of Susanna Hannig (Dickinson), in which she denounced all of the claims made by Cannon and proclaimed him "a colossal fraud."[79]

4.37
Santiago Rabia, 1997
From his handwritten journal

We set out for Monclova on the 1st of February, 1836, and arrived on the 4th. We set out for the Río Grande on the 8th and arrived on the 12th. We set out for San Antonio de Béjar on the 16th and arrived on the 23rd of the month that is expressed above. The enemy was saturated with 3 cannonadings lasting, in alteration, for 15 days, and the fortification of the alamo was given the attack on the 6th day of March between 4 and 6 in the morning. The battalions which took part in the aforesaid attack were the following: [ ]adara, Aldama, Toluca, Ma[tamoras], San Luis, cavalry, Regiment of Dolores and 20 men from Tampico. The force that was at the aforesaid Alamo was composed of 200, 50 [250?] Americans, 4 women - who were killed, and only one man and the women were set free. The dead and wounded of the Mexican troops were [ ] 500 men.[80]

The Santiago Rabia journal has been part of the collection of the Daughters of the Republic Library at the Alamo since 1990, when it was donated to the library by Odel Myers of Oswigo, Illinois. The fact that it contained a brief description of the Alamo battle was made public by Thomas R. Lindley in 1997.

4.38
Joaquin Ramirez y Sesma, 1998
From his after action reports on the battle of the Alamo, written on March 11, 1836

…[In] the occupation of Bejar at which only the 1st division of the army attended all that I commanded complied with their duty, and those who distinguished themselves, Señor colonel commandant of the Battalion of San Luis don Juan Morales, and the second lieutenants of cazadores of the Battalion of Matamoras Señor Alonzo Gonzales and Don Jose Maria Souza since their valor is held in high esteem of this chief, and marked of the two mentioned officers who did their duty so that in few moments the enemy were entirely reduced to the fortifications of the Alamo. In the blockhouse that before the assault sustained this point they worked with the greatest perseverance and always at risk the mentioned chief the captain of cazadores of the Battalion Jimenez. Don José Frias the Lieutenant Colonel of Matamoras Don Manuel Gonzales, of equal rank commander of the Battalion Jimenez Don Mariano Salas and the captains of the regiment of Dolores Don Jose Fato, and Don Ramon Valera.

In the assault my division corps was augmented by other brigades, and as from that [time] we took Bejar I left the plaza in order to cover the camp of the sentry box. The first column was commanded by Señor colonel Morales who is able to report to the Government that which he conveyed to His Excellency President General in chief; the second was commanded by the Señor General Cos, but his second was the Señor General Amador, and therefore he was able to inform with accuracy about the individuals who were in that [column.] [T]he third was by the Señor Colonel Don Jose Maria Romero but his second was the Señor Colonel Francisco Duque whose Chief is in that capital; and the reserve commanded by the Señor Colonel Don Augustin Amat who also is found in the Army; and with respect to the Cavalry I enclose to you the report that I made to His Excellency the President when I served when he requested of me very few days after the assault.

[The report followed as a separate document]

...[Once] the fire started and laid waste the enemy's first line of fortification as described to you, many of them thought to withdraw securely leaving by the small fort on his right and got loose in enough number that they marched organized to the plain trying to avail themselves of the adjoining brush country. As soon as I observed this I ordered a company of the Dolores Regiment with my assistants Lieutenant Colonel D. Juan Herrera, captain don Cayetano Montero, the Lieutenant of Dolores in the grade of Lieutenant Colonel don Juan Palacios, and standard bearer don Jose Maria Medrano so the enemy paid for that part of the brush country and the lancers' gallant officers charged, as well as the troop that they commanded charged and slashed in moments despite the desperate resistance they did not hesitate or falter one moment. Another band of about fifty men got loose then from the center of the fort, and I ordered the company of lancers of the Regiment of Dolores to charge under the orders of brevet Lieutenant Colonel D. Ramon Valera, Lieutenant don Santos Castillo and second lieutenant D. Leandro Ramirez and don Tomas Viveros and as the enemy saw their movement they seized an irrigation ditch making a defense so vigorous that I had to order Lieutenant D. Franco Molina with twenty Lancers of Tampico and twelve of Veracruz that aided this force, although none faltered I feared that they would be repelled, and to the Captain of Rio Grande D. Manuel Barragan, and Lieutenant of the same company don Pedro Rodriguez with fifteen men on foot. All these officers carried out the movement with such determination and exactness that some men truly sheltered behind a parapet in that position resolved to sell their lives very dearly[,] they were swept away in a few minutes and suffered the knife. Then the Captains classified as Lieutenant Colonels of the Regiment of Dolores don Manuel Montellano, don Jose Fato and standard bearer d. Jose Guijarro were detained with another company to charge those who got loose from the fort on the left, and that they were also killed showing those officers and troops were not to be exceeded by their companions; as the rest of the cavalry under the command of General don Ventura Marar colonel of the Regiment of Dolores, sergeant major Venvenuto Lopez, Captain don Antonio Valdez[,] Lieutenant don Telesfero Carrion, and standard bearer don Manuel Ruis employed to cover the other flank of the fortification, and that troop left nothing to be desired: Ultimately, Your excellency, the cavalry surrounded the fortification of the alamo at a distance of fifteen paces in environs under the fire of the enemy, and complied with my orders so that I am able to assure you that the troops on this day under my command left nothing to be desired — The desperate resistance of those men, as has been showed to you since they had been in the middle of the danger dictating my orders and have been a better eye witness than any of the other facts. The enthusiasm was so great that it was impossible to single out without offending, and for the same I believe that the valiant officers who had been well patronized in this memorable and important military expedition that are so worthy of the consideration of the Supreme government, as the gratitude of their fellow countrymen, so that only I take the liberty to recommend to you the mother of the corporal of the regiment of Dolores Jose Hernandez who was killed as the charge was made to take possession of the ditch, who has no other support than her son, and lives in the town of Santiago Tlaguinterco....[81]

General Joaquin Ramirez y Sesma led the vanguard of the Mexican army on its advance to San Antonio and later commanded the lancers who surrounded the Alamo during the battle of March 6. His account first came to light in 1998. It was uncovered by William C. Davis in the Archivo Historical Mexicano Militar during research for his book *Three Roads to the Alamo*. Davis's discovery was significant in a number of ways. Ramirez y Sesma's reports confirm information detailed, or at least hinted at, in other accounts that many of the Alamo defenders were driven outside of the fort once the Mexican army gained the walls. His find also is an achievement since the Mexican Archives traditionally have been tough nuts to crack for Alamo researchers and historians. His discovery keeps hope alive that untapped information on the Alamo is still out there waiting to be uncovered.

Later Davis's discovery lost some of its wonder. As it turned out, Texan researcher and artist Jack Jackson found a typescript of these very same reports right in the Center for American History at the University of Texas at Austin, unnoticed and never used by historians.[82] (For other accounts that support the fact that Texan defenders were driven from the Alamo during the battle see #1.5, 2.2, 2.7, 3.21, 4.10, 4.30, and 4.34.)

The story of the battle of the Alamo has been told and retold for the past 160 years in the form of books, articles, films, reenactments, plays, speeches, etc., all based to one degree or another on the variety of eyewitness or alleged eyewitness accounts presented here. Very few of the tellings have resembled one another due to the variations of the sources and depending on which accounts a later writer, historian, filmmaker, or artist had access to, favored, or chose to ignore. Based on the number of conflicting reports and the variety of ways these reports may be used together, there is almost no limit to the way the story of the Alamo can be told.

Firsthand accounts of the battle of the Alamo have continued to surface over the years, and there is no reason to doubt that more will appear in the future. If some of the accounts from the latter half of the twentieth century are any indication, some "eyewitness accounts" may be in the process of being created right now. Ultimately it will be up to future historians and writers to determine who actually did or did not remember the Alamo.

The Alamo 1836

Painting by Joseph Musso (Courtesy of the
Texas Adventure Theater, San Antonio, Texas

Chapter Five

THE ALAMO

It should seem that there is, perhaps nothing on which so little reliance is to be placed as facts, especially when related by those who saw them.

— James Russell Lowell

The Alamo stands today in the center of modern San Antonio, Texas. Its familiar facade and the unmistakable carved parapet wall added on by the U.S. Army in 1847-1848, make it one of the most easily recognized buildings in the world. It is maintained as a shrine to the defenders of the Alamo by the Daughters of the Republic of Texas as well as a museum. It is one of the most visited tourist attractions in the United States. The familiar modern day Alamo originally was the church of the San Antonio de Valero mission. It later served as the main building of the Alamo fortress.

What confuses many visitors to the Alamo today, despite a number of very detailed maps, diagrams, and dioramas on display, is the fact that this building was only a small corner (the southeast corner) of the original mission/fortress complex. The front door of the modern Alamo is the main entrance to the Alamo grounds. In 1836 the fortress spread out across approximately three acres *in front* of this building. Its front door opened to the interior of the fortress.

When we speak of the Alamo as the 1836 fortress, we are speaking of this large area to the west of today's Alamo church building. Many of the "firsthand" accounts of the Alamo from the late nineteenth century raise questions as to their authenticity since they focus on the Alamo church, the only building still intact and recognizable at the time these accounts were given. It is unknown if some of the witnesses giving these accounts may have been concocting them using the only piece of the Alamo they had available to them as a reference, or if their words were merely misinterpreted by others to fit their descriptions of the larger Alamo fortress to the remaining church.

If the Alamo chapel was only a small corner of the Alamo fortress, then the Alamo fortress was only a small part of the Alamo battlefield. When we speak of the Alamo battlefield we must go beyond the fortress itself. The Alamo battlefield encompasses the whole town of San Antonio de Bexar and any locations around the town or the Alamo fortress where the Mexican army encamped, set up artillery positions, or mobilized for the attack.

I. The Alamo
A Main entrance of the Alamo fortress
B Inner courtyard
C Alamo church (in some accounts referred to as the chapel)
D Main Plaza
E Hospital and barracks
F Horse quartel
G Wooden palisade
H Southwest artillery position
I Low barracks
J Cattle pen
K Conjectural position of wells
L West wall with series of small rooms
M Long barracks
N Low wall
O Irrigation ditch

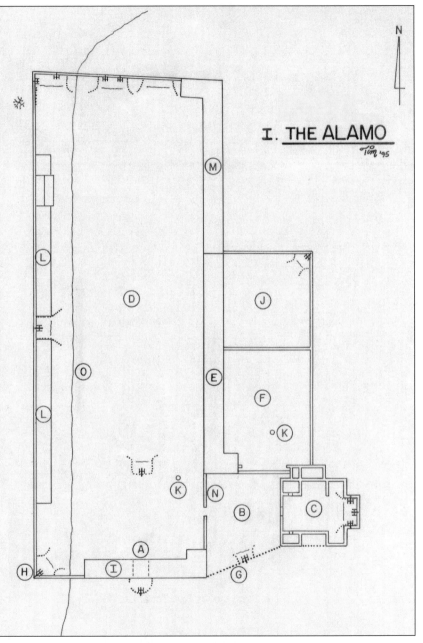

Original artwork by Rod Timanus

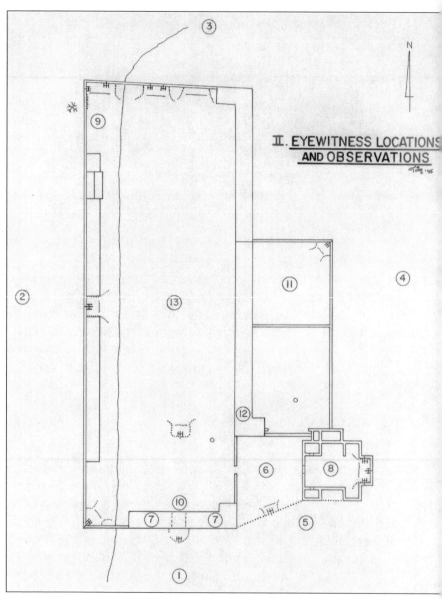

Original artwork by Rod Timanus

II. Eyewitness Locations and Observations

1 The south front

Manuel Loranca described Col. José Vincente Miñón with the infantry battalion as forming up on the south. Felix Nuñez claimed that Gen. Castrillón was responsible for this area. The de la Peña account states that Col. Morales and one hundred or so cazadores (chaussers) were to take the entrance [10] and the entrenchments that defended it. Gen. Filisola passed on the information that Cols. Miñón and Morales and their men seized a cannon at the southwest corner. Ramón Caro also was of the opinion that Miñón and Morales overcame this position.

2 The west front

This wall of the Alamo faced the San Antonio River and beyond that the town of San Antonio de Bexar. Loranca stated that Col. Mariano Salas and the Aldama battalion were responsible for the attack on this front. Nuñez remembered General Woll as being on the west side. The de la Peña account states that Gen. Cos with the Aldama battalion and three companies of the San Luis battalion had the west wall as their target. Maria Jesusa Peña told of witnessing the executions of Alamo defenders from a jacal toward the west of the Alamo.

3 The north front

Loranca remembered Col. Juan Baptisto Morales and the battalion "Firmas" of San Luis Potosi as attacking on the north. Francisco Becerra stated that Gen. Castrillón's column made "a lodgement" in the upper part [the north] of the Alamo. Nuñez recalled that Santa Anna, himself, was responsible for the north front. The de la Peña account states that it was Col. Duque with the battalion under his command [the Toluca] and three companies of the San Luis battalion that were responsible for the north. Francisco Ruiz recalled that Travis's body was found near one of the batteries on the north. Gen. Ampudia, Col. Duque, and Col. Amat all praised the actions of Lt. de la Peña in this area. Gen. Filisola passed on the information that

Gen. Amador was one of the first to reach the goal of climbing this wall. Ramón Caro reported that Gens. Amador, Ampudia, Col. Mora, and Lt. Col. Aquirre all gained a foothold on the north wall.

4   The east front

Loranca stated that Gen. Joaqiun Ramirez y Sesma and the Lancers guarded the east side of the Alamo and that Gen. Santa Anna positioned himself to the east of the fort with the band of the Dolores regiment. He also said that at least sixty-two Alamo defenders sallied from the fort in this direction during the battle in an unsuccessful attempt to escape. Nuñez stated that General Vincente Filisola was responsible for the east. The de la Peña account states that it was Col. Romero with the fusiliers of the battalions of Matamoras and Jimínez. In 1876 Susanna Hannig (Dickinson) stated that the Mexican scaling ladders were first raised on this side of the fort.

5   The southeast section of the Alamo

In an 1899 newspaper article about her life, it is said that Madam Candelaria identified Travis as the first Texan killed in the battle and that he died in this area.

6   The courtyard of the Alamo church

This enclosed area may have been the "small fort" described by Ruiz in 1860 in which he claimed to have found Crockett's body. In Morphis's 1875 *History of Texas*, Susanna Dickinson is said to have described this area as being covered with heaps of dead and dying. She also reported seeing Crockett's mutilated body "between the church and the two story barrack building." Her description could mean this area or the one directly to the north of it.

7   The low barracks

Ruiz described Bowie's body as being discovered in "one of the rooms on the South side." In 1901 Enrique Esparza remembered himself and others as being sheltered in rooms to either side of the main entrance [10].

8   The Alamo church

Several accounts such as those by Nuñez, Bledsoe, Cannon, and Madam Candelaria focused on this building as the scene of most of the action of the battle. It is the centerpiece of the Alamo Shrine today.

9   The northwest corner

Juana Alsbury in the John Ford Papers described herself, her son, and her sister as being in a building in this area of the fort during the siege and battle.

10 The main entrance to the Alamo

Loranca described Travis's and Bowie's bodies as being found in a room to the right of the entrance, but it is unclear if he was speaking of this main entrance or of the front doors of the Alamo church. Nuñez spoke of Travis's servant and two Mexican women as being found in a room to the right of the main entrance and a man in a room to the left. Once again it is uncertain as to whether he was speaking of the main entrance to the fort or the church.

11 The cattle pen

John Sutherland's account in the John Ford Papers stated that a herd of cattle were driven into this area by the Texans.

12 The hospital and long barracks

Much of Becerra's and de la Peña's description of the Alamo battle describes action in these buildings.

13 The main plaza

Nuñez claimed that almost all of the walls of the Alamo had been battered down by cannon fire and that all of the Americans had taken refuge in the church [8]. Zuber's tale of Apolinario Saldigna had the Mexican army burning the bodies of the Texans within the Alamo itself, despite the fact that the Mexican army would reoccupy the Alamo after the battle.

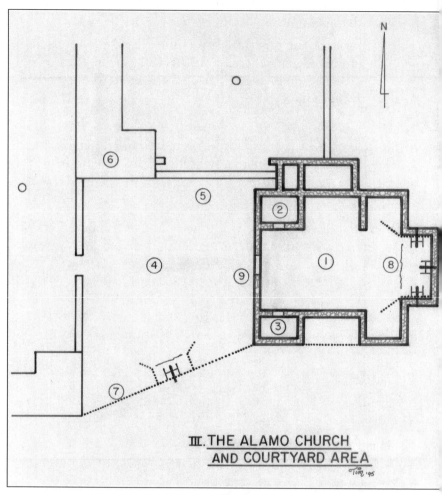

Original artwork by Rod Timanus

III. The Alamo Church and Courtyard

1   The Alamo church, known also as the chapel, is the most
    prominent building of the San Antonio de Valero mission,
    the Alamo fortress, and the present-day Alamo shrine. The
    west face of this building makes it one of the most easily
    recognizable buildings in the world. In 1881 Susanna
    Hannig (Dickinson) reported that she remained in a "little

dark room with an arch and window" in the rear of this building. Enrique Esparza's later accounts indicate that he and his family were also in the church during the battle. Madam Candelaria also claimed to have been in the church during the siege and battle. Nuñez's account centered most of the action of the battle around the church.

Nuñez and Bledsoe stated that the church was roofed over at the time of the battle. Madam Candelaria claimed that the roof had been destroyed by cannon fire before the siege. Esparza stated that the roof had been taken off.

2 Formerly the confessional of the mission church. Madam Candelaria reported that Bowie was housed in this room. In 1907 Esparza reported that Bowie was in a room on the north side of the church, but he was not clear if it was this room or not.

3 Formerly the baptismal of the mission church. Esparza reported in 1907 that the noncombatants were huddled in this room after the battle had ended. John Sutherland claimed that the garrison's ammunition was stored here.

4 The courtyard of the Alamo church. In 1888 Madam Candelaria reported the Crockett was one of the first to fall in the battle, shot down while unarmed and advancing from the church building "towards the wall or rampart running from the end of the stockade...."

5 Susanna (Dickinson) Hannig described seeing Crockett's mutilated body after the battle in James M. Morphis's *History of Texas* in 1875. Her description may have been of this area.

6 Formerly the convent of the mission, this two-story building served as the Alamo's hospital. In 1907 Esparza described some cannon as being in this building.

7 Wooden palisade connecting the low barracks and the church. An account attributed to John Sutherland claims that Travis assigned Crockett and his men to cover this position.

8   Earthen ramp over the apse of the chapel with three cannon positioned to fire over the wall. Esparza spoke of cannon as well as Travis on the roof of the church. In Morphis's *History of Texas* Susanna Hannig also described Travis as being on the top of the church. Loranca merely stated that there were Texans on top of the church. Becerra specified eleven Texans. The de la Peña account describes this position as a "space for high gentlemen."

9   The front doors of the Alamo church. Loranca stated that Gen. Tolza's command forced entry to these doors. Nuñez stated that the doors were open and that Travis worked a cannon just outside of them. His description of an unnamed defender whose death awed the Mexican soldiers took place just within these doors. Esparza claimed that Crockett died just outside of this position. Madam Candelaria's later tale described these doors as being sandbagged, and her description of Crockett's death changed to have him defending these doors inside of the church.

The Alamo—If only these walls could speak.

(Photo by Bill Groneman)

Notes

The following abbreviations will be used in these sources:

BRBML   Bieneke Rare Book and Manuscript Library, Yale University, New Haven, Connecticut

CAH   Center For American History, University of Texas at Austin

DRTL   Daughters of the Republic of Texas Library at the Alamo, San Antonio

GLO   Texas General Land Office

JPML   John Peace Memorial Library, University of Texas at San Antonio

NLB   Nettie Lee Benson Latin American Collection, University of Texas at Austin

TSA   Texas State Archives

UTA   University of Texas at Austin

Introduction

1   Elizabeth Loftus, Ph.D. and Katherine Ketcham, *Witness for the Defense* (New York: St. Martin's Press, 1991), 17. Also see, Sharon Begley and Martha Brant, "You Must Remember This," *Newsweek*, 26 September 1994, 68-69.

2   John Steinbeck, *Cannery Row* (New York: Viking Press, 1945), xiii-iv.

Chapter 1 The Siege

1   William B. Travis to Andrew Ponton, 23 February 1836, Yale Collection of Western Americana, BRBML. For more on Travis's writings see, Martha Anne Turner, *William Barret Travis — His Sword and His Pen* (Waco, Texas: Texian Press, 1972).

2   Henry Stuart Foote, *Texas and the Texans* Vol. II (n.p., 1841; reprint, Austin: The Steck Company, 1935), 224 (page reference is to reprint edition).

3   James Bowie to Commander of the invading forces below Bejar, 23 February 1836, Yale Collection of Western Americana, BRBML. Transcription in John H. Jenkins, *Papers of the Texas Revolution 1835-1836* Vol. IV (Austin: Presidial Press, 1973), 414.

4   Jose Batres to James Bowie, 23 February 1836, Archivo General de Mexico Papers, CAH. Translation in Jenkins, *Papers of the Texas Revolution* Vol. IV, 415.

5   William B. Travis to the People of Texas & All Americans in the world, 24 February 1836, TSA.

6   Michael R. Green, "To the People of Texas and All Americans in the World," *Southwestern Historical Quarterly* 91 (April 1988): 506-507.

7   "Important from Texas," *Arkansas Gazette*, 29 March 1836; "To the People of Texas and all Americans in the World," *Telegraph and Texas Register*, 5 March 1836; "Meeting of the Citizens of San Felipe," Broadside, 27 February 1836, #132 Streeter Collection, BRBML; and "To the Citizens of Texas," Broadside #185 Streeter Collection.

8   Launcelot Smither to All the Inhabitants of Texas, 24 February 1836, Army Papers, TSA.

9   Albert Martin to the People of Texas, 25 February 1836, Davidson Collection, TSA. This note was added as a postscript to Travis's letter of Feb. 24. See Green, "To the People of Texas," 493.

10 William B. Travis to Sam Houston, 25 February 1836, printed in the *Arkansas Gazette* April 12, 1836.

11 Umberto Daniel Filisola, "The Correspondence of Santa Anna" (MA thesis, UTA, 1939), printed in Jenkins, *Papers*, Vol. IV, 447-449.

12 Philip Dimitt to James Kerr, 28 February 1836, Army Papers, TSA.

13 Jenkins, *Papers* 4, 469; and Wallace Woolsey, *The History of the War in Texas by Don Vicente Filisola* Vol. II (Austin: Eakin Press, 1987), 172-173. Woolsey offers a different translation of this message.

14 William B. Travis to the Convention, 3 March 1836, printed in the *Telegraph and Texas Register*, 24 March 1836.

15 William B. Travis to a friend, 3 March 1836, printed in the *Telegraph and Texas Register*, 24 March 1836.

16 Juan Valentine Amador to the Generals, Chiefs of sections, and commanding officers, 5 March 1836, Archivo General de Mexico Papers, CAH, printed in Jenkins, *Papers*, Vol. IV, 518-519.

17 Ibid., 519; and Reuben M. Potter, "Fall of the Alamo," *Magazine of American History* (January 1878), reprint, in book form,

(Hillsdale, New Jersey: Otterden Press, 1977), 57 (page reference is to reprint edition).

18 Thomas Ricks Lindley, "Storming the Alamo," *Alamo Journal* 117 (June 2000): 11-18.

19 Antonio Lopez de Santa Anna to Jose Maria Tornel, 6 March 1836, printed in Jenkins, *Papers* Vol. V, 11-12.

20 Thomas Ricks Lindley, "A Correct List of Alamo Patriots," *The Alamo Journal* 89 (December 1993): 3-7.

Chapter 2 1836

1   *Telegraph and Texas Register*, 24 March 1836.

2   *El Mosquito Mexicano*, 5 April 1836. For a slight variation in this translation see, John F. Rios, compiler and editor, *Readings on the Alamo* (New York: Vantage Press, 1987), 115-117.

3   "Extract of a Letter from a Friend to the Editor," *New Orleans Commercial Bulletin*, 11 April 1836, printed in the *Portland (Maine) Advertiser*, 3 May 1836.

4   Ibid.

5   "Fall of San Antonio and its One Hundred and Eighty Seven Gallant Defenders," *Memphis (Tennessee) Enquirer*, 12 April 1836.

6   Ibid.

7   William Parker to the editor of the *Free Trader*, printed in Jenkins, *Papers*, Vol. 6: 122.

8   Correspondent of the Fredericksburg Arena, "Letter from Texas," *Frankfort (Kentucky) Commonwealth*, 25 May 1836.

9   Ibid.

10 Juan Nepomuceno Almonte, "Journal of the Mexican Campaign," printed in the *New York Herald*, 21 to 30 June 1836; also published in the *Southwestern Historical Quarterly* 48 (July 1944): 10-32.

11 *New York Herald*, 27 June 1836.

12 *Davy Crockett's Own Story — as written by himself* (New York: The Citadel Press, 1955), 357-73. This book incorporates the spurious *Col. Crockett's Exploits and Adventures in Texas* published in 1836 with *A Narrative of the Life of David Crockett... Written by Himself*, and *An Account of Col. Crockett's Tour to the North and Down East* both published in 1834.

13 Constance Rourk, *Davy Crockett* (New York: Harcourt, Brace and Company, 1934), 268-69.

14　Virgil E. Baugh, *Rendezvous at the Alamo — Highlights in the Lives of Bowie, Crockett, and Travis* (New York: Pageant Press, Inc., 1960), 236-37.

15　Henry Steel Commager and Allan Nevins, editors, *The Heritage of America* (Boston: Little, Brown and Company, 1939; enlarged edition, 1949), 592; Stephen Ambrose & Douglas Brinkley, *Witness to America* (New York: Harpercollins Publishers, A Lou Reda Book, 1999), 162; and David Colbert, editor, *Eyewitness to the American West — From the Aztec Empire to the Digital Frontier in the Words of Those Who Saw It Happen* (New York: Viking, 1998), 95.

16　For more detailed explanations of *Exploits and Adventures* see: James Atkins Shackford, *David Crockett The Man and the Legend*, edited by John B. Shackford (Chapel Hill, North Carolina: University of North Carolina Press, 1956; reprint Westport Connecticut: Greenwood Press, Publishers, 1981), 273-281 (page reference is to reprint edition; Richard Boyd Hauck, *Crockett: A Bio-Bibliography* (Westport, Connecticut and London, England: Greenwood Press, 1982), 51-52, 80, 83-85, 125; Paul Andrew Hutton, introduction to *A Narrative of the Life of David Crockett of the State of Tennessee Written by Himself* (Lincoln, Nebraska and London, England: University of Nebraska Press, 1987), xxxcii; Mark Derr, *The Frontiersman — The Real Life and the Many Legends of Davy Crockett* (New York: William Morrow and Company, Inc., 1993), 255-56; and William Bedford Clark, "Col. Crockett's Exploits and Adventures in Texas: Death and Transfiguration," *Studies in American Humor* 1 (June 1982): 66-72.

17　*Morning Courier and New York Enquirer*, 9 July 1836.

18　Billings Hayward, New York to David G. Burnett, Texas, 4 March 1836, Domestic Correspondence, TSA, printed in Jenkins, *Papers*, 511-512; Frederic Hudson, *Journalism in the United States — from 1690 to 1872* (New York: Harper & Brothers, Publishers, 1873), 424; and Frank M. O'Brien, *The Story of the Sun* (New York and London: D. Appleton and Company, 1928), 34.

19　Hayward to Burnett, 4 March 1836; and O'Brien, *The Story of the Sun*, 84.

20　Marilyn McAdams Sibley, "Thomas Jefferson Green: Recruiter for the Texas Army, 1836," *Texas Military History* 3 (Fall 1963): 129-145; Leo Hershkowitz, "'The Land of Promise': Samuel Swartwout and Land Speculation in Texas, 1830-1838," *New York Historical Society Quarterly* 48 (October 1964): 308,

312-316; and James E. Winston, "New York and the Independence of Texas," *Southwestern Historical Quarterly* 18 (July 1914 to April 1915): 368-385.

21 James Gordon Bennett, *Memoirs of James Gordon Bennett and his Times* (New York: Stringer & Townsend, 1855), 182-183; James Stanford Bradshaw, "George W. Wisner and the New York Sun," *Journalism History* 6: 4 (Winter 1979-80): 118; and John D. Stevens, *Sensationalism and the New York Press* (New York: Columbia University Press, 1991), 22-23.

22 George M. Dolson, Galveston Island to his brother, Detroit, 19 July 1836, printed in the *Detroit Democratic Free Press*, 7 September 1836.

23 Ibid.

24 Ibid.

25 Samuel Swartwout, New York to James Morgan, Galveston Island, 29 June 1836, James Morgan Papers, Rosenburg Library, Galveston, Texas, mentioned in Jenkins, *Papers* Vol. 7, 311.

Chapter 3 19th Century

1 Antonio Lopez de Santa Anna, *Manifesto que de sus operaciones en la Campana de Tejas dirige a sus Conciudadanos* (Vera Cruz: Imprenta Liberal a cargo de Antonio Maria Valdez, 1837), translated and printed in Carlos E. Castañeda, translator and editor, *The Mexican Side of the Texas Revolution* (Dallas: P.L. Turner Co., 1928), 13-15.

2 Ramon Martinez Caro, *Verdadera Idea de la Primera Campaña de Tejas y sucesos ocurridos después de la accion de San Jacinto* (Mexico: Imprenta de Santiago Perez, 1837), printed in Castañeda, *Mexican Side*, 101-104.

3 *El Mosquito Mexicano*, 21 February 1837. These letters are also printed in J. Sanchez Garza, *La Rebelion de Texas — Manuscrito Inedito de 1836 por un Oficial de Santa Anna* (Mexico: A. Frank de Sanchez, 1955), 235-7.

4 Chester Newell, *History of the Revolution in Texas* (New York: Wiley & Putnam, 1838; reprint, New York: Arno Press, 1973), 88-89 (page reference is to reprint edition).

5 Ibid., v.

6 Col. Edward Stiff, *The Texan Emigrant* (Cincinnati: George Conclin, 1840), 313-315.

7 Ibid., 312.

8 Ibid., 313-315.

9   Wallace Woolsey, trans., *Memoirs for the History of the War in Texas by General Vicente Filisola*, Vol. II (Austin: Eakin Press, 1987), 170-174.

10 Ibid., x-xi, and Translator's note, page 174; and John H. Jenkins, *Basic Texas Books: An Annotated Bibliography of Selected Works for a Research Library* (Austin: Texas State Historical Association, 1988), 160-162. Woolsey translated and published the version of Filisola's work originally published by R. Rafael in 1848-49, but he added parts of the version published by Ignacio Cumplido published in 1849.

11 Woolsey, *Memoirs for the History of the War in Texas*, 174-181.

12 Memorial No. 131, files 81-82, Amelia Williams Papers, CAH, University of Texas at Austin.

13 Thomas Ricks Lindley, "The Revealing of Dr. John Sutherland," DRTL.

14 Juan N. Seguin, *Personal Memoirs of Juan N. Seguin*, 3, typescript copy in the DRTL.

15 Jesús F. de la Teja, *A Revolution Remembered — the Memoirs and Selected Correspondence of Juan N. Seguin* (Austin: State House Press, 1991), vii.

16 Francisco Esparza, Deposition, 26 August 1859, Court of Claims Voucher File #2558, (heirs of Gregorio Esparza), GLO.

17 Candelario Villanueva, Deposition, 26 August 1859, Court of Claims Voucher File #2558 (heirs of Gregorio Esparza), GLO.

18 Nicholas Labadie, "San Jacinto Campaign" *Texas Almanac* (1859); also printed in James M. Day, compiler, *The Texas Almanac 1857-1873 — A compendium of Texas History* (Waco, Texas: Texian Press, 1967), 174.

19 Labadie, "San Jacinto Campaign" in Day, *Texas Almanac*, 175; Groneman, *Defense of a Legend*, 51-54; Bill Groneman, "Some Problems with the Urriza Account," *Alamo Journal* 87 (July 1993): 6-7; and Bill Groneman, *Death of a Legend: The Myth and Mystery Surrounding the Death of Davy Crockett* (Plano, Texas: Republic of Texas Press, 1999), 60-63.

20 Francis Antonio Ruiz, "Fall of the Alamo and Massacre of Travis and His Brave Associates," *Texas Almanac* (1860): 80-81.

21 Daughters of the Republic of Texas, *The Alamo — Long Barrack Museum* (Dallas: Taylor Publishing Co., 1986), 42; Groneman, *Defense of a Legend*, 108; and Groneman, *Death of a Legend*, 88-91.

22 Brigidio Guerrero, Petition, 4 January 1861, Court of Claims Voucher File #3416 (Brigdio Guerrero). GLO.

23 Jake Ivey, "The Problem of the Two Guerreros," *Alamo Lore and Myth Organization Newsletter* 4, no. 1 (March 1982): 12-13.

24 William P. Zuber, "An Escape from the Alamo" *Texas Almanac* (1873): 80-85.

25 W.P. Zuber, "Rose's Escape from the Alamo," *Southwestern Historical Quarterly* 6 (July 1902 - April 1903): 68.

26 William P. Zuber to General William Steele, September 14, 1877, TSA; and W.P. Zuber, "The Escape of Rose From the Alamo," read at the annual reunion of the Texas Veterans and Daughters of the Republic at Austin, April 20, 1901, printed as W.P. Zuber, *The Escape of Rose From the Alamo* (Houston: The Union National Bank, 1928), 8.

27 R.B. Blake, "A Vindication of Rose and His Story," printed in J. Frank Dobie, et al, editors, *In The Shadow of History* (Austin: Texas Folk-Lore Society, 1839; reprint, Detroit: Folklore Associates, 1971), 39 (page reference is to reprint edition).

28 Thomas Ricks Lindley puts forth the theory that Rose was part of an attempt to relieve the Alamo in his unpublished, *Alamo Traces: An Investigative Case Book*. For more about the Zuber, Rose and line story see, Groneman, *Defense of a Legend*, 72, 75; Bill Groneman, "Travis and the Line," *Alamo News, Newsletter of Alamo International* 40 (March 1984), 2-10; and Steven G. Kellman, "The Yellow Rose of Texas," *Journal of American Culture* 2 (Summer 1982): 45-48.

29 J.M. Morphis, *History of Texas from its Discovery and Settlement* (New York: United States Publishing Company, 1875), 174-177.

30 Walter Prescott Webb, *The Handbook of Texas* Vol. 2 (Austin: Texas State Historical Association, 1952), 236.

31 John S. Ford, "Memoirs of John S. Ford — 1815-1836," 122-124, CAH.

32 For more on Juana Alsbury see, Crystal Sasse Ragsdale, *Women and Children of the Alamo* (Austin: State House Press, 1994), 27-40; and Bill Groneman, *Alamo Defenders* (Austin: Eakin Press, 1990), 5-6.

33 "Testimony of Mrs. Hannig Touching on the Alamo Massacre," 23 September 1876, TSA.

34 Ibid.; and Walter Lord, *A Time to Stand* (New York: Harper & Row, Publishers, 1961), 228.

35 "Santa Anna's Last Effort," *San Antonio Express*, 23 June 1878.

36 Ibid.

37 Lord, *A Time To Stand*, 161, 229.

38 "Dusty Attic Brings Forth Epic Story of Mrs. Dickinson. Her Photo Found by History Professor," *San Antonio Express*, (n.d.) 1929.

39 Ibid.

40 For more information on Anthony Wolf see, Bill Groneman "Tracing an Alamo Defender," *Journal of South Texas* 3, (Spring 1990): 24-35.

41 The Survivor of the Alamo," *San Antonio Express*, 28 April 1881.

42 Ibid.

43 *Houston Daily Post*, 1 March 1882, printed in Andrew Jackson Sowell, *Rangers and Pioneers of Texas* (San Antonio: 1884), 146-149; and in Edward G. Rohrbough, "How Jim Bowie Died," in Dobie, *In the Shadow of History*, 48-52.

44 Dobie, *In the Shadow of History*, 52.

45 [John S. Ford], "The Fall of the Alamo," *Texas Mute Ranger*, April 1882, 168-172.

46 Francisco Becerra, *A Mexican Sergeant's Recollections of the Alamo & San Jacinto*, with an Introduction by Dan Kilgore (Austin: Jenkins Publishing Company, 1980), 13.

47 Ibid., 8.

48 Ibid., 13.

49 Katherine W. Ellison and Robert Buckhout, *Psychology and Criminal Justice*, (Harper & Row Publishers, 1981), 106-110.

50 John S. Ford, *Origin and Fall of the Alamo* (San Antonio: Johnson Brothers Printing Co., 1894), 22.

51 [Ford], "The Fall of the Alamo," 172

52 Ibid.

53 Ibid.

54 Ibid.

55 "Statement by Mrs. S.A. Hannig Wife of Almaron Dic[k]enson (or Dickerson)," Adjutant General's Miscellaneous papers, TSA.

56 Ibid.; and Lord, *A Time to Stand*, 201-204. Walter Lord brings out the fact that survivors did not start to speak of a line until after the Zuber story broke, but he places some credence on this particular story since it did not have "the ring of a coached remark."

He also states that this account was dated September 23, 1876, but there is actually no date entered on this document.

57 Sowell, *Rangers and Pioneers of Texas*, 138-39.

58 Ibid., 137-38.

59 Juan Seguin, Laredo de Tamaulipas, to Hamilton P. Bee, 28 March 1889, TSA.

60 Ibid; and Daughters of the Republic of Texas, *The Alamo — Long Barrack Museum*, (Dallas: Taylor Publishing Co., 1986), 43.

61 Felix Nuñez, "Fall of the Alamo," *Fort Worth Gazette*, 23 June 1889.

62 Stephen L. Hardin, "The Felix Nuñez Account and the Siege of the Alamo: A Critical Appraisal," *Southwestern Historical Quarterly* 94 (July 1990): 65-84.

63 Juan Seguin, Nuevo Laredo, to William Winston Fontaine, 7 June 1890, CAH.

64 Ibid.; and Webb, *Handbook of Texas* Vol. 1, 615-616.

65 William Corner, editor and compiler, *San Antonio de Bexar — a Guide and History* (San Antonio: Bainbridge & Corner, 1890), 117-119.

66 Ibid.; Maurice Elfer, *Madam Candelaria — Unsung Heroine of the Alamo* (Houston: The Rein Company, 1933); Webb, *Handbook of Texas* Vol. 1, 288-289; and Ragsdale, *Women and Children of the Alamo*, 41-52.

67 John Henry Brown, *Indian Wars and Pioneers of Texas* (Austin, 1896), 137-138.

68 Amelia M. Williams, "A Critical Study of the Siege of the Alamo and of the Personnel of its Defenders," Ph.D. diss., University of Texas 1931, published in abridged form, *Southwestern Historical Quarterly* 36 and 37 (1933-1934), 311-312.

69 "Fall of the Alamo — Historical Reminiscences of the Aged Madam Candelaria," *San Antonio Express*, 6 March 1892.

70 The Account of Antonio Cruz Arrocha, box SM-2, Gentilz Collection, DRTL.

71 Ibid.; Dorothy Steinbomer Kendall and Carmen Perry, *Gentilz — Artist of the Old Southwest*, Austin and London: University of Texas Press, 1974), 22; and Sam DeShong Ratcliff, *Painting Texas History to 1900*, (Austin: University of Texas Press, 1992), 27-32.

72 "The Alamo by Dr. Sutherland," John S. Ford papers, CAH.

73 Lindley, "The Revealing of Dr. John Sutherland." For other versions of Sutherland's story see, *Dallas Morning News*, 5 and 12 February 1911; James T. DeShields, *Tall Men With Long Rifles* (San Antonio: The Naylor Co., 1935), 150-168; Dr. John Sutherland, *The Fall of the Alamo*, ed. by Annie B. Sutherland (San Antonio: The Naylor Co., 1936; and Howard R. Driggs and Sarah S. King, *Rise of the Lone Star* (New York: Frederick A. Stokes Co., 1936), 199-212.

74 "Another Story of the Alamo — The Battle Described by an Alleged Eye Witness," *San Antonio Express*, 12 April 1896.

75 Ibid.

76 Mary A. Maverick, *The Fall of The Alamo*, (n.p., 1898).

77 Webb, *Handbook of Texas*, Vol. 2, 160-161.

78 "Alamo Massacre as told by the late Madam Candaleria [sic]," *San Antonio Light*, 19 February 1899.

79 Ibid.

Chapter 4 20th Century

1 A.J. Sowell, *Early Settlers and Indian Fighter of Southwest Texas* (Austin: Ben C. Jones & Co., 1900), 9-10.

2 Ibid.; Webb, *Handbook of Texas*, 808-809; and Groneman, *Alamo Defenders*, 60-61.

3 "Children of the Alamo," *Houston Chronicle*, 9 November 1901; and "Adina De Zavala — Alamo Crusader," *Texas Highways*, March 1995, 14-21.

4 Ibid.; and "Children of the Alamo," *Houston Chronicle*, 8 November 1901.

5 [Enrique Esparza], *San Antonio Express*, 22 November 1902.

6 Ibid.; and "Story of the Massacre of Heroes of the Alamo" *San Antonio Daily Express*, 7 March 1904, typescript by Richard D. Esparza, DRTL.

7 W.P. Zuber, Iola, Texas to Charlie Jeffries, Winkler, Texas, 17 August 1904, printed in Charlie Jeffries, "Inventing Stories About the Alamo," in Dobie, *In the Shadow of History*, 45-46.

8 Ibid., 42, 45.

9 Ibid., 46-47.

10 "Battle of the Alamo from Survivor's Lips," *San Antonio Express*, 23 August 1904.

11 Ibid.

12 Charles Merritt Barnes, "Aged Citizen Describes Alamo Fight and Fire," *San Antonio Daily Express*, 1 July 1906.

13 Ibid.

14 "Was in the Alamo Conflict," *San Antonio Express*, 4 May 1907.

15 Ibid.

16 Charles Merritt Barnes, "The Alamo's Only Survivor," *San Antonio Express*, 12 and 19 May 1907.

17 Ibid.; Branda, *Handbook of Texas — a Supplement*, 60; and Etna Scott, "Information — Enrique Esparza — Evidence that he was born in 1828," 1984, DRTL.

18 Antonio Menchaca, *Memoirs* (San Antonio: Yanaguana Society, 1937), 22-23.

19 Frederick C. Chabot, foreword to Menchaca *Memoirs*; and George O. Coalson, "José Antonio Menchaca," in Ron Tyler, editor, *The New Handbook of Texas* Vol. 4, (Austin: Texas State Historical Association, 1996), 617.

20 "Witnessed Last Struggle of the Alamo Patriots," *San Antonio Express*, 19 July 1907.

21 Ibid.

22 "As A Boy, Juan Díaz, venerable San Antonian witnessed the Attack on the Alamo," *San Antonio Light*, 1 September 1907.

23 Ibid.; and James T. DeShields, *Tall Men With Long Rifles* (San Antonio: The Naylor Co., 1935, reprint, 1971), 178-179 (page reference is to reprint edition).

24 "This Man Heard Shots Fired at Battle of Alamo," *San Antonio Light*, 31 October 1909, 10.

25 William Fairfax Gray, *From Virginia to Texas* (Houston: Gray, Dillaye & Co., Printers, 1909, reprint, Houston: Fletcher Young Publishing Co., 1965), 137-138 (page reference is to reprint edition).

26 Ibid.

27 Louis de Nette, "This Man Was Old When Santa Anna Spilled Blood in Alamo and Built Texans' Funeral Pyre," *San Antonio Light*, 3 April 1910.

28 Ibid.

29 Charles Merritt Barnes, "Builders' Spades Turn Up Soil Baked by Alamo Funeral Pyres," *San Antonio Express*, 26 March 1911.

30 Ibid.

31 Ibid.; and Francisco Esparza Deposition, 26 August 1859, Court of Claims Voucher File #2558, (heirs of Gregorio Esparza) GLO.

32 Charles Merritt Barnes, "Men Still Living Who Saw the Fall of the Alamo," *San Antonio Express*, 27 August 1911.

33 Ibid.

34 "New Light on Alamo Massacre," interview of Andrés Coy, son of Trinidad Coy, *San Antonio Light*, 26 November 1911.

35 Timothy M. Matovina, *The Alamo Remembered* (Austin: University of Texas Press, 1995), 107; and Ron Jackson, *Alamo Legacy — Alamo Descendants Remember the Alamo* (Austin: Eakin Press, 1997), 105.

36 Adina de Zavala, *The Story of the Siege and Fall of The Alamo* (San Antonio: n.p., 1911), 13.

37 Ibid.; Branda, *Handbook of Texas — A Supplement*, 242-243; and Frank W. Jennings.

38 J.M. Rodriguez, *Rodriguez Memoirs of Early Texas* (San Antonio: n.p., 1913), 7-9.

39 Leonard Garza, "In Memoriam," in Rodriguez, *Rodriguez Memoirs of Early Texas*; and Webb, *Handbook of Texas* Vol. 2, 497.

40 "Bullet-Ridden and Tomahawk-Scarred San Antonio Home is being Demolished," *San Antonio Express*, 19 April 1914.

41 Ibid.; also see, Charles Merritt Barnes, "Remember Early Days," *San Antonio Express*, 15, 22 December 1907; "Builders' Spades;" and "Men Still Living Who Saw the Fall of the Alamo," *San Antonio Express*, 17 August 1911.

42 Rena Maverick Green, editor, *Memoirs of Mary A. Maverick* (San Antonio: Alamo Printing Co., 1921), 135-136.

43 Ibid., 135.

44 Colonel William G. Smith, "Life of William Sanders Oury 1817-1887," 1930, typescript, p. 5, CAH.

45 Ibid.; C.C. Smith, "The History of the Oury Family," typescript, Arizona Historical Society, and Cornelius Cole Smith Jr., *William Sanders Oury — History-Maker of the Southwest* (Tucson, Arizona: University of Arizona Press).

46 DeShields, *Tall Men With Long Rifles*, 183-185.

47 Ibid., viii; and Webb, *Handbook of Texas* Vol. 2, 715.

48 DeShields, *Tall Men*, 174.

49 Ibid., 183.

50 Ibid., 175.

51 Ibid.

52 Ibid., 180.

53 Ibid., 178-182.

54 Ibid., 182.

55 Ibid.

56 Howard R. Driggs and Sarah S. King, *Rise of the Lone Star* (New York: Frederick A. Stokes Co., 1936), 220-231.

57 Ibid., 213.

58 "Early Days in San Antonio Recalled by a Pioneer Resident of the City," *San Antonio Light*, 4 February 1917.

59 Carlos Sanchez-Navarro [y Peón], *La Guerra de Tejas — Memorias de un Soldado* (Mejico: Editorail Polis, 1938), 148-152. Translation by Bill Groneman. For a different translation of this account see; C.D. Huneycutt, trans., *At the Alamo — The Memoirs of Captain Navarro* (New London, North Carolina: Gold Star Press, 1988), 62-66.

60 "Last Survivor of the Alamo Dead: Saw End of Defenders," *San Antonio Express*, 21 December 1917; and [Obituary of Alejo E. Perez], [San Antonio] *La Prensa*, 20 October 1918.

61 José Juan Sanchez-Navarro, "Ayudantia de Inspeccion de Nuevo León y Tamaulipas," NLB; Sanchez Navarro [y Peón], *La Guerra de Tejas*; Lon Tinkle, *13 Days to Glory — The Siege of the Alamo* (New York, Toronto and London: McGraw-Hill Book Co., Inc., 1958), 249.

62 Helen Hunnicutt, "A Mexican View of the Texan War: Memoirs of a Veteran of the Two Battles of the Alamo," *Library Chronicle of the University of Texas* 4 (Summer 1951): 59-74; and Charles H. Harris, *A Mexican Family Empire — The Latifundio of the Sanchez-Navarros, 1765-1867* (Austin & London: University of Texas Press, 1975), xxviii.

63 Ralph L. Elder, UTA to Bill Groneman, New York, 15 July and 26 October 1991, originals in the possession of the author.

64 For more information on the Sanchez-Navarro journal see, Groneman, *Defense of a Legend*, 63, 95-98, 101-106, and 146; and *Death of a Legend*, 69-73.

65 Sanchez Garza, *La Rebelion de Texas*, 58-71. Translation by Bill Groneman. In translating this I have tried to keep the translation as literal as possible. For a variation on this translation see Carmen Perry, trans. and ed., *With Santa Anna in Texas — A Per-*

sonal Narrative of the Revolution by José Enrique de la Peña (College Station, Texas: Texas A & M University Press, 1975), 43-56.

66 Sanchez Garza, *La Rebelion de Texas*, XI-XXVI; and Perry, *With Santa Anna in Texas*, xi-xiv.

67 Lately a great deal of renewed attention has been focused on the de la Peña "dairy." See, Groneman, *Defense of a Legend*; Bill Groneman, "The Diary of José Enrique de la Peña," *Journal of Southern History* 7 (1994): 28-51; "The Controversial Alleged Account of José Enrique de la Peña," and "Publish or Perish — Regardless: Jim Crisp and the de la Peña Diary," *Military History of the West* (Fall 1995); "Crossing the Border — Writing Western History as a Nonacademic Historian," *Roundup Magazine*, December 1995; James E. Crisp, "The Little Book That Wasn't There: The Myth and Mystery of the de la Peña Diary," *Southwestern Historical Quarterly* 98 (October 1994): 260-296; "Texas History — Texas Mystery," *Sallyport — The Magazine of Rice University*, February/March 1995, 13-21; "When Revision Becomes Obsession: Bill Groneman and the de la Peña Diary," *Military History of the West* (Fall 1995).

68 Don Carlton, "Welcome and Introductions," Introduction to the symposium; and James E. Crisp, "The Peña Narrative as History," paper presented at the symposium, *Eyewitness to the Texas Revolution — José Enrique de la Peña and His Narrative*, Center for American History, University of Texas at Austin, 29 April 2000, videotaped by Cynthia Wolf, copy in possession of the author; and Thomas Ricks Lindley, "At the Alamo Walls Again," *Alamo Journal* 119 (December 2000): 3.

69 Jackson Burke, "The Secret of the Alamo," *Man's Illustrated*, August 1956, 36.

70 Ibid.

71 Isaac Millsaps, the Alamo, San Antonio de Bexar to [Mary Millsaps, Gonzales, Texas], 3 March 1836, University of Houston, Houston, Texas.

72 Gregory Curtis, "Forgery Texas Style," *Texas Monthly*, March 1989, 105; C. Dorman David, Interview by Brian Huberman, 15 January 1999, transcript in possession of the author; and William Simpson, Interview by Brian Huberman, 5 January 1999, transcript in possession of the author.

73 Ann Fears Crawford, *The Eagle — The Autobiography of Santa Anna* (Austin: Pemberton Press, 1967; reprint, State House Press, 1988), 50-51 (page reference is to reprint edition). Printed with

permission of Ann Fears Crawford and Tom Munnerlyn of State House Press.

74 Ibid., v-vii, xii-xv.

75 "Bn. Activo de Sn Luis 1st division de operaciones sobre Texas. Ytinerares de las jornadas q. la ha hecho el espresado cuerpo desde la cuidad de Sn Luis Potosí el dia 17 de Nobiembre de 1835," element 5 of packet 3, de la Peña Papers, CAH.

76 James E. Crisp, Introduction to Carmen Perry, Trans., *José Enrique de la Peña — With Santa Anna in Texas — A Personal Narrative of the Revolution* Expanded Edition (College Station, Texas: Texas A&M University Press, 1997), xxiv.

77 [Rewritten diary], element 10 of packet 1, de la Peña Papers, CAH. No original copy of de la Peña's alleged "diary" exists. This supposedly is de la Peña's rewritten copy of his original "diary." Professor James E. Crisp has called this the "rewritten diary." Thomas R. Lindley calls it the "clean diary."

78 William James Cannon, Austin to J.S. Hogg, Austin, 9 June 1893, printed in Thomas Ricks Lindley, "A New Alamo Account," *Alamo Journal* 94 (December 1994): 4-7.

79 Statement of Mrs. Susan Griffith Sterling, 17 February 1926, Claims to Property, Box 2-23/591, TSA, printed in *Alamo Journal* 98 (October 1995): 25.

80 Santiago Rabia, *The Journal of Sergeant Santiago Rabia*, Santiago Rabia Collection #6070 DRTL, Trans. by Ned F. Brierley.

81 Joaquin Ramirez y Sesma to Antonio Lopez de Santa Anna, 11 March 1836, and Ramirez y Sesma to Santa Anna, 23 August 1836, Box 335 2Q 174, CAH.

82 William C. Davis, *Three Roads to the Alamo — The Lives and Fortunes of David Crockett, James Bowie, and William Barret Travis* (New York: HarperCollins Publishers, 1998), xiii-xv, and 736-37.

Sources

Archival Material

Amador, Juan Valentine, to the generals, chiefs of sections, and commanding officers, 5 March 1836. Archivo General de Mexico Papers, UTA.

Batres, José, to James Bowie, 23 February 1836. Archivo General de Mexico Papers, UTA.

Bowie, James, to commander of the invading forces below Bejar, 23 February 1836. Yale Collection of Western Americana, BRBML.

Cruz y Arrocha, Antonio. Interview by Theodore Gentilz. Typescript translation, Box SM-2, Gentilz Collection, DRTL.

De la Peña Papers. CAH.

Dimitt, Philip, to James Kerr, 28 February 1836. Army Papers, TSA.

Esparza, Francisco. Deposition, 26 August 1859. Court of Claims Voucher File #2558 (heirs of Gregorio Esparza). GLO.

_____. Petition, 24 August 1860. Court of Claims Voucher File #2557, GLO.

Filisola, Umberto Daniel. "The Correspondence of Santa Anna." MA Thesis, University of Texas, 1939.

Ford, John S. "The Alamo by Dr. Sutherland." John S. Ford Papers, CAH.

_____. "Memoirs of John S. Ford — 1815-1836." John S. Ford Papers, CAH.

Guerrero, Brigidio. Petition, 4 January 1861. Court of Claims Voucher File #3416, GLO.

Hannig, Mrs. S.A. "Statement by Mrs. S.A. Hannig wife of Almaron Dic[k]enson (or Dickerson)," n.d. Adjutant General's Miscellaneous Papers. TSA.

Hannig, Susanna. "Testimony of Mrs. Hannig touching on the Alamo Massacre," 23 September 1876. TSA.

Martin, Albert, to the People of Texas, 25 February 1836. Davidson Collection, TSA.

"Meeting of the Citizens of San Felipe," 27 February 1836. Broadside #132, Streeter Collection, BRBML.

Millsaps, Isaac, the Alamo, San Antonio de Bexar, to [Mary Millsaps, Gonzales], 3 March 1836. University of Houston, Houston, Texas.

Rabia, Santiago. *The Journal of Sergant Santiago Rabia*. Santiago Rabia Collection #6070. DRTL.

Ruiz, Francisco. Deposition, 16 April 1861. Court of Claims Voucher File #5026 (heirs of Toribio Losoya). GLO.

Sanchez-Navarro, José Juan. "Ayudantia de Inspeccion de Nuevo León y Tamaulipas." NLB.

Seguin, Juan N., Laredo de Tamaulipas, to Hamilton Bee, 28 March 1889. TSA.

_____, Nuevo Laredo, to William Winston Fontaine, 7 June 1890. CAH.

_____. "Personal Memoirs of Juan N. Seguin. Typescript copy, DRTL.

Smither, Launcelot, to All the inhabitants of Texas, 24 February 1836. Army Papers, TSA.

Sterling, Susan Griffith. "Statement of Mrs. Susan Griffith Sterling," 17 February 1926. Claims to Property, Box 2-23/591, TSA.

Sutherland, John. Deposition, 1854. Memorial No. 131, Files 81-82, Amelia Williams Papers, CAH.

Travis, William B., to Andrew Ponton, 23 February 1836. Yale Collection of Western Americana, BRBML.

_____, to the People of Texas & All Americans in the World, 24 February 1836. TSA.

Villanueva, Candelario. Deposition, 26 August 1859. Court of Claims Voucher File #2558 (heirs of Gregorio Esparza). GLO.

Zuber, William P., to General William Steele, 14 September, 1877. TSA.

Articles

Almonte, Juan N. "The Private Journal of Juan Nepomuceno Almonte." *Southwestern Historical Quarterly* 48 (July 1944): 10-31.

Begley, Sharon and Martha Brant. "You Must Remember This." *Newsweek*, 26 September 1994, 68-69.

Bradshaw, James Stanford. "George W. Wisner and the *New York Sun*." *Journalism History* 6:4 (Winter 1979-80): 112.

Burke, Jackson. "The Secret of the Alamo." *Man's Illustrated*, August 1956, 36.

Clark, William Bedford. "Col. Crockett's Exploits and Adventures in Texas: Death and Transfiguration." *Studies in American Humor* 1 (June 1982): 66-76.

Connelly, Thomas Lawrence. "Did David Crockett Surrender at the Alamo? A Contemporary Letter." *Journal of Southern History* 26 (1960): 368-376.

Crisp, James E. "The Little Book That Wasn't There: The Myth and Mystery of the de la Peña Diary." *Southwestern Historical Quarterly* 98 (October 1994): 260-296.

_____. "Texas History — Texas Mystery." *Sallyport — The Magazine of Rice University*, February/March 1995, 13-21.

_____. "When Revision Becomes Obsession: Bill Groneman and the de la Peña Diary." *Military History of the West* (Fall 1995).

Curtis, Gregory. "Forgery Texas Style." *Texas Monthly*, March 1989, 105.

[Ford, John S.]. "The Fall of the Alamo." *Texas Mute Ranger*, April 1882.

Green, Michael R. "To the People of Texas & All Americans in the World." *Southwestern Historical Quarterly* 91 (April 1988): 483-508.

Groneman, Bill. "Anthony Wolf — Tracing an Alamo Defender." *Journal of South Texas* 3 (Spring 1990): 24-35.

_____. "The Controversial Alleged Account of José Enrique de la Peña." *Military History of the West* (Fall 1995).

_____. "Crossing the Border — Writing Western History as a Non-academic Historian." *Roundup Magazine*, December 1995.

_____. De la Peña and the Alamo Mystery Victim." *Alamo Journal* 85 (February 1993): 6-8.

_____. "The Diary of José Enrique de la Peña." *Journal of South Texas* 7 (1994): 28-51.

_____. "Publish of Perish — Regardless: Jim Crisp and the de la Peña 'Diary.'" *Military History of the West* (Fall 1995).

_____. "Some Comparisons to the de la Peña 'Diary.'" *Alamo Journal* 92 (July 1994): 8-9.

_____. "Some Problems With the Almonte Account." *Alamo Journal* 90 (February 1994): 3-5.

_____. "Some Problems With the Urriza Account." *Alamo Journal* 67 (July 1993): 6-7.

_____. "Travis and the Line." *Alamo News — Newsletter of Alamo International* 40 (March 1984): 2-10.

_____. "A Witness to the Executions?" *Alamo Journal* 88 (October 1993): 3-6.

Hardin, Stephen L. "The Felix Nuñez Account and the Siege of the Alamo: A Critical Appraisal." *Southwestern Historical Quarterly* 94 (July 1990): 65-84.

Henson, Margaret Swett. "Politics and the Treatment of the Mexican Prisoners after the Battle of San Jacinto." *Southwestern Historical Quarterly* 94 (Oct. 1990): 189-230.

Hershkowitz, Leo. "'The Land of Promise: Samuel Swarthout and Land Speculation in Texas 1830-1838." *New York Historical Society Quarterly* 48 (October 1964): 307-325.

Hunnicutt, Helen. "A Mexican View of the Texas War." *Library Chronicle* 4 (Summer 1951): 59-74.

Ivey, Jake. "The Problem of the Two Guerreros." *Alamo Lore and Myth Organization Newsletter* 4, no. 1 (March 1982): 10-12.

Jennings, Frank W. "Adina De Zavala — Alamo Crusader." *Texas Highway* (March 1995): 14-21.

Kellman, Steven G. "The Yellow Rose of Texas." *Journal of American Culture* 2 (Summer 1982): 45-48.

Labadie, Nicholas. "San Jacinto Campaign." *Texas Almanac* (1859).

Lindley, Thomas Ricks. "A Current List of Alamo Patriots." *Alamo Journal* 89 (December 1993): 3-7.

_____. "At the Alamo Walls Again." *Alamo Journal* 119 (December 2000): 3-9.

_____. "Documents of the Texian Revolution." *Alamo Journal* 98 (October 1995): 25.

_____. "Killing Crockett — It's All In The Execution." *Alamo Journal* 96 (May 1995): 3-12.

_____. "Killing Crockett — Lindley's Opinion." *Alamo Journal* 98 (October 1995): 9-24.

_____. "Killing Crockett — Theory Paraded as Fact." *Alamo Journal* 97 (July 1995): 3-14.

_____. "A New Alamo Account." *Alamo Journal* 94 (December 1994): 4-7.

_____. "Storming the Alamo." *Alamo Journal* 117 (June 2000): 11-18.

Ruiz, Francis Antonio. "Fall of the Alamo and Massacre of Travis and his Brave Associates." *Texas Almanac* (1860).

Sibley, Marilyn McAdams. "Thomas Jefferson Green: Recruiter for the Texas Army." *Texas Military History* 3 (Fall 1963): 129-145.

Wade, John Donald. "The Authorship of David Crockett's 'Autobiography.'" *Georgia Historical Quarterly* VI (September 1922): 265-268.

Williams Amelia M. "A Critical Study of the Siege of the Alamo and of the Personnel of its Defenders." Ph.D. diss., University of Texas 1931. Published in abridged form. *Southwestern Historical Quarterly* 36 and 37 (1933-1934).

Winston, James E. "New York and the Independence of Texas." *Southwestern Historical Quarterly* 18 (July 1914 - April 1915): 368-385.

Zuber, William P. "An Escape from the Alamo." *Texas Almanac* (1873).

_____. "Rose's Escape from the Alamo." *Southwestern Historical Quarterly* (July 1902 - April 1903): 67-69.

Books

Ambrose, Stephen & Douglas Brinkley. *Witness to America*. New York: HarperCollins Publishers. A Lou Reda Book, 1999.

Baugh, Virgil E. *Rendezvous at the Alamo*. New York: Pageant Press, 1960.

Becerra, Francisco. *A Mexican Sergeant's Recollections of the Alamo & San Jacinto*. With an Introduction by Dan Kilgore. Austin: Jenkins Publishing Co., 1980.

Bennett, James Gordon. *Memoirs of James Gordon Bennett and His Times*. New York: Stringer & Townsend, 1855.

Branda, Eldon Stephen., ed. *The Handbook of Texas — A Supplement*. Vol. 3. Austin: Texas State Historical Assoc., 1976.

Burleson, Georgia, comp. and publ. *The Life and Writings of Rufus C. Burleson*. n.p., 1901.

Caro, Ramon Martinez. *Verdadera Idea de la Primera Compaña de Tejas y Sucesos Occuridos Despues de la Accion de San Jacinto*. Mexico: Imprenta de Santiago Perez, 1837.

Castañeda, Carlos E. *The Mexican Side of the Texas Revolution*. Dallas: P.L. Turner Co., 1928; reprint, New York: Arno Press, 1976.

Colbert, David, Editor. *Eyewitness to America*. New York: Pantheon Books, 1997.

_____. *Eyewitness to the American West*. New York: Viking, 1998.

Commager, Henry Steele and Allan Nevins. *The Heritage of America*. Boston: Little, Brown & Company, 1939; revised and enlarged edition, 1949.

Corner, William, ed. and comp. *San Antonio de Bexar — Guide and History*. San Antonio: Bainbridge & Corner, 1890.

Crawford, Ann Fears. *The Eagle — the Autobiography of Santa Anna*. Austin: Pemberton Press, 1967; reprint, State House Press, 1988.

Daughters of the Republic of Texas. *The Alamo — Long Barracks Museum*. Dallas: Taylor Publishing Co., 1986.

Day, James M., comp. *The Texas Almanac 1857-1873 — A Compendium of Texas History*. Waco, Texas: Texian Press, 1967.

De la Teja, Jesús, ed. *A Revolution Remembered — The Memoirs and Selected Correspondence of Juan Seguin*. Austin: State House Press, 1991.

Derr, Mark. *The Frontiersman — The Real Life and the Many Legends of Davy Crockett*. New York: William Morrow and Company, Inc., 1993.

DeShields, James T. *Tall Men With Long Rifles*. San Antonio: Naylor Co., 1935; reprint 1971.

De Zavala, Adina. *The Story of the Siege and Fall of the Alamo*. San Antonio: n.p., 1911.

Dobie, J. Frank, Mody C. Boatright, and Harry H. Ransom, eds. *In the Shadow of History*. Austin: Texas Folk Lore Society, 1939; reprint, Detroit: Folklore Associates, 1971.

Driggs, Howard R. and Sarah S. King. *Rise of the Lone Star*. New York: Frederick A. Stokes Co., 1936.

Edmondson, J. R. *The Alamo Story — From Early History to Current Conflicts*. Plano, Texas: Republic of Texas Press, 2000.

Elfer, Maurice. *Madam Candelaria — Unsung Heroine of the Alamo*. Houston: The Rein Company, 1933.

Ellison, Katherine W. and Robert Buckhout. *Psychology and Criminal Justice*. Harper & Row Publishers, 1981.

Feely, Thomas F., & Nancy E. Nagle. *Crockett's Last Stand — A Diorama*. Ridgefield Park, New Jersey: Historical Dioramas, 1995.

Filisola, General Vicente. *Memoirs for the History of the War in Texas*. Vol. II. Translated by Wallace Woolsey. Austin: Eakin Press, 1987.

Foote, Henry Stuart. *Texas and the Texans* Vol. 2. n.p., 1841; reprint, Austin: The Steck Company, 1935.

Ford, John S. *Origins and Fall of the Alamo*. San Antonio: Johnson Brother Printing Co., 1894.

Garza, J. Sanchez. *La Rebelion de Texas*. Mexico: A. Frank de Sanchez, 1955.

Gray, William F. *From Virginia to Texas*, 1835. Houston: Gray, Dillaye & Co., 1909; Reprint, Houston: Fletcher Young Publishing Co., 1965.

Green, Rena Maverick, ed. *Memoirs of Mary A. Maverick*. San Antonio: Alamo Printing Co., 1921.

Groneman, Bill. *Alamo Defenders*. Austin: Eakin Press, 1990.

_____. *Death of a Legend — The Myth and Mystery Surrounding the Death of Davy Crockett*. Plano, Texas: Republic of Texas Press, 1999.

_____. *Defense of a Legend — Crockett and the de La Peña Diary*. Plano, Texas: Republic of Texas Press, 1994.

Harris, Charles H. *A Mexican Family Empire — The Latifundio of the Sanchez Navarros, 1765-1867*. Austin and London: University of Texas Press, 1975.

Hauck, Richard Boyd. *Crockett a Bio-Bibliography*. Westport, Connecticut, London, England: Greenwood Press, 1973.

Hudson, Frederick. *Journalism in the United States from 1690 to 1872*. New York: Harper & Brothers Publishers, 1873.

Huffines, Alan C. *Blood of Noble Men — The Alamo Siege & Battle — An Illustrated Chronology*. Austin: Eakin Press, 1999.

Huneycutt, C.D., trans. *At the Alamo: The Memoirs of Capt. Navarro*. New London, North Carolina: Gold Star Press, 1988.

Hutton, Paul Andrew. *Introduction to A Narrative of the Life of David Crockett*. Lincoln, Nebraska and London, England: University of Nebraska Press, 1987.

Jenkins, John H. *Basic Texas Books: An Annotated Bibliography of Selected Works for a Research Library*. Austin: Texas State Historical Association, 1988.

_____, ed. *Papers of the Texas Revolution 1835-1836*. 10 Vols. Austin: Presidial Press, 1973.

Kendal, Dorothy Steinbomer and Carmen Perry. *Gentilz — Artist of the Old Southwest*. Austin and London: University of Texas Press, 1974.

Kilgore, Dan. *How Did Davy Die?* College Station, Texas, and London: Texas A&M University Press, 1978.

King, C. Richard. *Susanna Dickinson — Messenger of the Alamo*. Austin: Shoal Creek Publ. Co., 1976.

Loftus, Elizabeth, Ph.D. and Katherine Ketcham. *Witness for the Defense — The Accused, the Eyewitness, and the Expert Who Puts Memory on Trial*. New York: St. Martin's Press, 1991.

Lord, Walter. *A Time to Stand*. New York: Harper & Row, Publishers, 1961.

Lozano, Ruben Rendon. With new material added by Mary Ann Noonan Guerra. *Viva Tejas — The Story of the Tejanos, The Mexican-born Patriots of the Texas Revolution*. San Antonio: The Alamo Press, 1985.

Matovina, Timothy M. *The Alamo Remembered — Tejano Accounts and Perspectives*. Austin: University of Texas Press, 1995.

Maverick, Mary A. *The Fall of the Alamo*. n.p.: n.p., 1898.

Morphis, J.M. *History of Texas*. New York: United States Publishing Co., 1875.

Newell, Chester. *History of the Revolution in Texas*. New York: Wiley & Putnam, 1838; reprint, Arno Press, 1973.

Nofi, Albert A. *The Alamo and the Texas War of Independence, September 30, 1835 to April 21, 1836*. Conshocken, Pennsylvania: Combined Books, 1992.

O'Brien, Frank. *The Story of the Sun*. New York and London: D. Appleton and Company, 1928.

Perry, Carmen, trans. and ed. *With Santa Anna in Texas — a Personal Narrative of the Revolution by José Enrique de la Peña*. College Station, Texas: Texas A&M University Press, 1975.

_____, with an introduction by James E. Crisp. *José Enrique de la Peña — With Santa Anna in Texas — a Personal Narrative of the Revolution*. Expanded Edition. College Station, Texas: Texas A&M University Press, 1997.

Potter, Reuben M. *The Fall of the Alamo*. San Antonio: Herald Steam Press, 1860.

_____. "The Fall of the Alamo." *Magazine of American History*. January 1878; reprint in book form, Hillsdale, New Jersey: Otterden Press, 1977.

Ragsdale, Crystal Sasse. *Women & Children of the Alamo*. Austin: State House Press, 1994.

Ratcliffe, Sam DeShong. *Painting Texas History to 1900*. Austin: University of Texas Press, 1992.

Rios, John F., ed. *Readings on the Alamo*. New York: Vantage Press, Inc., 1987.

Rodriguez, J.M. *Rodriguez Memoirs of Early Texas*. San Antonio: n.p., 1913.

Rourke, Constance. *Davy Crockett*. New York: Harcourt, Brace and Company, 1934.

Sanchez-Navarro y Peón, Carlos. *La Guerra de Tejas — Memorias de un Soldado*. Mexico: Editorial Polis, 1938.

Santa Anna, Antonio Lopez de. *Manifesto que de sus Operaciones en la Campana de Tejas dirige a sus Conciudadanos*. Vera Cruz: Imprenta Liberal a Cargo de Antonio Maria Valdez, 1837.

Shackford, John Atkins. Edited by John B. Shackford. *David Crockett: The Man and the Legend*. Westport, Connecticut: Greenwood Press, Publishers, 1956.

Smith, Cornelius C. *William Sanders Oury — History Maker of the Southwest*. Tucson, Arizona: University of Arizona Press, 1967.

Sowell, Andrew Jackson. *Early Settlers and Indian Fighters of Southwest Texas*. Austin: Ben C. Jones & Co., 1900.

_____. *Rangers and Pioneers of Texas*. San Antonio, 1884.

Steinbeck, John. *Cannery Row*. New York: Viking Press, 1945.

Stevens, John D. *Sensationalism and the New York Press*. New York: Columbia University Press, 1991.

Stiff, Col. Edward. *The Texan Emigrant*. Cincinnati: George Conclin, 1840.

Sutherland, Dr. John. *The Fall of the Alamo*. Edited by Annie B. Sutherland. San Antonio: The Naylor Co., 1936.

Tinkle, Lon. *13 Days to Glory — The Siege of the Alamo*. New York, Toronto and London: McGraw-Hill Book Co., Inc., 1958.

Todish, Tim J. & Terry Todish. *Alamo Sourcebook 1836: A Comprehensive Guide to the Alamo and the Texas Revolution*. Austin: Eakin Press, 1998.

Turner, Martha Anna. *William Barret Travis — His Sword and His Pen*. Waco, Texas: Texian Press, 1972.

Tyler, Ron, Douglas E. Barnett, Roy R. Barkley, Penelope C. Anderson, Mark F. Odintz. eds. *The New Handbook of Texas*. 6 Vols. Austin: The TSHA, 1996.

Webb, Walter Prescott, ed. *The Handbook of Texas* Vols. 1 & 2. Austin: Texas State Historical Assoc., 1952.

Woolsey, Wallace. *The History of the War in Texas by Don Vicente Filisola* Vol. II. Austin: Eakin Press, 1987.

Zuber, W.P. *The Escape of Rose from the Alamo*. Houston: The Union National Bank, 1928.

Correspondence

Elder, Ralph T., UTA, to Bill Groneman, New York, 15 July and 26 October 1991. Originals in possession of the author.

Interviews

David, C. Dorman. Interview by Brian Huberman, 15 January 1999. Transcript in possession of the author.

Simpson, William. Interview by Brian Huberman, 5 January 1999. Transcript in possession of the author.

Newspapers

"Alamo Massacre — as told by the Late Madam Candelaria." *San Antonio Light*, 22 February 1899.

Almonte, Juan Nepomuceno. "Journal of the Mexican Campaign." *New York Herald*, 21 June to [?] July 1836.

"Another Story of the Alamo — The Battle Described by an Alleged Eyewitness." *San Antonio Express*, 12 April 1896.

"As a Boy, Juan Diaz, Venerable San Antonian Witnessed the Attack on the Alamo." *San Antonio Light*, 1 September 1907.

Barnes, Charles Merritt. "Aged Citizen Describes Alamo Fight and Fire." *San Antonio Express*, 1 July 1906.

_____. "The Alamo's Only Survivor." *San Antonio Express*, 12 and 19 May 1907.

_____. "Builders' Spades Turn Up Soil Baked by Alamo Funeral Pyres." *San Antonio Express*, 29 March 1911.

_____. "Men Still Living Who Saw the Fall of the Alamo." *San Antonio Express*, 27 August 1911.

_____. "Remember Early Days." *San Antonio Express*, 15, 22 December 1907.

"Battle of the Alamo From Survivor's Lips." *San Antonio Express*, 23 August 1904.

"Bullet-Ridden and Tomahawk-Scarred San Antonio Home is Being Demolished." *San Antonio Express*, 19 April 1914.

"Children of the Alamo." *Houston Chronicle*, 8 and 9 November 1901.

Correspondent of the *Fredericksburg Arena*. "Letter From Texas." *Frankfort (Kentucky) Commonwealth*, 25 May 1836.

Correspondent of the *New York Courier* and *Enquirer*, Galveston Bay, 9 June 1836. "Texas." *Frankfort (Kentucky) Commonwealth*, 27 July 1836.

De Nette, Louis. "This Man Was Old When Santa Anna Spilled Blood in Alamo and Built Texans' Funeral Pyre." *San Antonio Light*, 3 April 1910.

DeShields, James T. "[Dr. John Sutherland]." *Dallas Morning News*, 5 and 12 February 1911.

"Early Days in San Antonio Recalled by a Pioneer Resident of the City." *San Antonio Light*, 4 February 1917.

Dolson, George M. "Texas — Extract from a letter written by Mr. George M. Dolson, an officer in the Texian army to his brother in this city: Dated Galveston Island, Camp Trevos [sic] July 19, 1836." *(Detroit) Democratic Free Press*, 7 September 1836.

"Dusty Attic Brings Forth Epic Story of Mrs. Dickinson. Her Photo Found by History Professor." *San Antonio Express*, n.d. 1929.

El Mosquito Mexicano, 5 April 1836.

"[Enrique Esparza]." *San Antonio Express*, 22 November 1902.

Esparza, Enrique. "Alamo's Only Survivor." Interview by Charles Merritt Barnes. *San Antonio Express*, 12, 19 May 1907.

"Extract of a letter from a friend to the Editor." *New Orleans Commercial Bulletin*, 11 April 1836.

"Extract of a letter from a friend to the Editor." *Portland (Maine) Advertiser*, 3 May 1836.

"Fall of the Alamo — Historical Reminiscences of the Aged Madam Candelaria." *San Antonio Express*, 6 March 1892.

"Fall of San Antonio and its One Hundred and Eighty Seven Gallant Defenders." *Columbia Tennessee Observer*, 14 April 1836.

"Fall of San Antonio and its One Hundred and Eighty Seven Gallant Defenders." *Memphis Tennessee Enquirer*, 12 April 1836.

[Gray, William F.] "Letter From Texas — Correspondence of the Fredricksburg Arena — Groce's Retreat, March 30th, 1836." *Frankfort (Kentucky) Commonwealth*, 25 May 1836.

Houston Daily Post, 1 March 1882.

"Important from Texas." *Arkansas Gazette*, 29 March 1836.

"Last Survivor of the Alamo Dead: Saw End of Defenders." *San Antonio Express*, 21 December 1917.

Loranca, Manuel. "Santa Anna's Last Effort." *San Antonio Express*, 28 June 1878.

"Men Still Living Who Saw the Fall of the Alamo." *San Antonio Express*, 17 August 1911.

"Texas." *Morning Courier and New York Enquirer*, 9 July 1936.

Nuñez, Felix. "Fall of the Alamo." *Fort Worth Gazette*, 23 June 1889.

[Obituary of Alejo E. Perez Jr.]. *(San Antonio) La Prensa*, 20 October 1918.

"Story of the Massacre of the Heroes of the Alamo." *San Antonio Express*, 7 March 1904. Typescript of Article by Richard D. Esparza. DRTL.

"The Survivor of the Alamo." *San Antonio Express*, 28 April 1881.

"This Man Heard Shots Fired at Battle of the Alamo." *San Antonio Light*, 31 October 1909.

"To the People of Texas and All Americans in the World." *Telegraph and Texas Register*, 5 March 1836.

Travis, William B., to the Convention, 3 March 1836. *Telegraph and Texas Register*, 24 March 1836.

_____, to a Friend, 3 March 1836. *Telegraph and Texas Register*, 24 March 1836.

_____, to Sam Houston, 25 February 1836. *Arkansas Gazette*, 12 April 1836.

"Was in the Alamo Conflict." *San Antonio Express*, 4 May 1907.

"Witnessed Last Struggle of the Alamo Patriots." *San Antonio Express*, 19 July 1907.

Papers

Carlton, Don. "Welcome and Introductions." Introduction to the symposium, *Eyewitness to the Texas Revolution — José Enrique de la Peña and His Narrative*, 29 April 2000. Center for American History, University of Texas at Austin.

Crisp, James E. "The Peña Narrative as History." Paper given at the symposium, *Eyewitness to the Texas Revolution — José Enrique de la Peña and His Narrative*, 29 April 2000. Center for American History, University of Texas at Austin.

Unpublished Manuscripts

Lindley, Thomas Ricks. *Alamo Traces: An Investigative Case Book.*

_____. "The Revealing of Dr. John Sutherland." DRTL.

Scott, Etna. "Information — Enrique Esparza — Evidence that he was born in 1828." DRTL.

Smith, C.C. "The History of the Oury Family." Typescript. Arizona Historical Society.

Smith, Colonel William G. "Life of William Sanders Oury 1817-1887," 1930. Typescript, CAH.

Index